AVENGERS

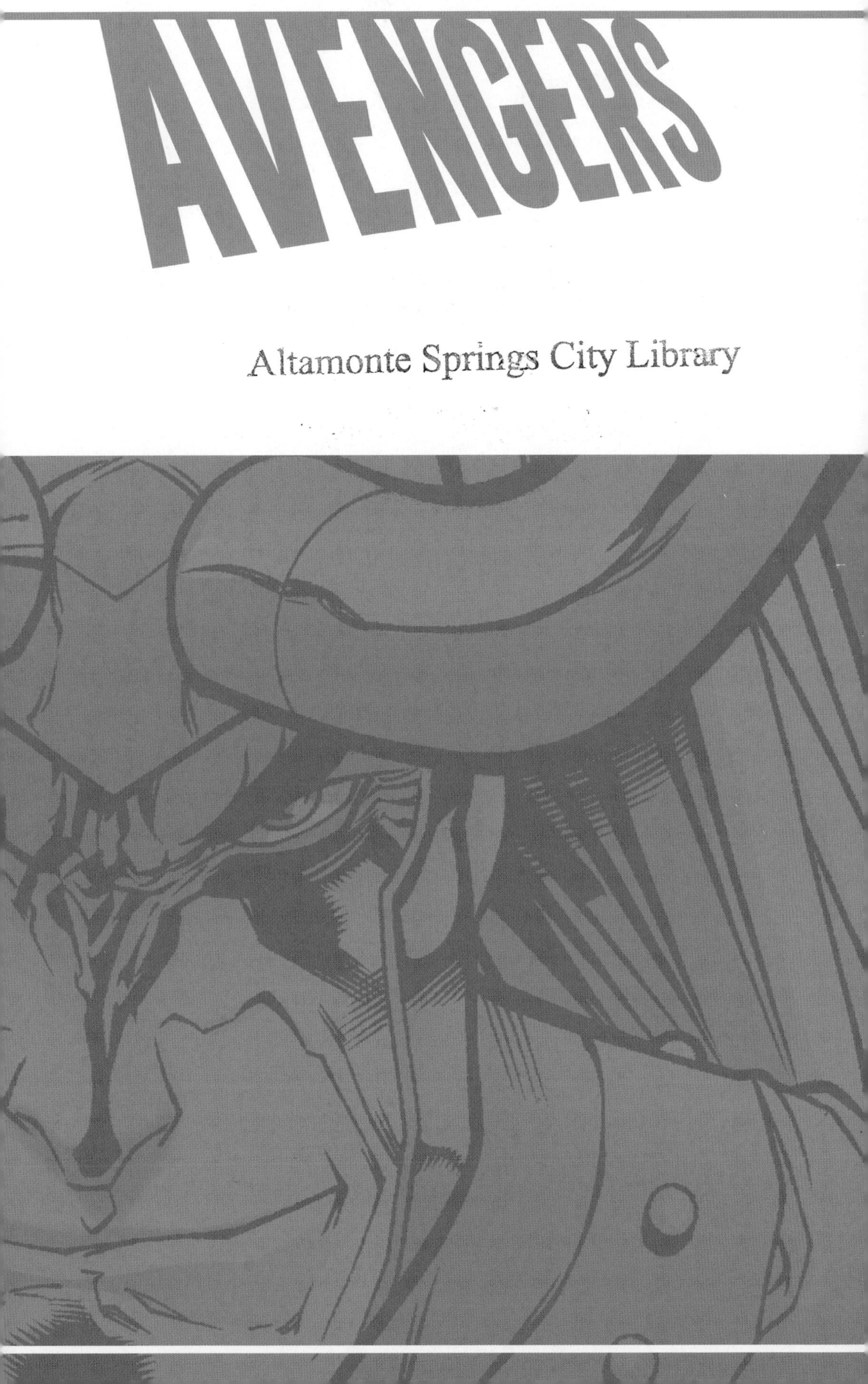

COLLECTION EDITOR: **JENNIFER GRÜNWALD**
ASSISTANT EDITORS: **ALEX STARBUCK & NELSON RIBEIRO**
EDITOR, SPECIAL PROJECTS: **MARK D. BEAZLEY**
SENIOR EDITOR, SPECIAL PROJECTS: **JEFF YOUNGQUIST**
SVP OF PRINT AND DIGITAL PUBLISHING SALES: **DAVID GABRIEL**
COVER & BOOK DESIGN: **JEFF POWELL**

EDITOR IN CHIEF: **AXEL ALONSO**
CHIEF CREATIVE OFFICER: **JOE QUESADA**
PUBLISHER: **DAN BUCKLEY**
EXECUTIVE PRODUCER: **ALAN FINE**

AVENGERS: SEASON ONE. Contains material originally published in magazine form as AVENGERS ASSEMBLE #1. First printing 2013. ISBN# 978-0-7851-6596-5. Published by MARVEL WORLDWIDE, INC., a subsidia

10 9 8 7 6 5 4 3 2 1

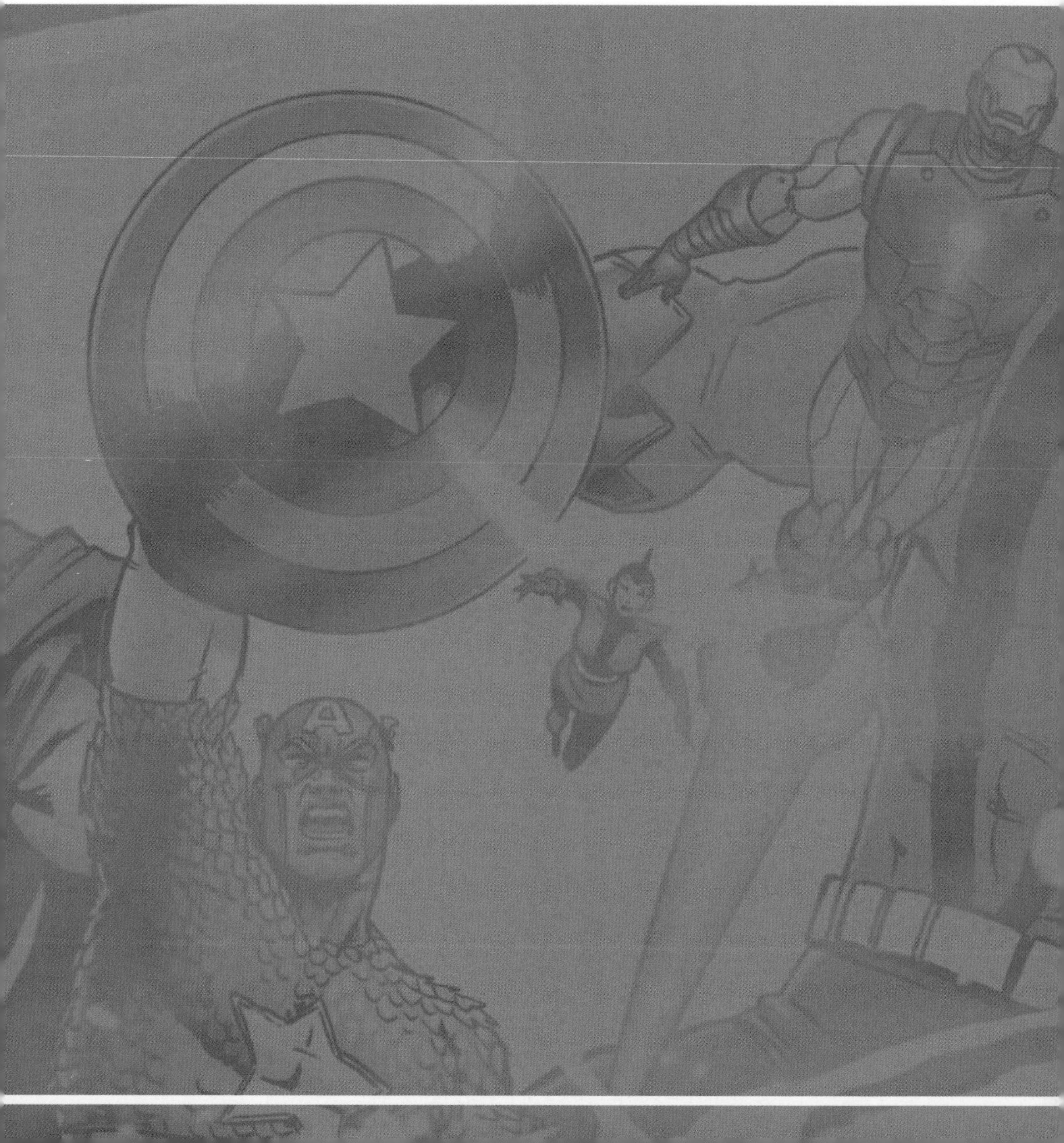

AVENGERS

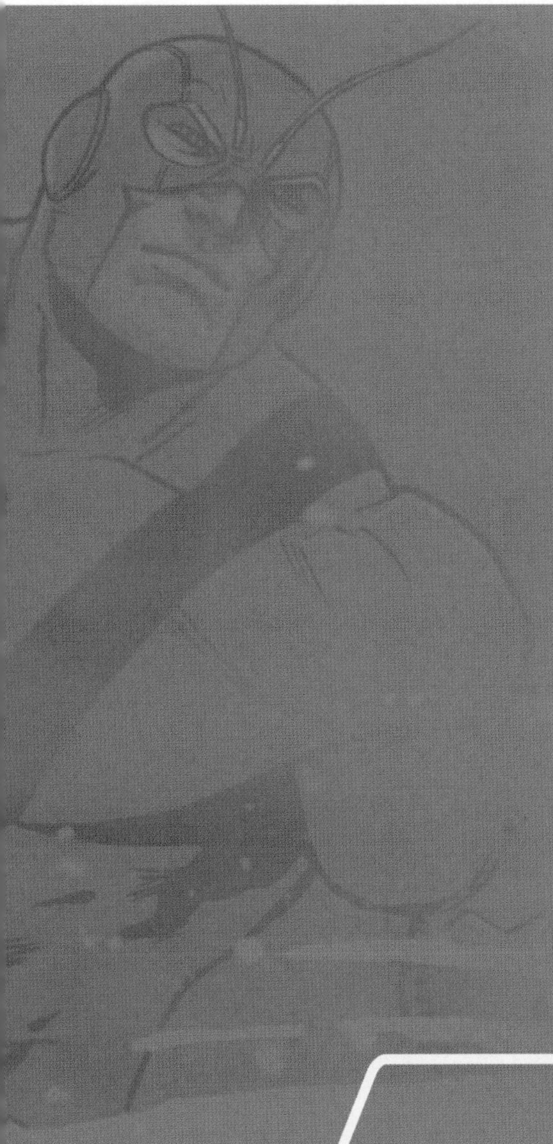

WRITER
PETER DAVID

ARTISTS
ANDREA DI VITO (PAGES 1-21 & 80-100)
JON BURAN (PAGES 22-41)
NIGEL RAYNOR (PAGES 42-59)
**MIKE BOWDEN &
WALDEN WONG** (PAGES 60-79)

COLOR ARTIST
WIL QUINTANA

LETTERER
VC'S CLAYTON COWLES

COVER ARTIST
JULIAN TOTINO TEDESCO

ASSISTANT EDITOR
JAKE THOMAS

ASSOCIATE EDITOR
LAUREN SANKOVITCH

EXECUTIVE EDITOR
TOM BREVOORT

SEASON ONE

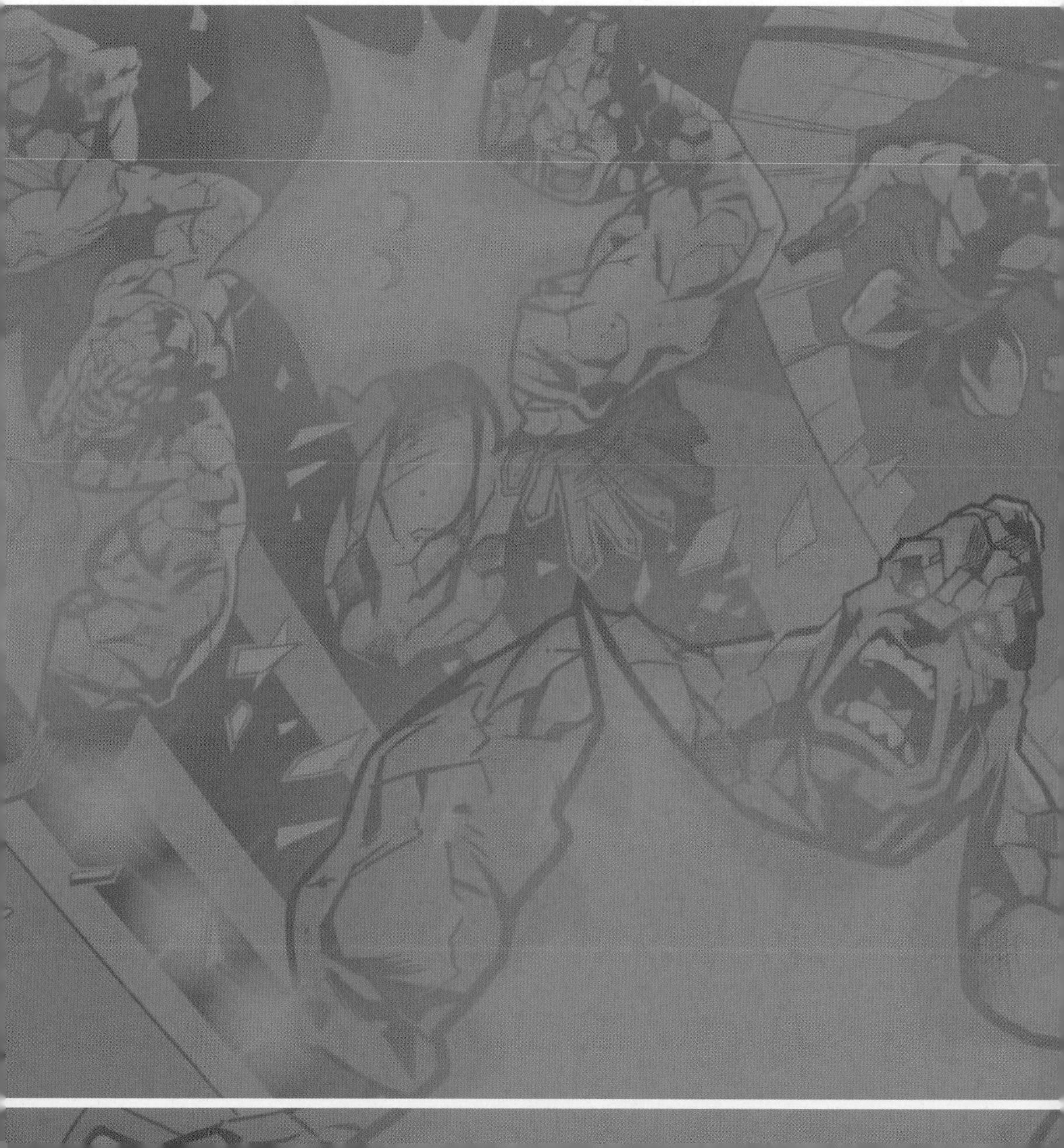

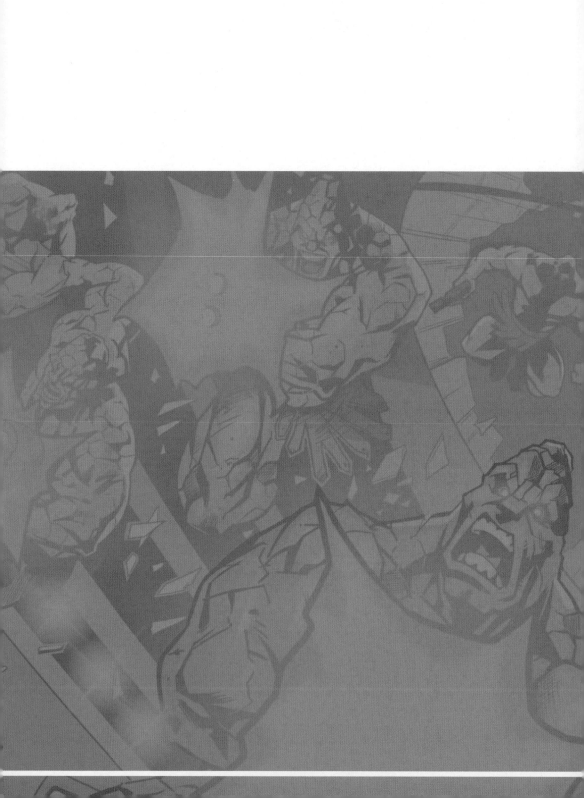

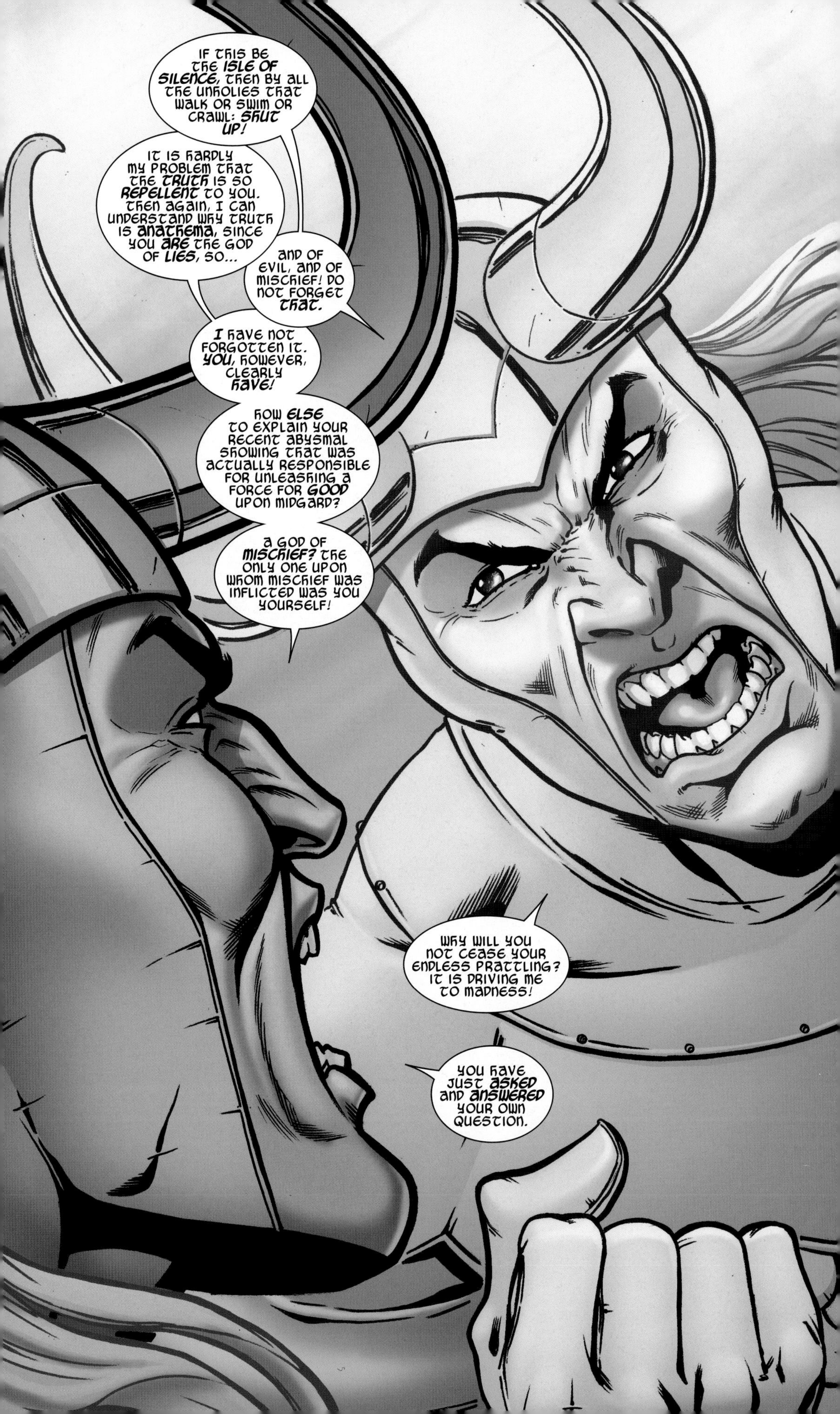
IF THIS BE THE ISLE OF SILENCE, THEN BY ALL THE UNHOLIES THAT WALK OR SWIM OR CRAWL: SHUT UP!
IT IS HARDLY MY PROBLEM THAT THE TRUTH IS SO REPELLENT TO YOU. THEN AGAIN, I CAN UNDERSTAND WHY TRUTH IS ANATHEMA, SINCE YOU ARE THE GOD OF LIES, SO...
AND OF EVIL, AND OF MISCHIEF! DO NOT FORGET THAT.
I HAVE NOT FORGOTTEN IT. YOU, HOWEVER, CLEARLY HAVE!
HOW ELSE TO EXPLAIN YOUR RECENT ABYSMAL SHOWING THAT WAS ACTUALLY RESPONSIBLE FOR UNLEASHING A FORCE FOR GOOD UPON MIDGARD?
A GOD OF MISCHIEF? THE ONLY ONE UPON WHOM MISCHIEF WAS INFLICTED WAS YOU YOURSELF!
WHY WILL YOU NOT CEASE YOUR ENDLESS PRATTLING? IT IS DRIVING ME TO MADNESS!
YOU HAVE JUST ASKED AND ANSWERED YOUR OWN QUESTION.

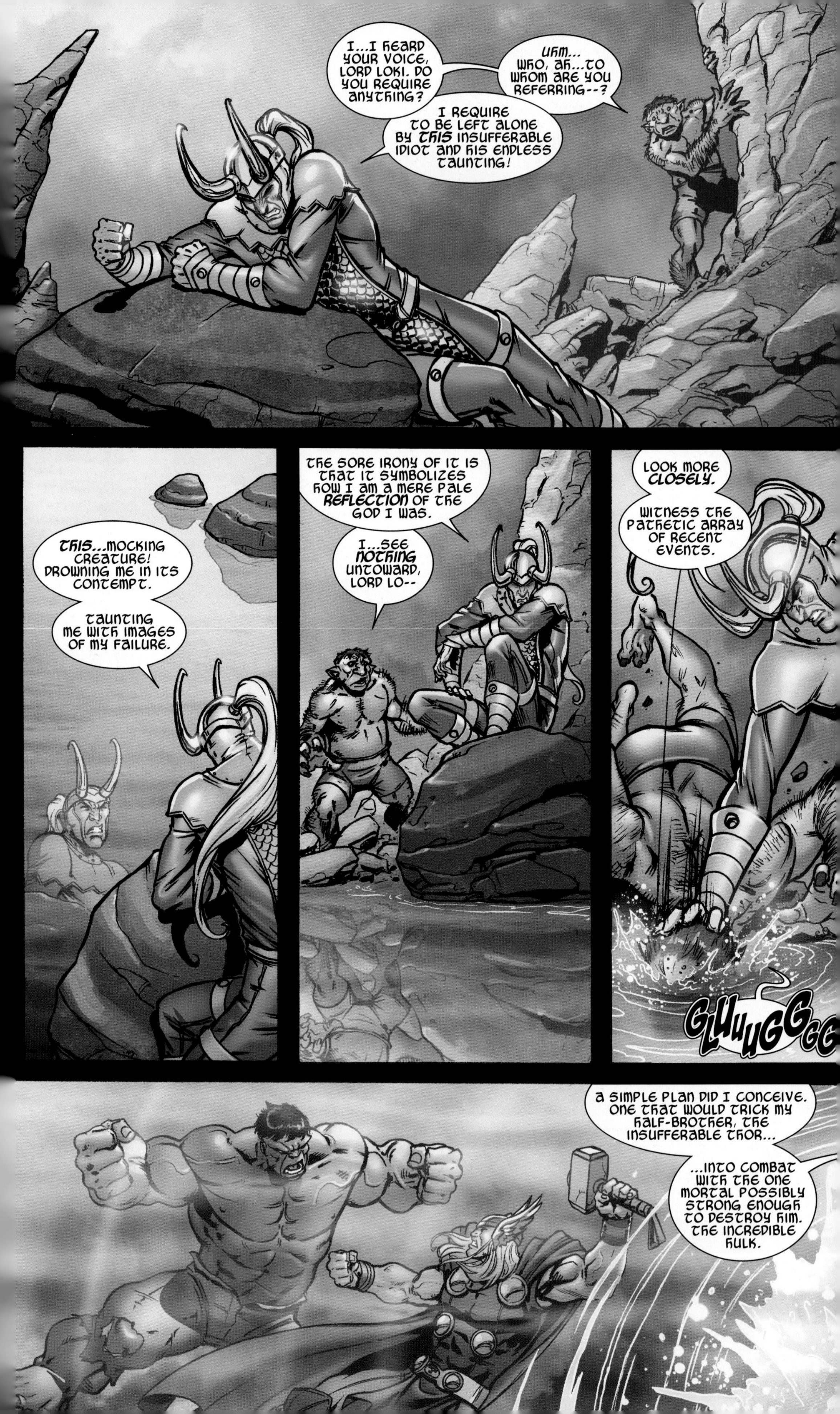

I...I HEARD YOUR VOICE, LORD LOKI. DO YOU REQUIRE ANYTHING?
UHM... WHO, AH...TO WHOM ARE YOU REFERRING--?
I REQUIRE TO BE LEFT ALONE BY THIS INSUFFERABLE IDIOT AND HIS ENDLESS TAUNTING!
THIS...MOCKING CREATURE! DROWNING ME IN ITS CONTEMPT.
TAUNTING ME WITH IMAGES OF MY FAILURE.
THE SORE IRONY OF IT IS THAT IT SYMBOLIZES HOW I AM A MERE PALE REFLECTION OF THE GOD I WAS.
I...SEE NOTHING UNTOWARD, LORD LO--
LOOK MORE CLOSELY.
WITNESS THE PATHETIC ARRAY OF RECENT EVENTS.
GLUUUGGGGE
A SIMPLE PLAN DID I CONCEIVE. ONE THAT WOULD TRICK MY HALF-BROTHER, THE INSUFFERABLE THOR...
...INTO COMBAT WITH THE ONE MORTAL POSSIBLY STRONG ENOUGH TO DESTROY HIM. THE INCREDIBLE HULK.

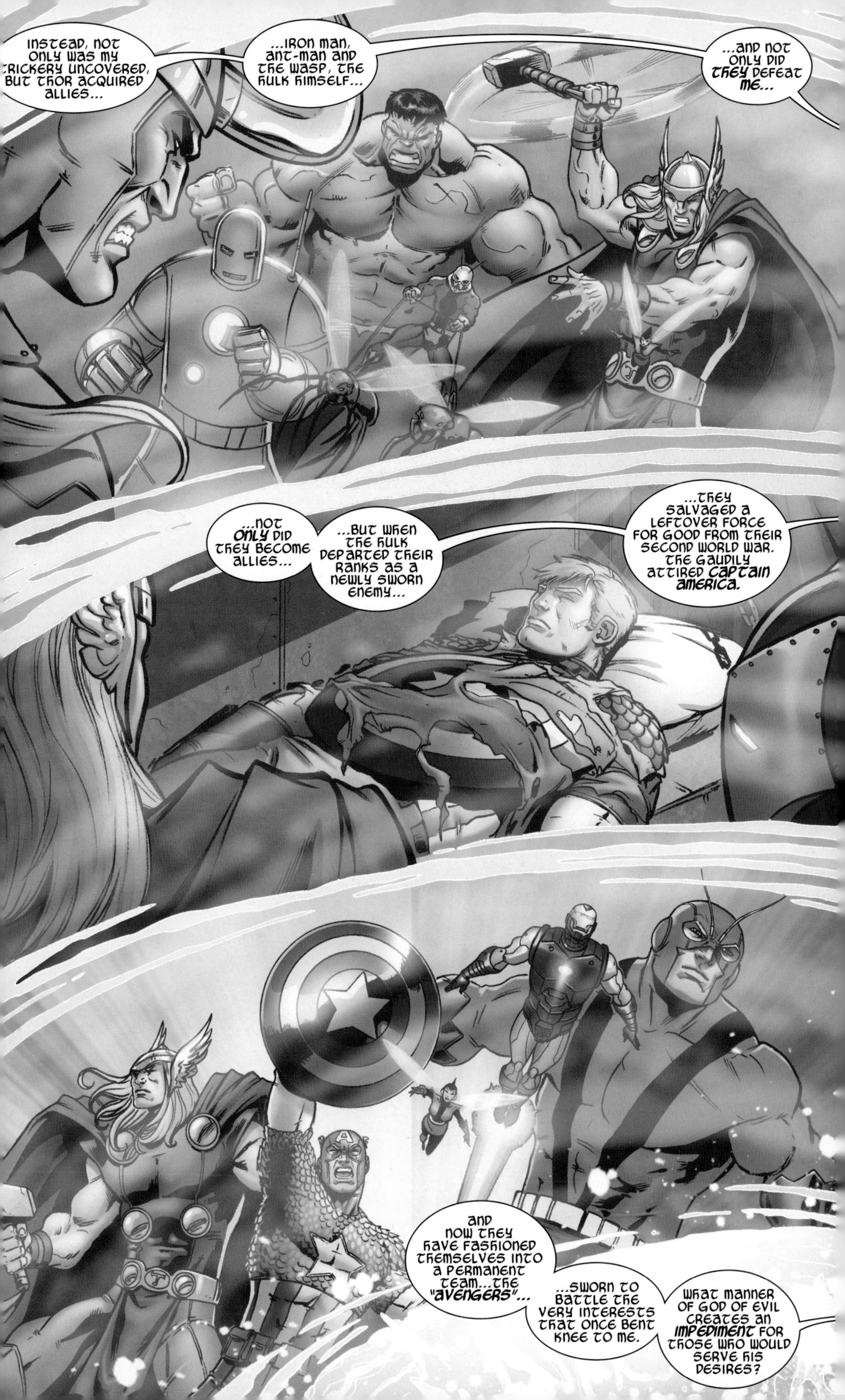
INSTEAD, NOT ONLY WAS MY TRICKERY UNCOVERED, BUT THOR ACQUIRED ALLIES...
...IRON MAN, ANT-MAN AND THE WASP, THE HULK HIMSELF...
...AND NOT ONLY DID THEY DEFEAT ME...
...NOT ONLY DID THEY BECOME ALLIES...
...BUT WHEN THE HULK DEPARTED THEIR RANKS AS A NEWLY SWORN ENEMY...
...THEY SALVAGED A LEFTOVER FORCE FOR GOOD FROM THEIR SECOND WORLD WAR. THE GAUDILY ATTIRED CAPTAIN AMERICA.
AND NOW THEY HAVE FASHIONED THEMSELVES INTO A PERMANENT TEAM...THE "AVENGERS"...
...SWORN TO BATTLE THE VERY INTERESTS THAT ONCE BENT KNEE TO ME.
WHAT MANNER OF GOD OF EVIL CREATES AN IMPEDIMENT FOR THOSE WHO WOULD SERVE HIS DESIRES?

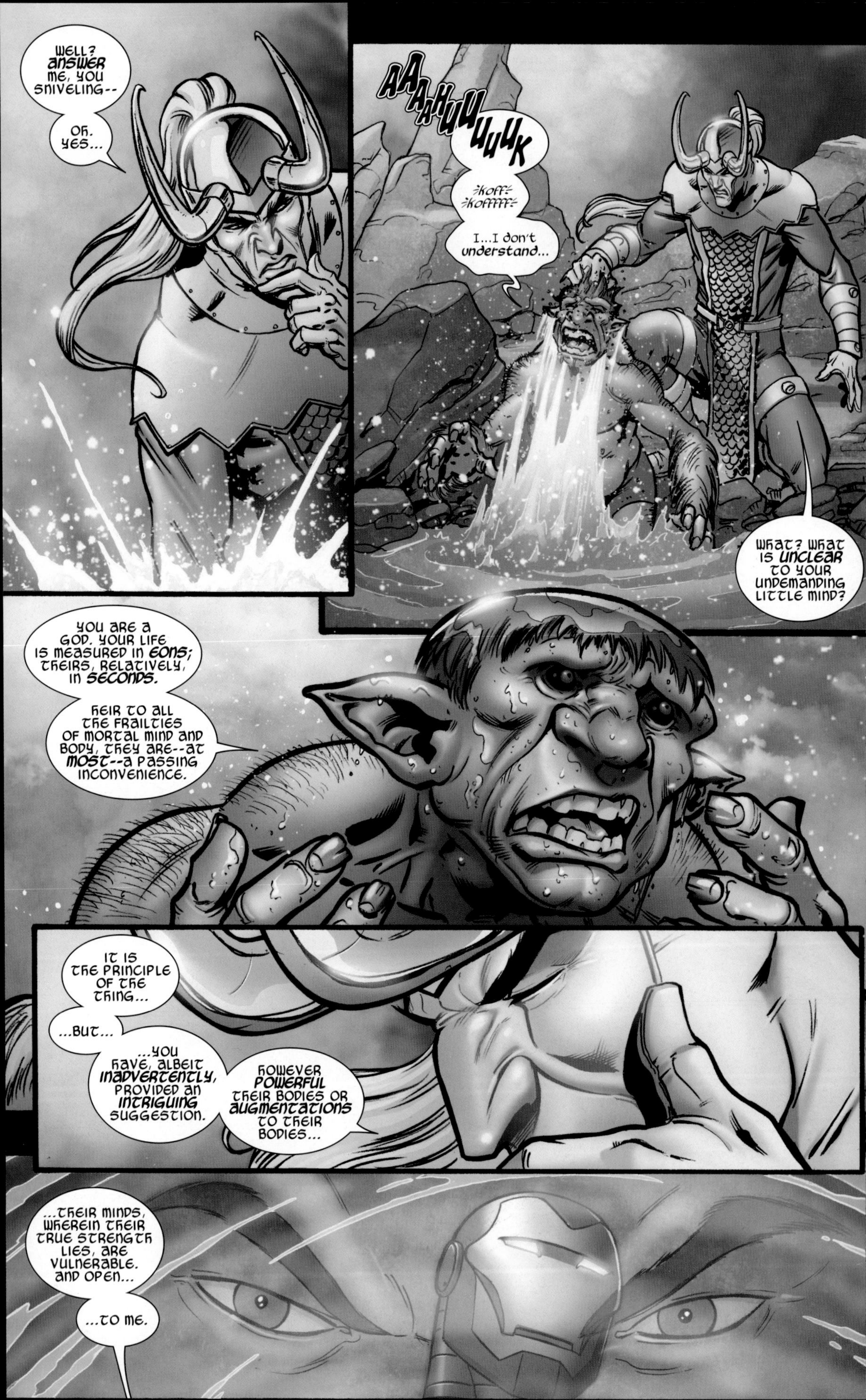
WELL? ANSWER ME, YOU SNIVELING--
OH. YES...
AAAAHUUUUUK
KOFF *KOFFFFF*
I...I don't understand...
WHAT? WHAT IS UNCLEAR TO YOUR UNDEMANDING LITTLE MIND?
YOU ARE A GOD. YOUR LIFE IS MEASURED IN EONS; THEIRS, RELATIVELY, IN SECONDS.
HEIR TO ALL THE FRAILTIES OF MORTAL MIND AND BODY, THEY ARE--AT MOST--A PASSING INCONVENIENCE.
IT IS THE PRINCIPLE OF THE THING...
...BUT...
...YOU HAVE, ALBEIT INADVERTENTLY, PROVIDED AN INTRIGUING SUGGESTION.
HOWEVER POWERFUL THEIR BODIES OR AUGMENTATIONS TO THEIR BODIES...
...THEIR MINDS, WHEREIN THEIR TRUE STRENGTH LIES, ARE VULNERABLE. AND OPEN...
...TO ME.

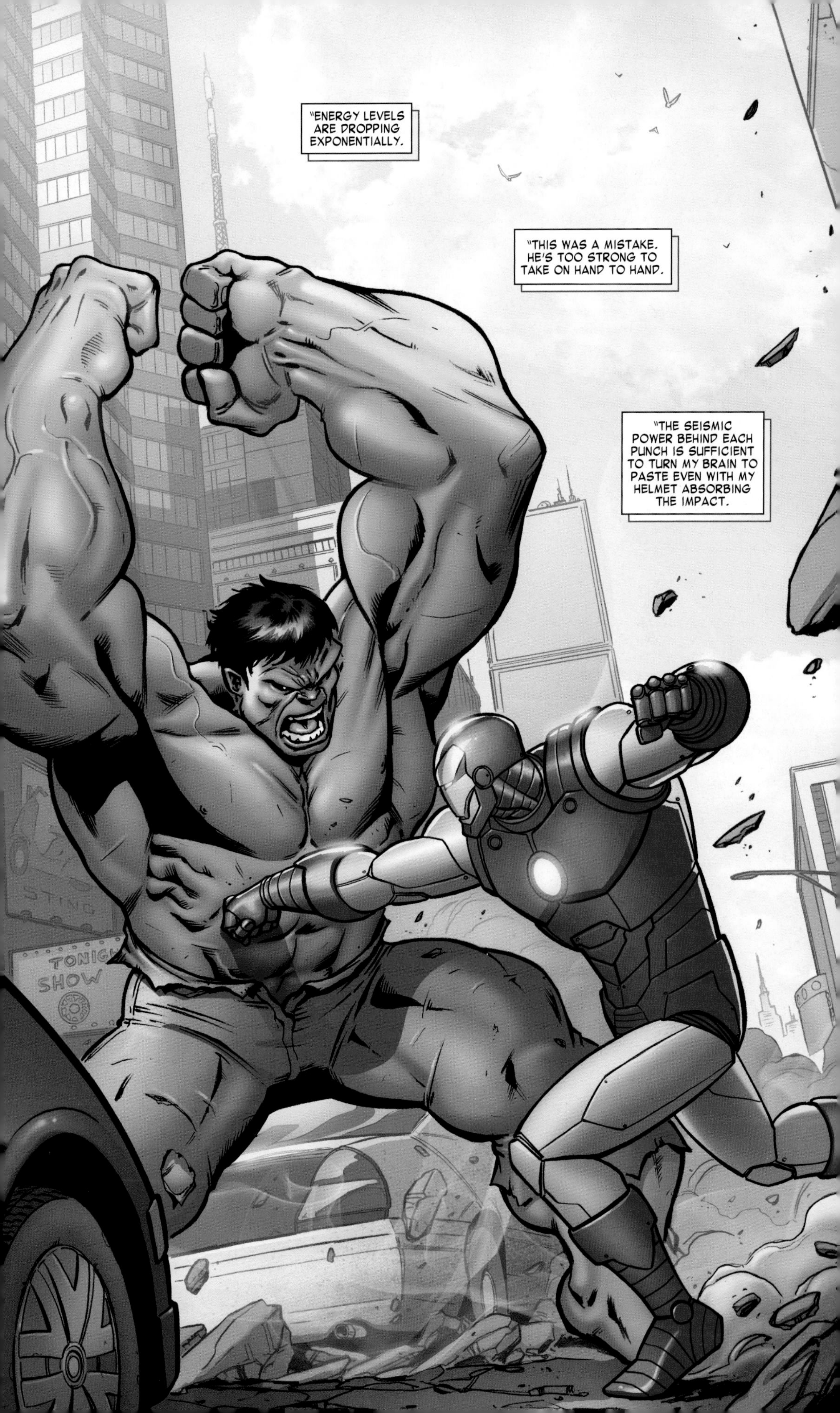
"ENERGY LEVELS ARE DROPPING EXPONENTIALLY.
"THIS WAS A MISTAKE. HE'S TOO STRONG TO TAKE ON HAND TO HAND.
"THE SEISMIC POWER BEHIND EACH PUNCH IS SUFFICIENT TO TURN MY BRAIN TO PASTE EVEN WITH MY HELMET ABSORBING THE IMPACT.
STING
TONIGH
SHOW

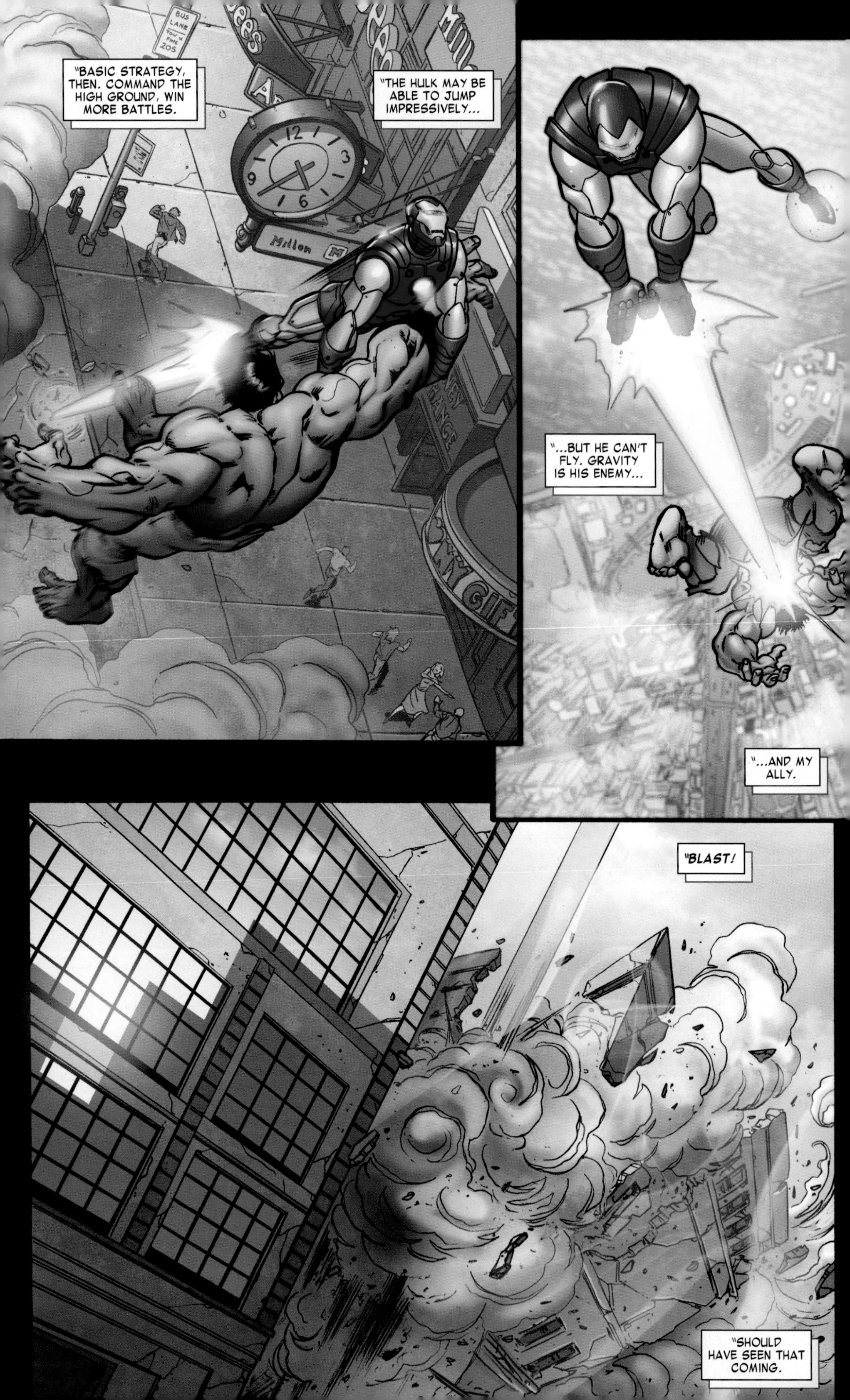
"BASIC STRATEGY, THEN. COMMAND THE HIGH GROUND, WIN MORE BATTLES.
"THE HULK MAY BE ABLE TO JUMP IMPRESSIVELY...
"...BUT HE CAN'T FLY. GRAVITY IS HIS ENEMY...
"...AND MY ALLY.
"BLAST!
"SHOULD HAVE SEEN THAT COMING.

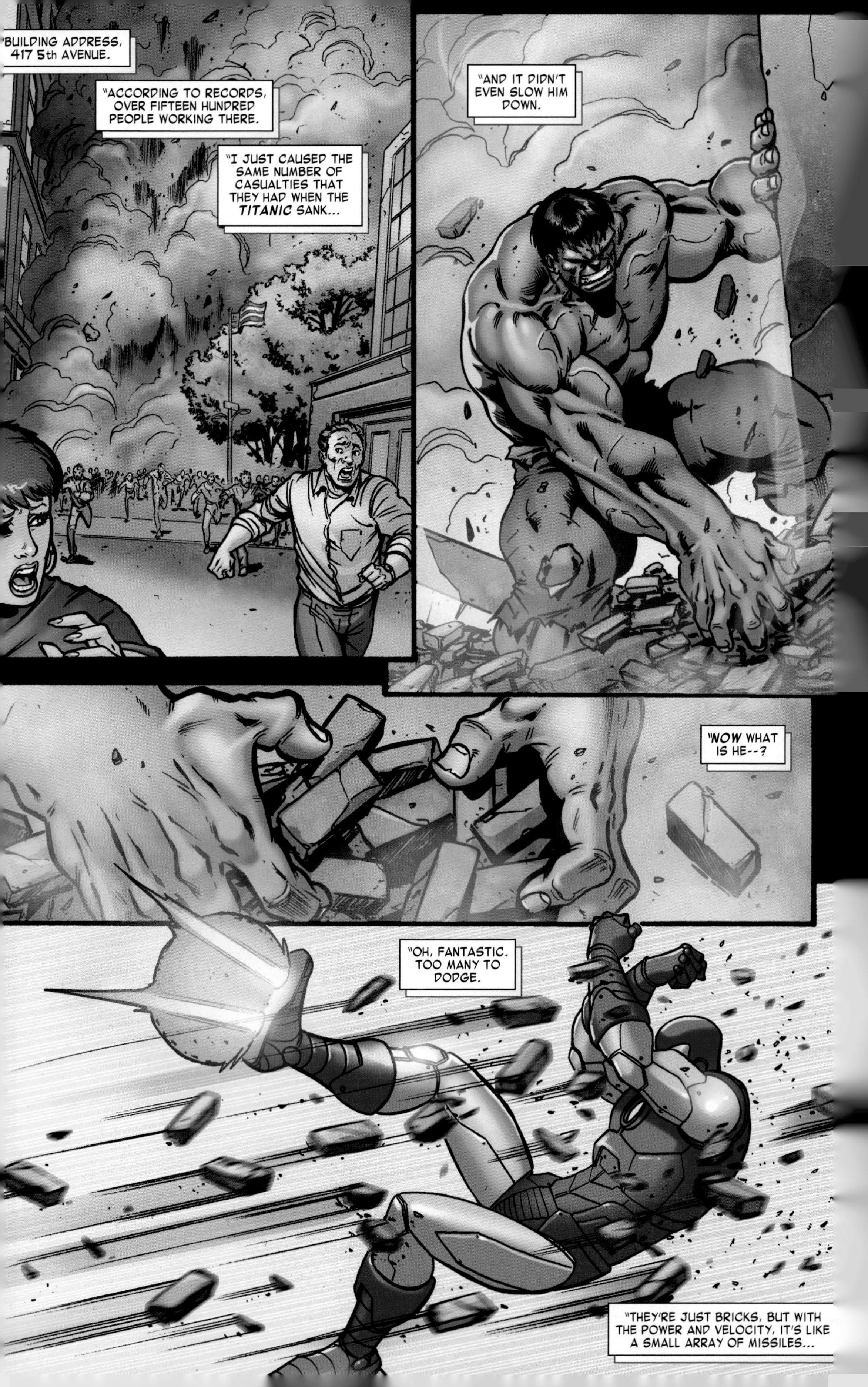
"BUILDING ADDRESS, 417 5th AVENUE.
"ACCORDING TO RECORDS, OVER FIFTEEN HUNDRED PEOPLE WORKING THERE.
"I JUST CAUSED THE SAME NUMBER OF CASUALTIES THAT THEY HAD WHEN THE *TITANIC* SANK...
"AND IT DIDN'T EVEN SLOW HIM DOWN.
"*NOW* WHAT IS HE--?
"OH, FANTASTIC. TOO MANY TO DODGE.
"THEY'RE JUST BRICKS, BUT WITH THE POWER AND VELOCITY, IT'S LIKE A SMALL ARRAY OF MISSILES...

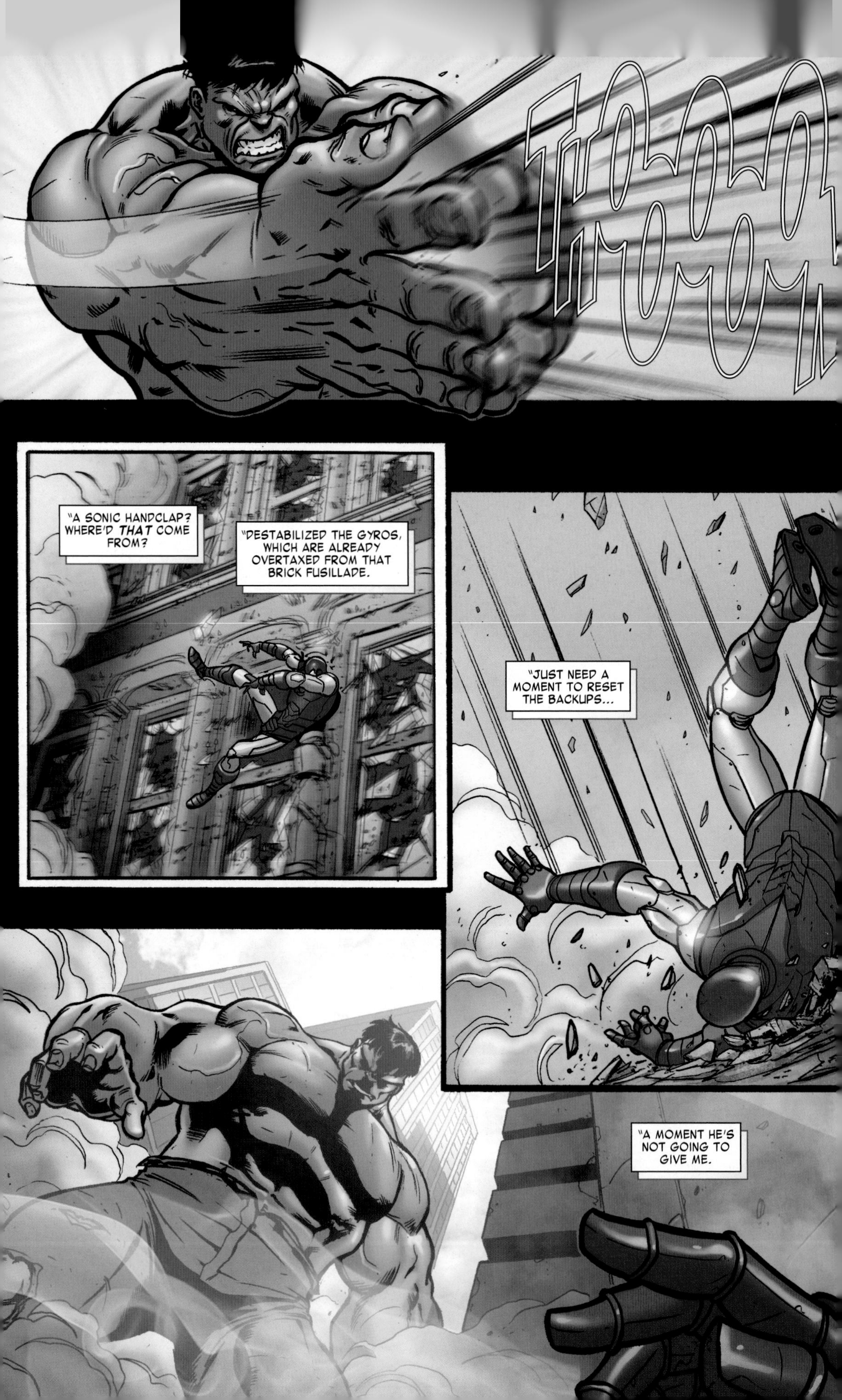

"A SONIC HANDCLAP? WHERE'D *THAT* COME FROM?
"DESTABILIZED THE GYROS, WHICH ARE ALREADY OVERTAXED FROM THAT BRICK FUSILLADE.
"JUST NEED A MOMENT TO RESET THE BACKUPS...
"A MOMENT HE'S NOT GOING TO GIVE ME.

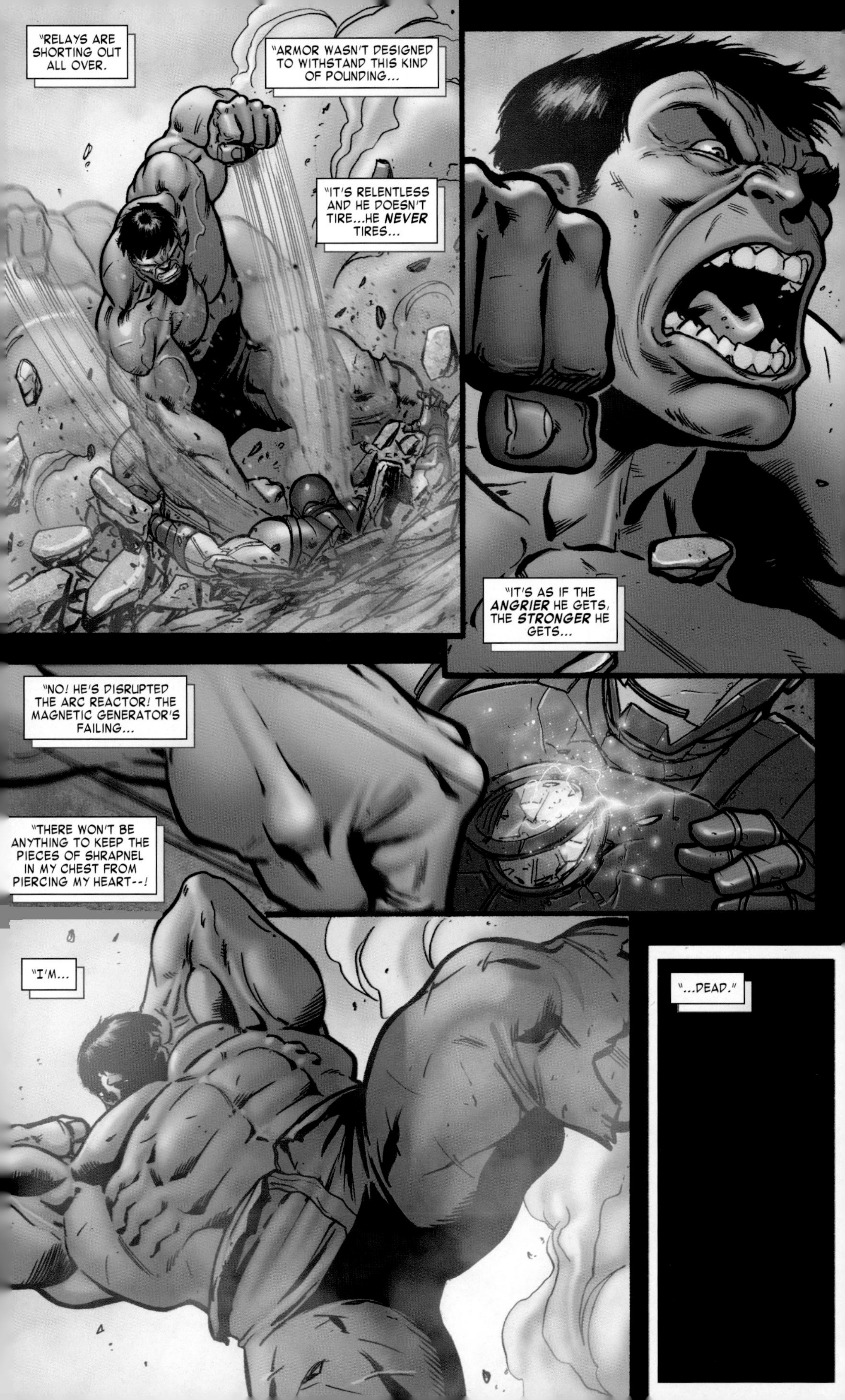
"RELAYS ARE SHORTING OUT ALL OVER.
"ARMOR WASN'T DESIGNED TO WITHSTAND THIS KIND OF POUNDING...
"IT'S RELENTLESS AND HE DOESN'T TIRE...HE NEVER TIRES...
"IT'S AS IF THE ANGRIER HE GETS, THE STRONGER HE GETS...
"NO! HE'S DISRUPTED THE ARC REACTOR! THE MAGNETIC GENERATOR'S FAILING...
"THERE WON'T BE ANYTHING TO KEEP THE PIECES OF SHRAPNEL IN MY CHEST FROM PIERCING MY HEART--!
"I'M...
"...DEAD."

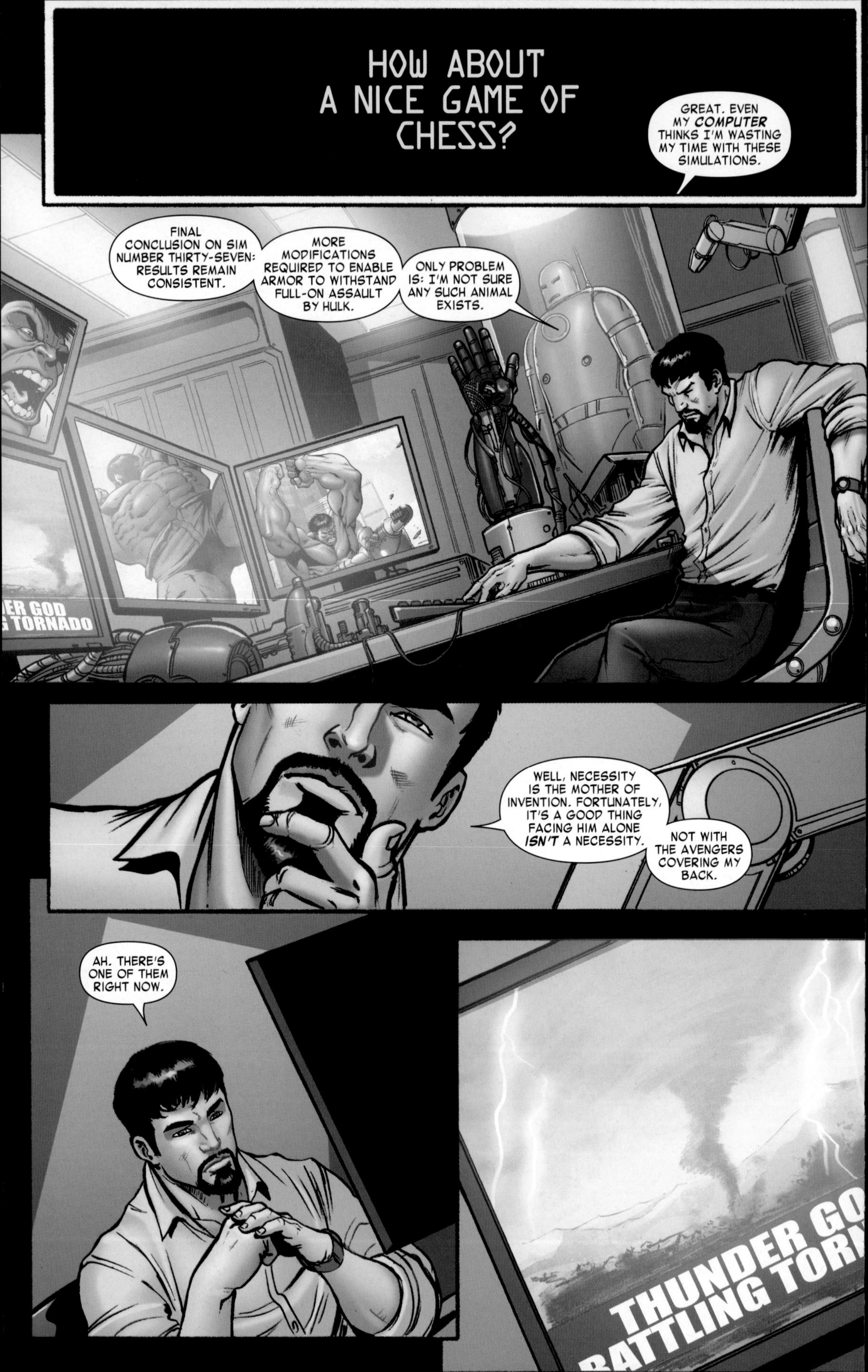
HOW ABOUT A NICE GAME OF CHESS?
GREAT. EVEN MY COMPUTER THINKS I'M WASTING MY TIME WITH THESE SIMULATIONS.
FINAL CONCLUSION ON SIM NUMBER THIRTY-SEVEN: RESULTS REMAIN CONSISTENT.
MORE MODIFICATIONS REQUIRED TO ENABLE ARMOR TO WITHSTAND FULL-ON ASSAULT BY HULK.
ONLY PROBLEM IS: I'M NOT SURE ANY SUCH ANIMAL EXISTS.
DER GOD
G TORNADO
WELL, NECESSITY IS THE MOTHER OF INVENTION. FORTUNATELY, IT'S A GOOD THING FACING HIM ALONE ISN'T A NECESSITY.
NOT WITH THE AVENGERS COVERING MY BACK.
AH. THERE'S ONE OF THEM RIGHT NOW.
THUNDER GO
BATTLING TOR

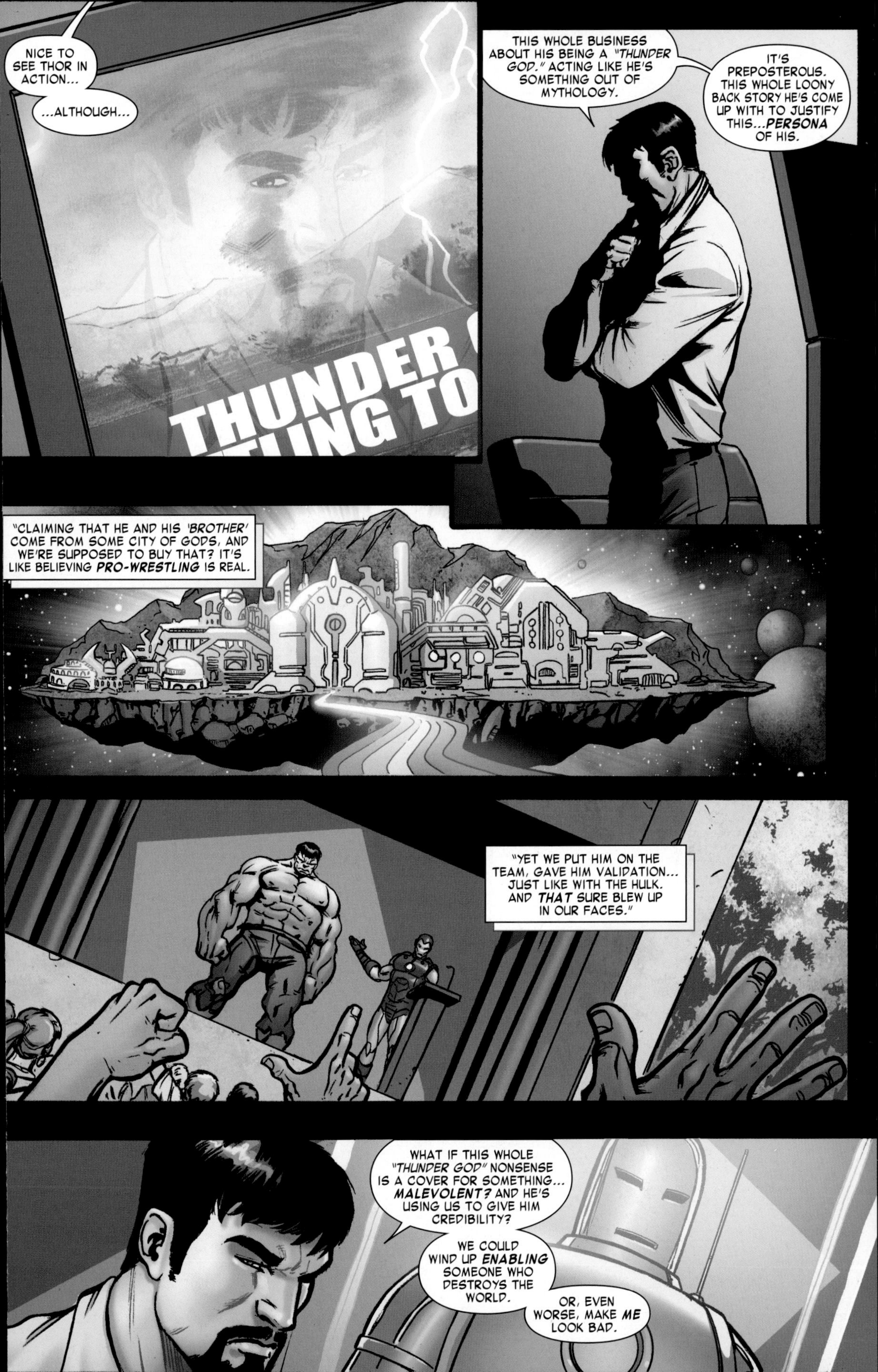
NICE TO SEE THOR IN ACTION...
...ALTHOUGH...
THUNDER
TLING TO
THIS WHOLE BUSINESS ABOUT HIS BEING A "THUNDER GOD." ACTING LIKE HE'S SOMETHING OUT OF MYTHOLOGY.
IT'S PREPOSTEROUS. THIS WHOLE LOONY BACK STORY HE'S COME UP WITH TO JUSTIFY THIS...PERSONA OF HIS.
"CLAIMING THAT HE AND HIS 'BROTHER' COME FROM SOME CITY OF GODS, AND WE'RE SUPPOSED TO BUY THAT? IT'S LIKE BELIEVING PRO-WRESTLING IS REAL.
"YET WE PUT HIM ON THE TEAM, GAVE HIM VALIDATION... JUST LIKE WITH THE HULK. AND THAT SURE BLEW UP IN OUR FACES."
WHAT IF THIS WHOLE "THUNDER GOD" NONSENSE IS A COVER FOR SOMETHING... MALEVOLENT? AND HE'S USING US TO GIVE HIM CREDIBILITY?
WE COULD WIND UP ENABLING SOMEONE WHO DESTROYS THE WORLD.
OR, EVEN WORSE, MAKE ME LOOK BAD.

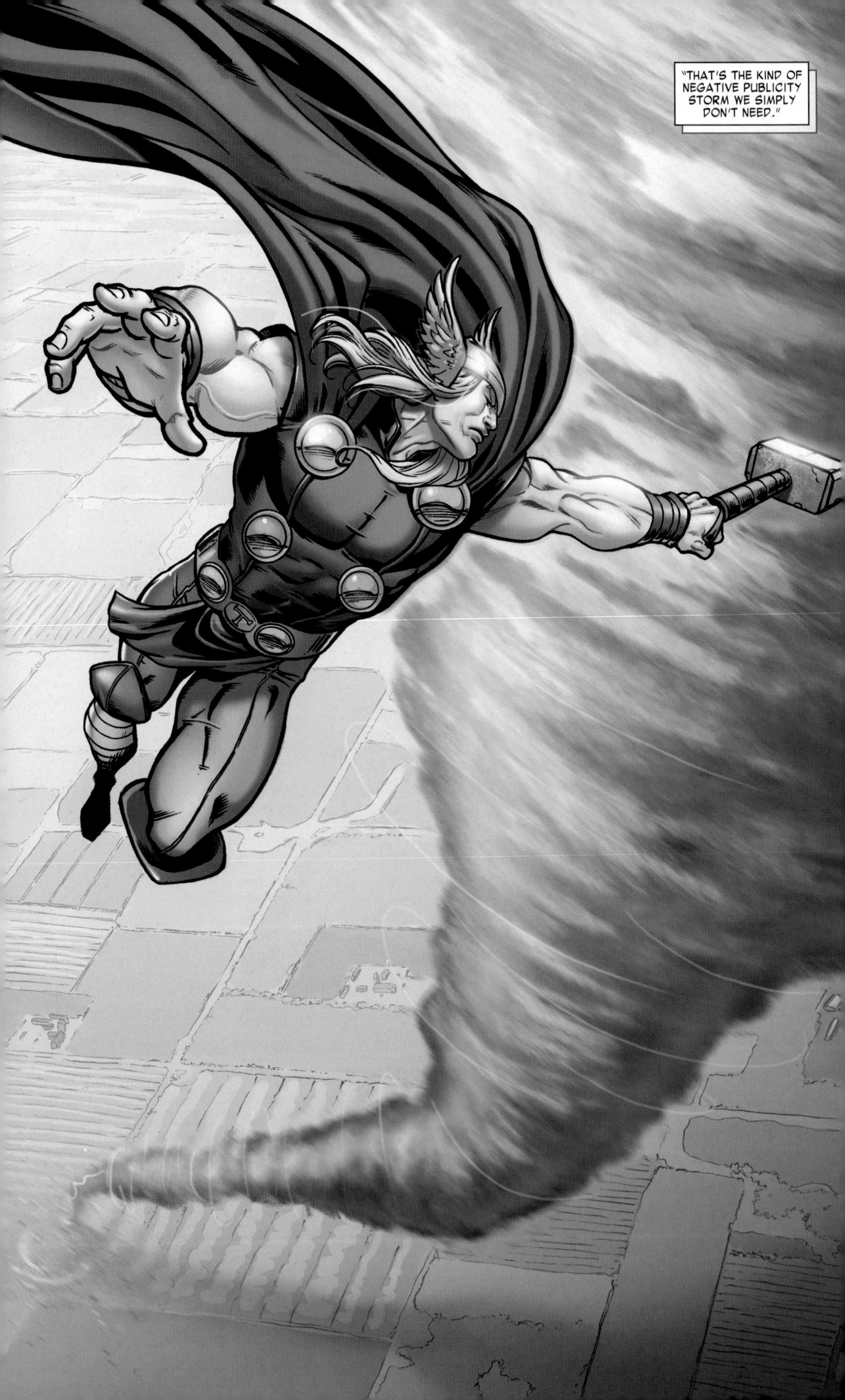
"THAT'S THE KIND OF NEGATIVE PUBLICITY STORM WE SIMPLY DON'T NEED."

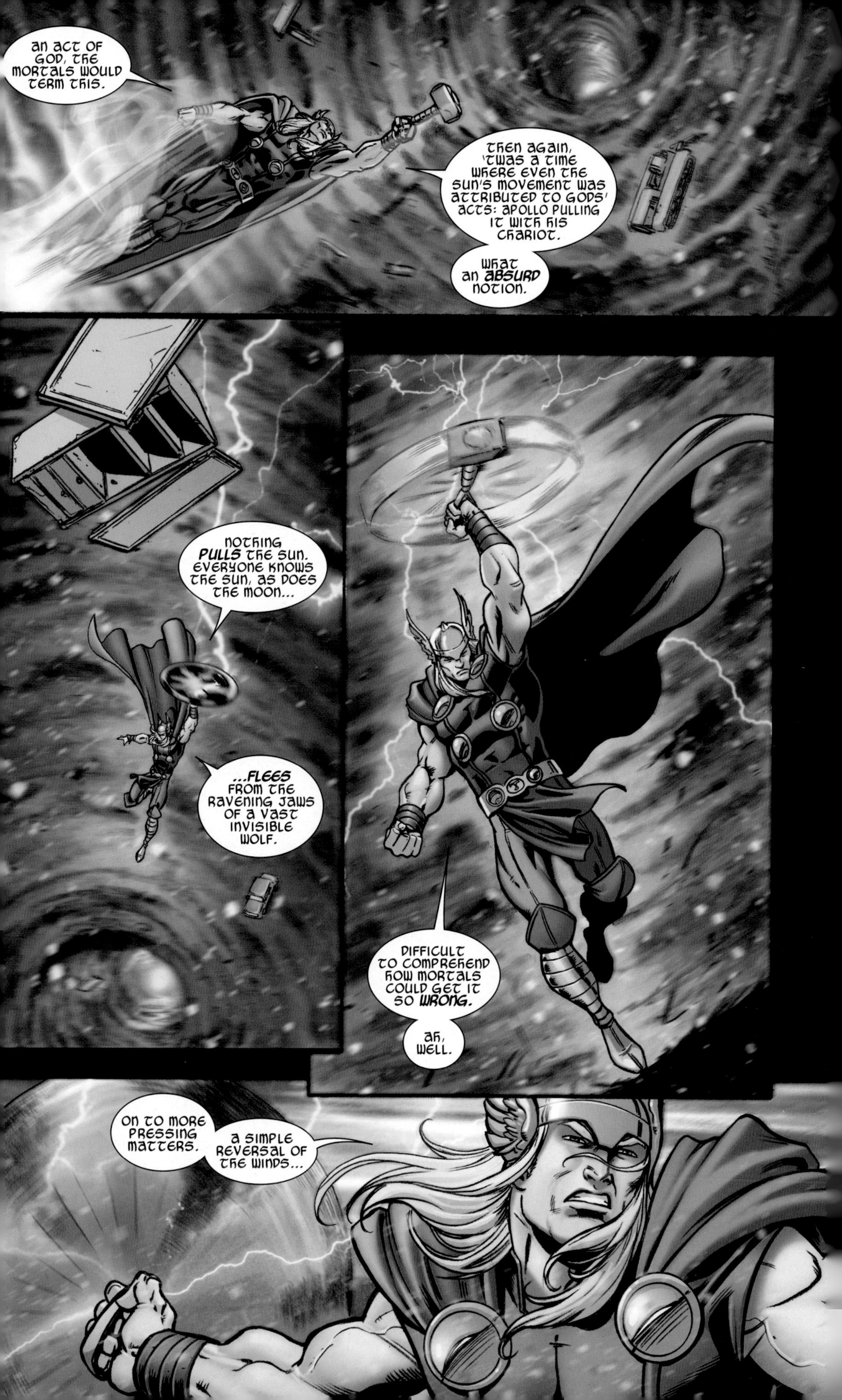

AN ACT OF GOD, THE MORTALS WOULD TERM THIS.
THEN AGAIN, 'TWAS A TIME WHERE EVEN THE SUN'S MOVEMENT WAS ATTRIBUTED TO GODS' ACTS: APOLLO PULLING IT WITH HIS CHARIOT.
WHAT AN ABSURD NOTION.
NOTHING PULLS THE SUN. EVERYONE KNOWS THE SUN, AS DOES THE MOON...
...FLEES FROM THE RAVENING JAWS OF A VAST INVISIBLE WOLF.
DIFFICULT TO COMPREHEND HOW MORTALS COULD GET IT SO WRONG.
AH, WELL.
ON TO MORE PRESSING MATTERS.
A SIMPLE REVERSAL OF THE WINDS...

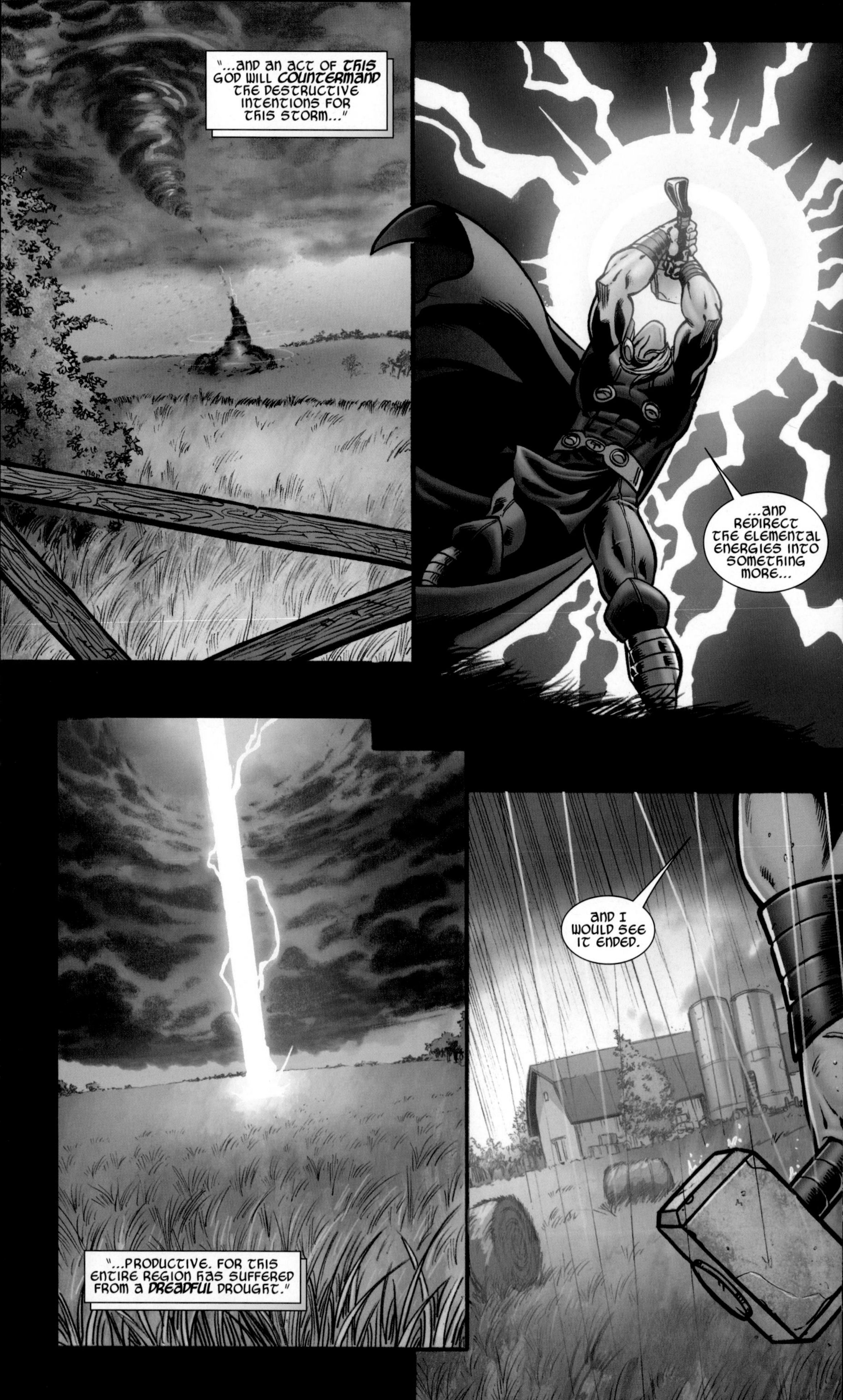
"...AND AN ACT OF THIS GOD WILL COUNTERMAND THE DESTRUCTIVE INTENTIONS FOR THIS STORM..."
...AND REDIRECT THE ELEMENTAL ENERGIES INTO SOMETHING MORE...
"...PRODUCTIVE. FOR THIS ENTIRE REGION HAS SUFFERED FROM A DREADFUL DROUGHT."
AND I WOULD SEE IT ENDED.

AN *EXCELLENT* RAIN, IF I SAY SO MYSELF.

DID...DID *YOU* DO THIS? GET RID OF THE TORNADO? MAKE IT RAIN?

YES, OLD ONE, 'TWAS I.

WE WERE HIDING DOWN IN OUR STORM CELLAR! THEN WE HEARD IT ALL JUST...JUST STOP--!

AND IMAGINE! A GOD STEPPED IN AND--!

EASY, GRANDPA. WE SHOULD GET YOU BACK INSIDE. WEATHER'S STILL ROUGH...

FORGET *THAT!* I COME FROM HARDY STOCK! MY DAD FOUGHT IN THE WAR TO END ALL WARS...

RAGNAROK?

AND *I* WAS IN DUBBYA DUBBYA TWO! EVEN SAW CAPTAIN AMERICA IN ACTION!

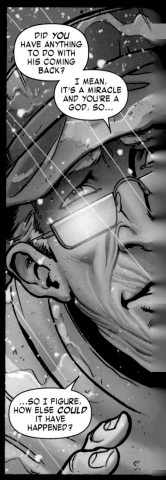

DID *YOU* HAVE ANYTHING TO DO WITH HIS COMING BACK?

I MEAN, IT'S A MIRACLE AND YOU'RE A GOD, SO...

...SO I FIGURE, HOW ELSE *COULD* IT HAVE HAPPENED?

INDEED...'TWOULD SEEM TO HAVE REQUIRED DIVINE INTERVENTION.

YOUR *PARDON*, OLD ONE. I MUST NEEDS *DEPART.*

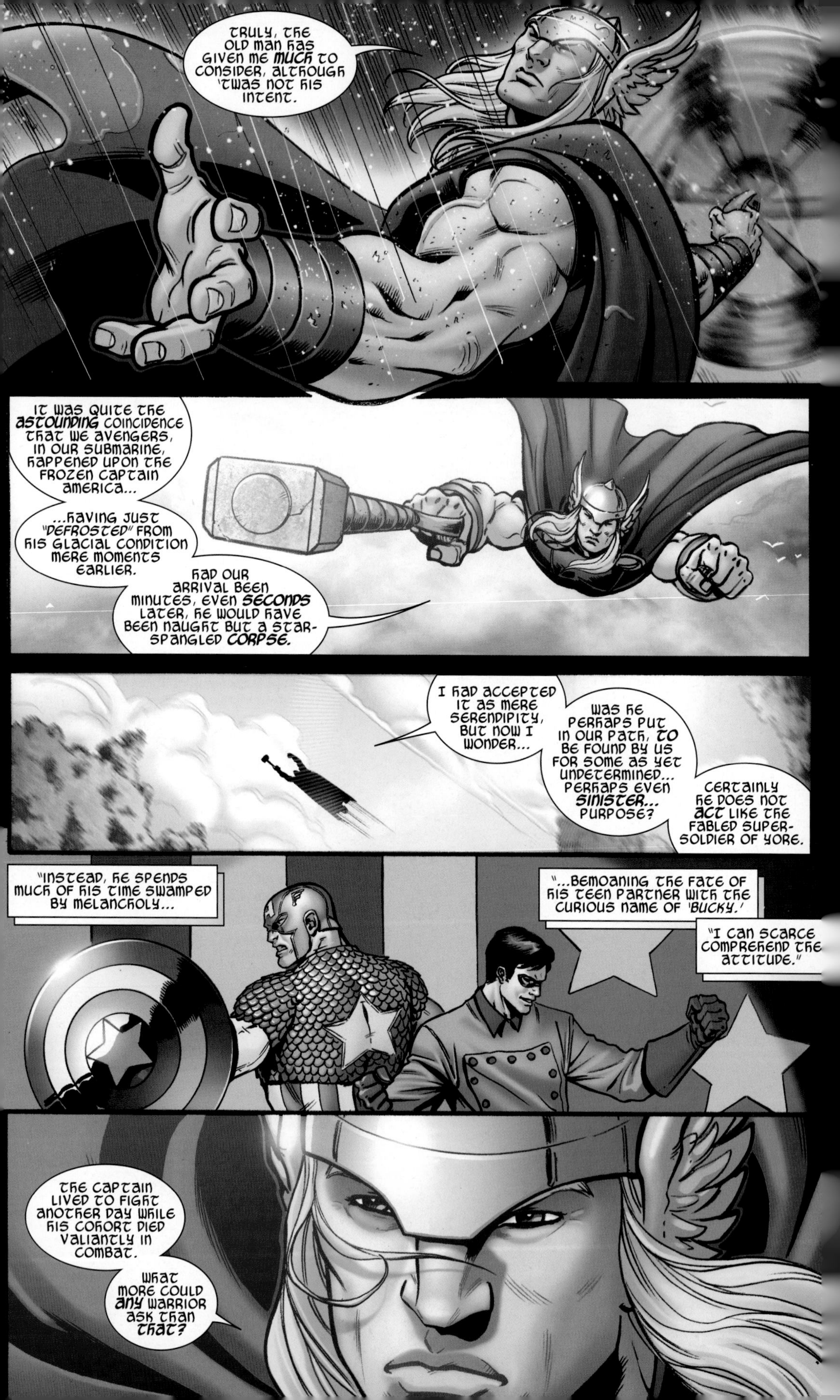
TRULY, THE OLD MAN HAS GIVEN ME MUCH TO CONSIDER, ALTHOUGH 'TWAS NOT HIS INTENT.
IT WAS QUITE THE ASTOUNDING COINCIDENCE THAT WE AVENGERS, IN OUR SUBMARINE, HAPPENED UPON THE FROZEN CAPTAIN AMERICA...
...HAVING JUST "DEFROSTED" FROM HIS GLACIAL CONDITION MERE MOMENTS EARLIER.
HAD OUR ARRIVAL BEEN MINUTES, EVEN SECONDS LATER, HE WOULD HAVE BEEN NAUGHT BUT A STAR-SPANGLED CORPSE.
I HAD ACCEPTED IT AS MERE SERENDIPITY, BUT NOW I WONDER...
WAS HE PERHAPS PUT IN OUR PATH, TO BE FOUND BY US FOR SOME AS YET UNDETERMINED... PERHAPS EVEN SINISTER... PURPOSE?
CERTAINLY HE DOES NOT ACT LIKE THE FABLED SUPER-SOLDIER OF YORE.
"INSTEAD, HE SPENDS MUCH OF HIS TIME SWAMPED BY MELANCHOLY...
"...BEMOANING THE FATE OF HIS TEEN PARTNER WITH THE CURIOUS NAME OF 'BUCKY.'
"I CAN SCARCE COMPREHEND THE ATTITUDE."
THE CAPTAIN LIVED TO FIGHT ANOTHER DAY WHILE HIS COHORT DIED VALIANTLY IN COMBAT.
WHAT MORE COULD ANY WARRIOR ASK THAN THAT?

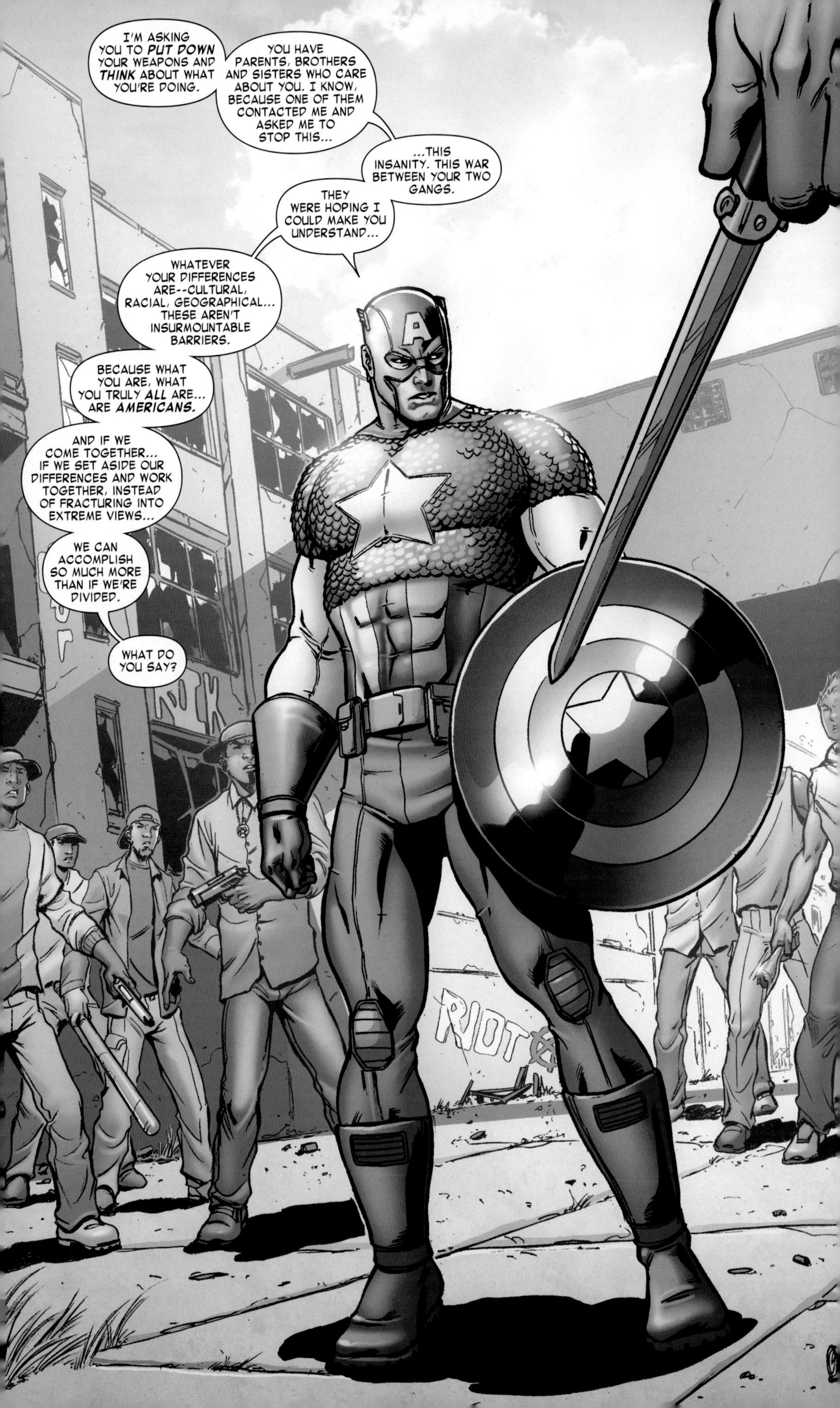
I'M ASKING YOU TO PUT DOWN YOUR WEAPONS AND THINK ABOUT WHAT YOU'RE DOING.
YOU HAVE PARENTS, BROTHERS AND SISTERS WHO CARE ABOUT YOU. I KNOW, BECAUSE ONE OF THEM CONTACTED ME AND ASKED ME TO STOP THIS...
...THIS INSANITY. THIS WAR BETWEEN YOUR TWO GANGS.
THEY WERE HOPING I COULD MAKE YOU UNDERSTAND...
WHATEVER YOUR DIFFERENCES ARE--CULTURAL, RACIAL, GEOGRAPHICAL... THESE AREN'T INSURMOUNTABLE BARRIERS.
BECAUSE WHAT YOU ARE, WHAT YOU TRULY ALL ARE... ARE AMERICANS.
AND IF WE COME TOGETHER... IF WE SET ASIDE OUR DIFFERENCES AND WORK TOGETHER, INSTEAD OF FRACTURING INTO EXTREME VIEWS...
WE CAN ACCOMPLISH SO MUCH MORE THAN IF WE'RE DIVIDED.
WHAT DO YOU SAY?
RIOT

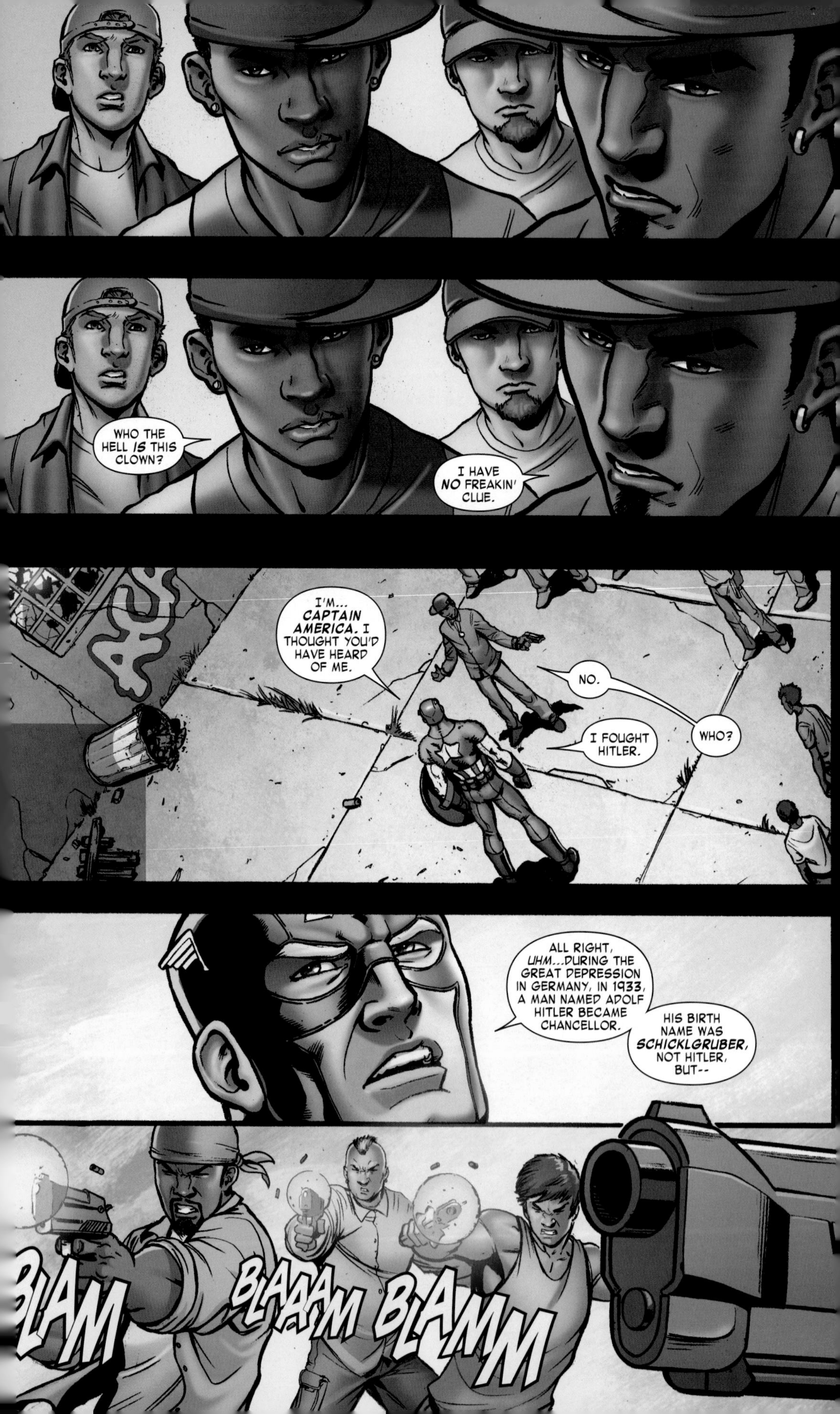
WHO THE HELL *IS* THIS CLOWN?
I HAVE *NO* FREAKIN' CLUE.
I'M... *CAPTAIN AMERICA.* I THOUGHT YOU'D HAVE HEARD OF ME.
NO.
WHO?
I FOUGHT HITLER.
ALL RIGHT, *UHM*...DURING THE GREAT DEPRESSION IN GERMANY, IN 1933, A MAN NAMED ADOLF HITLER BECAME CHANCELLOR.
HIS BIRTH NAME WAS *SCHICKLGRUBER*, NOT HITLER, BUT--
BLAM
BLAAAM
BLAMM

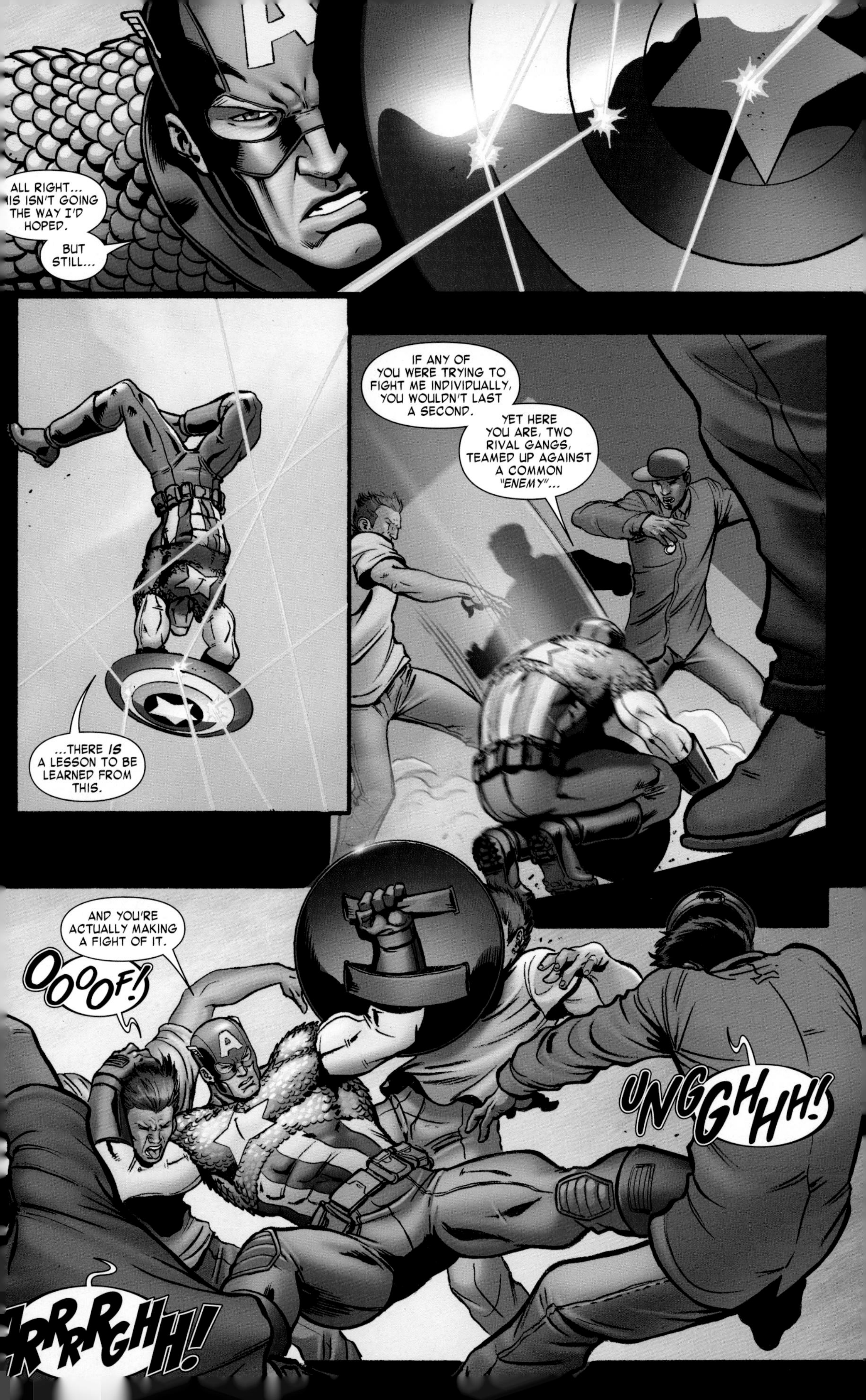
ALL RIGHT... HIS ISN'T GOING THE WAY I'D HOPED.
BUT STILL...
...THERE IS A LESSON TO BE LEARNED FROM THIS.
IF ANY OF YOU WERE TRYING TO FIGHT ME INDIVIDUALLY, YOU WOULDN'T LAST A SECOND.
YET HERE YOU ARE, TWO RIVAL GANGS, TEAMED UP AGAINST A COMMON "ENEMY"...
AND YOU'RE ACTUALLY MAKING A FIGHT OF IT.
OOOOF!
UNGGHHH!
RRRRGHH!

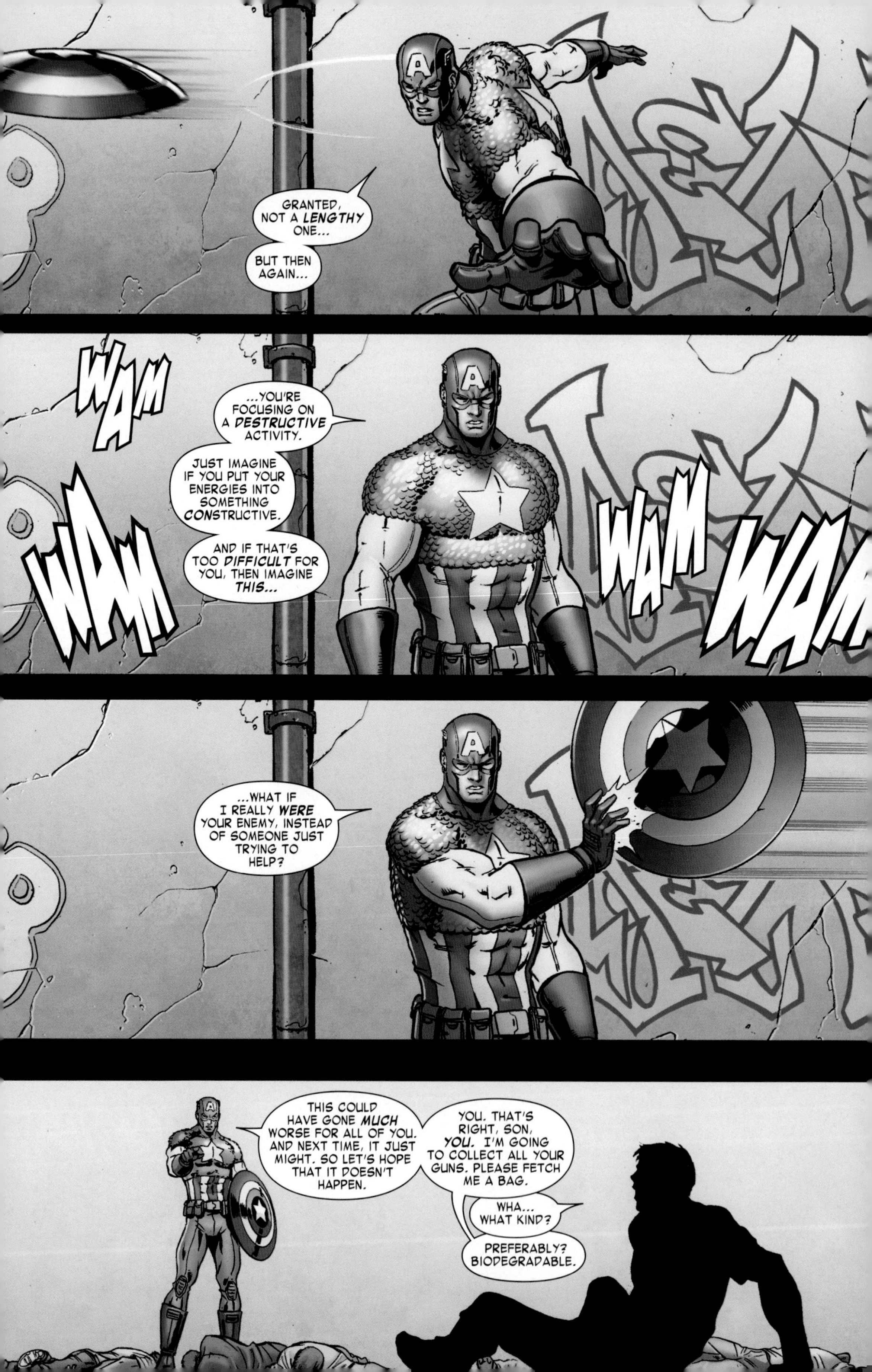
GRANTED, NOT A LENGTHY ONE...
BUT THEN AGAIN...
WAM
...YOU'RE FOCUSING ON A DESTRUCTIVE ACTIVITY.
JUST IMAGINE IF YOU PUT YOUR ENERGIES INTO SOMETHING CONSTRUCTIVE.
AND IF THAT'S TOO DIFFICULT FOR YOU, THEN IMAGINE THIS...
WAM
WAM
WAM
...WHAT IF I REALLY WERE YOUR ENEMY, INSTEAD OF SOMEONE JUST TRYING TO HELP?
THIS COULD HAVE GONE MUCH WORSE FOR ALL OF YOU. AND NEXT TIME, IT JUST MIGHT. SO LET'S HOPE THAT IT DOESN'T HAPPEN.
YOU. THAT'S RIGHT, SON, YOU. I'M GOING TO COLLECT ALL YOUR GUNS. PLEASE FETCH ME A BAG.
WHA... WHAT KIND?
PREFERABLY? BIODEGRADABLE.

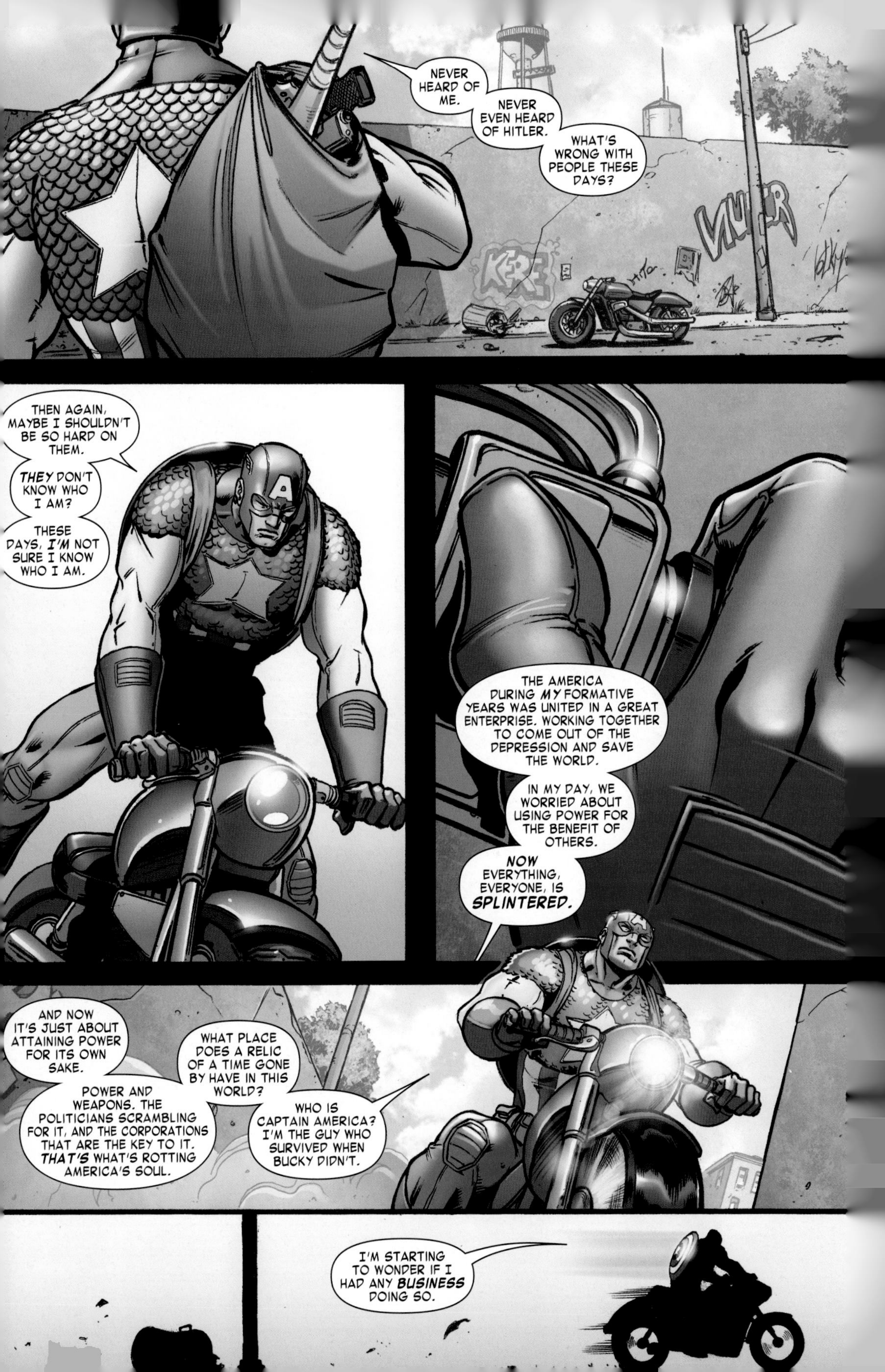
NEVER HEARD OF ME.
NEVER EVEN HEARD OF HITLER.
WHAT'S WRONG WITH PEOPLE THESE DAYS?
THEN AGAIN, MAYBE I SHOULDN'T BE SO HARD ON THEM.
THEY DON'T KNOW WHO I AM?
THESE DAYS, I'M NOT SURE I KNOW WHO I AM.
THE AMERICA DURING MY FORMATIVE YEARS WAS UNITED IN A GREAT ENTERPRISE. WORKING TOGETHER TO COME OUT OF THE DEPRESSION AND SAVE THE WORLD.
IN MY DAY, WE WORRIED ABOUT USING POWER FOR THE BENEFIT OF OTHERS.
NOW EVERYTHING, EVERYONE, IS SPLINTERED.
AND NOW IT'S JUST ABOUT ATTAINING POWER FOR ITS OWN SAKE.
POWER AND WEAPONS. THE POLITICIANS SCRAMBLING FOR IT, AND THE CORPORATIONS THAT ARE THE KEY TO IT. THAT'S WHAT'S ROTTING AMERICA'S SOUL.
WHAT PLACE DOES A RELIC OF A TIME GONE BY HAVE IN THIS WORLD?
WHO IS CAPTAIN AMERICA? I'M THE GUY WHO SURVIVED WHEN BUCKY DIDN'T.
I'M STARTING TO WONDER IF I HAD ANY BUSINESS DOING SO.

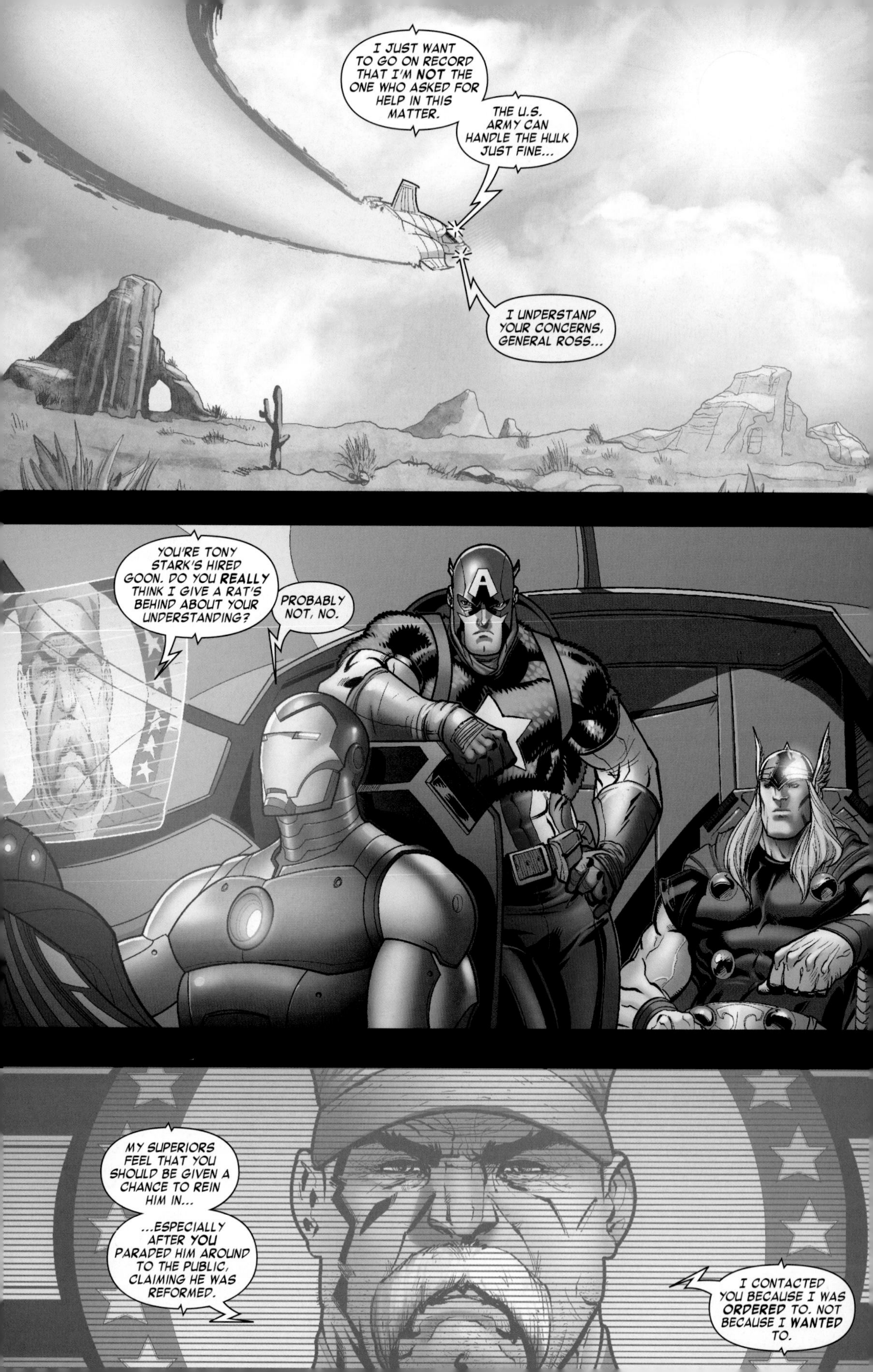
I JUST WANT TO GO ON RECORD THAT I'M NOT THE ONE WHO ASKED FOR HELP IN THIS MATTER.
THE U.S. ARMY CAN HANDLE THE HULK JUST FINE...
I UNDERSTAND YOUR CONCERNS, GENERAL ROSS...
YOU'RE TONY STARK'S HIRED GOON. DO YOU REALLY THINK I GIVE A RAT'S BEHIND ABOUT YOUR UNDERSTANDING?
PROBABLY NOT, NO.
MY SUPERIORS FEEL THAT YOU SHOULD BE GIVEN A CHANCE TO REIN HIM IN...
...ESPECIALLY AFTER YOU PARADED HIM AROUND TO THE PUBLIC, CLAIMING HE WAS REFORMED.
I CONTACTED YOU BECAUSE I WAS ORDERED TO. NOT BECAUSE I WANTED TO.

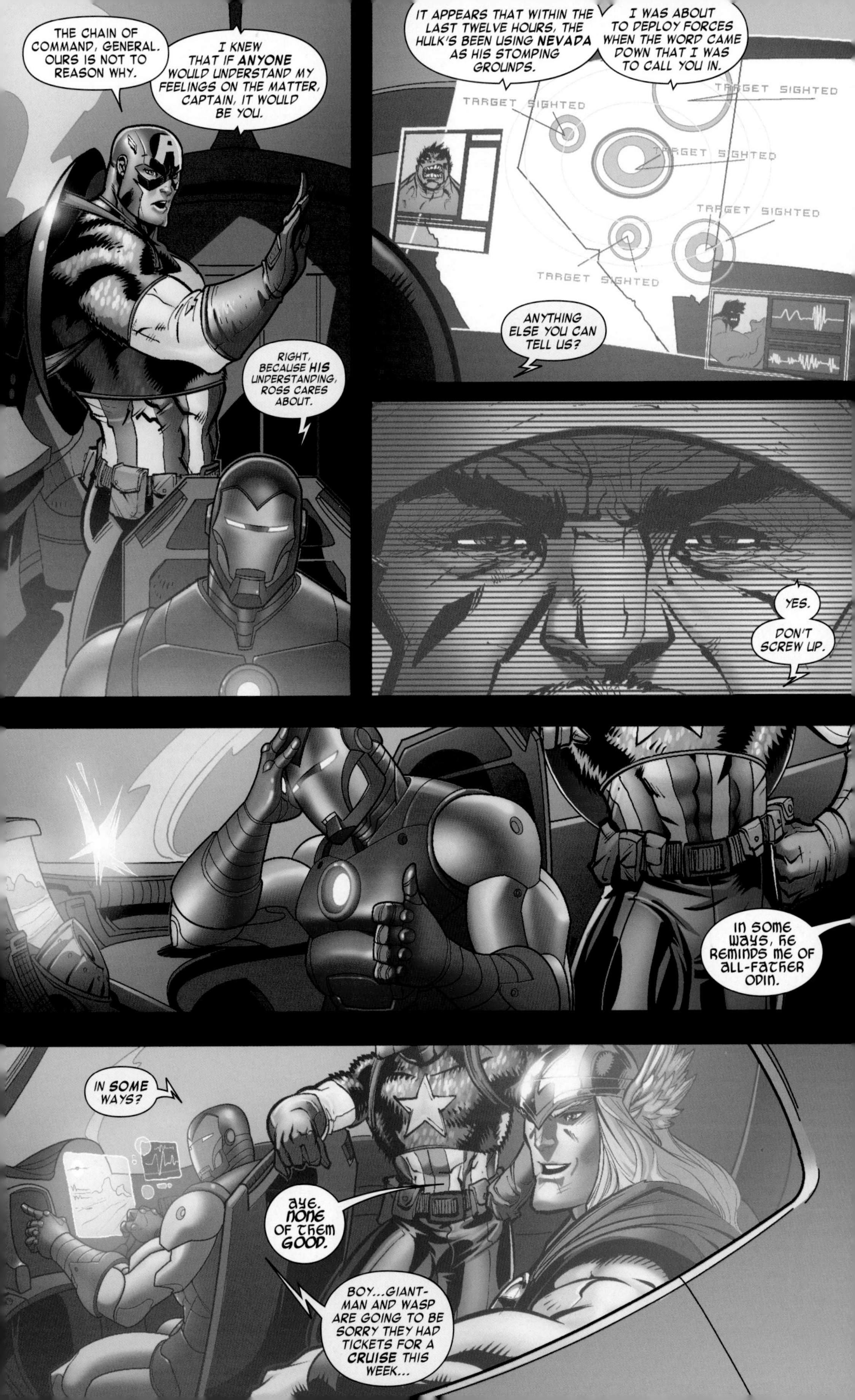
THE CHAIN OF COMMAND, GENERAL. OURS IS NOT TO REASON WHY.
I KNEW THAT IF ANYONE WOULD UNDERSTAND MY FEELINGS ON THE MATTER, CAPTAIN, IT WOULD BE YOU.
RIGHT, BECAUSE HIS UNDERSTANDING, ROSS CARES ABOUT.
IT APPEARS THAT WITHIN THE LAST TWELVE HOURS, THE HULK'S BEEN USING NEVADA AS HIS STOMPING GROUNDS.
I WAS ABOUT TO DEPLOY FORCES WHEN THE WORD CAME DOWN THAT I WAS TO CALL YOU IN.
TARGET SIGHTED
TARGET SIGHTED
TARGET SIGHTED
TARGET SIGHTED
TARGET SIGHTED
ANYTHING ELSE YOU CAN TELL US?
YES.
DON'T SCREW UP.
IN SOME WAYS, HE REMINDS ME OF ALL-FATHER ODIN.
IN SOME WAYS?
AYE. NONE OF THEM GOOD.
BOY...GIANT-MAN AND WASP ARE GOING TO BE SORRY THEY HAD TICKETS FOR A CRUISE THIS WEEK...

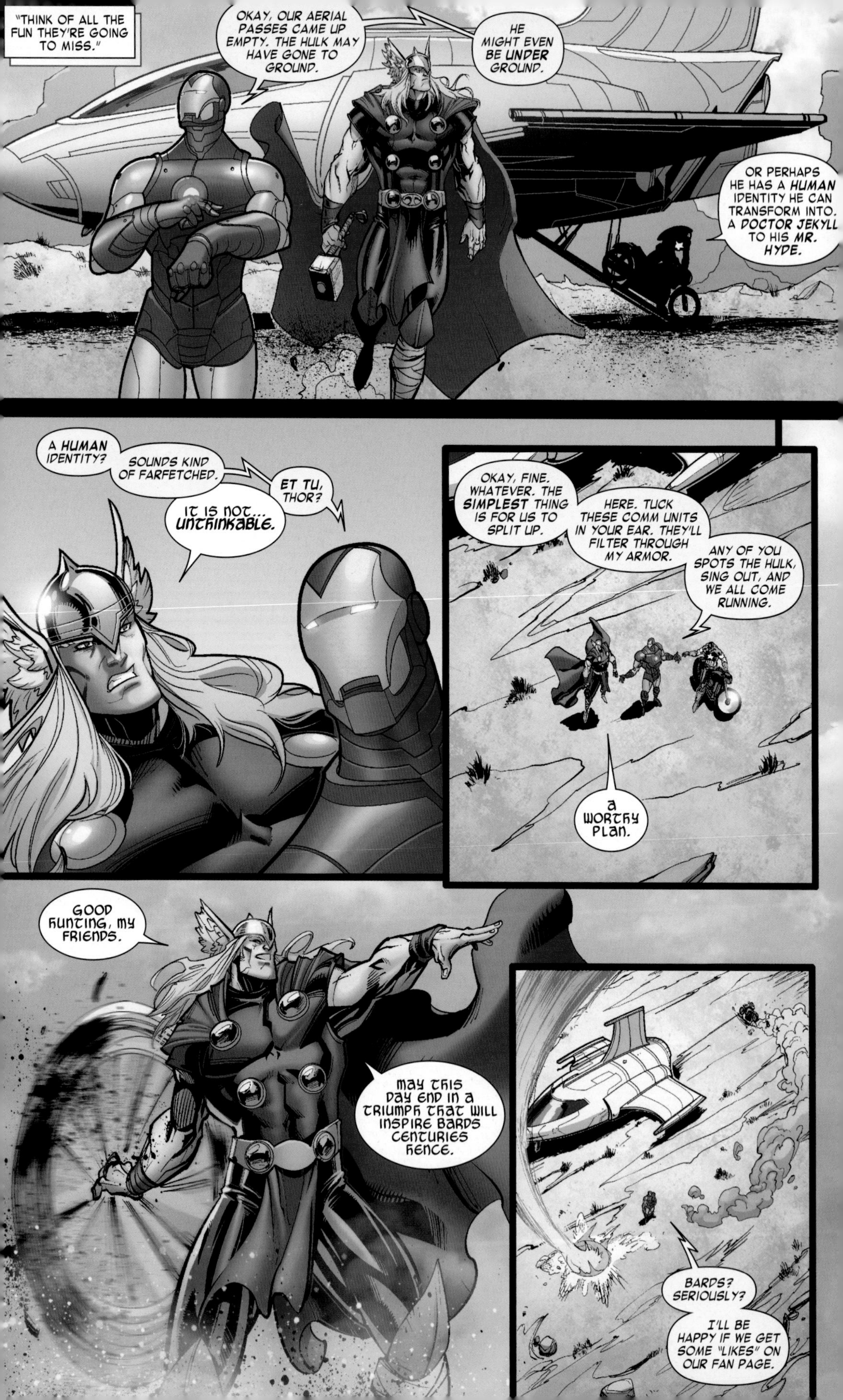
"THINK OF ALL THE FUN THEY'RE GOING TO MISS."
OKAY, OUR AERIAL PASSES CAME UP EMPTY. THE HULK MAY HAVE GONE TO GROUND.
HE MIGHT EVEN BE UNDER GROUND.
OR PERHAPS HE HAS A HUMAN IDENTITY HE CAN TRANSFORM INTO. A DOCTOR JEKYLL TO HIS MR. HYDE.
A HUMAN IDENTITY?
SOUNDS KIND OF FARFETCHED.
IT IS NOT... UNTHINKABLE.
ET TU, THOR?
OKAY, FINE. WHATEVER. THE SIMPLEST THING IS FOR US TO SPLIT UP.
HERE. TUCK THESE COMM UNITS IN YOUR EAR. THEY'LL FILTER THROUGH MY ARMOR.
ANY OF YOU SPOTS THE HULK, SING OUT, AND WE ALL COME RUNNING.
A WORTHY PLAN.
GOOD HUNTING, MY FRIENDS.
MAY THIS DAY END IN A TRIUMPH THAT WILL INSPIRE BARDS CENTURIES HENCE.
BARDS? SERIOUSLY?
I'LL BE HAPPY IF WE GET SOME "LIKES" ON OUR FAN PAGE.

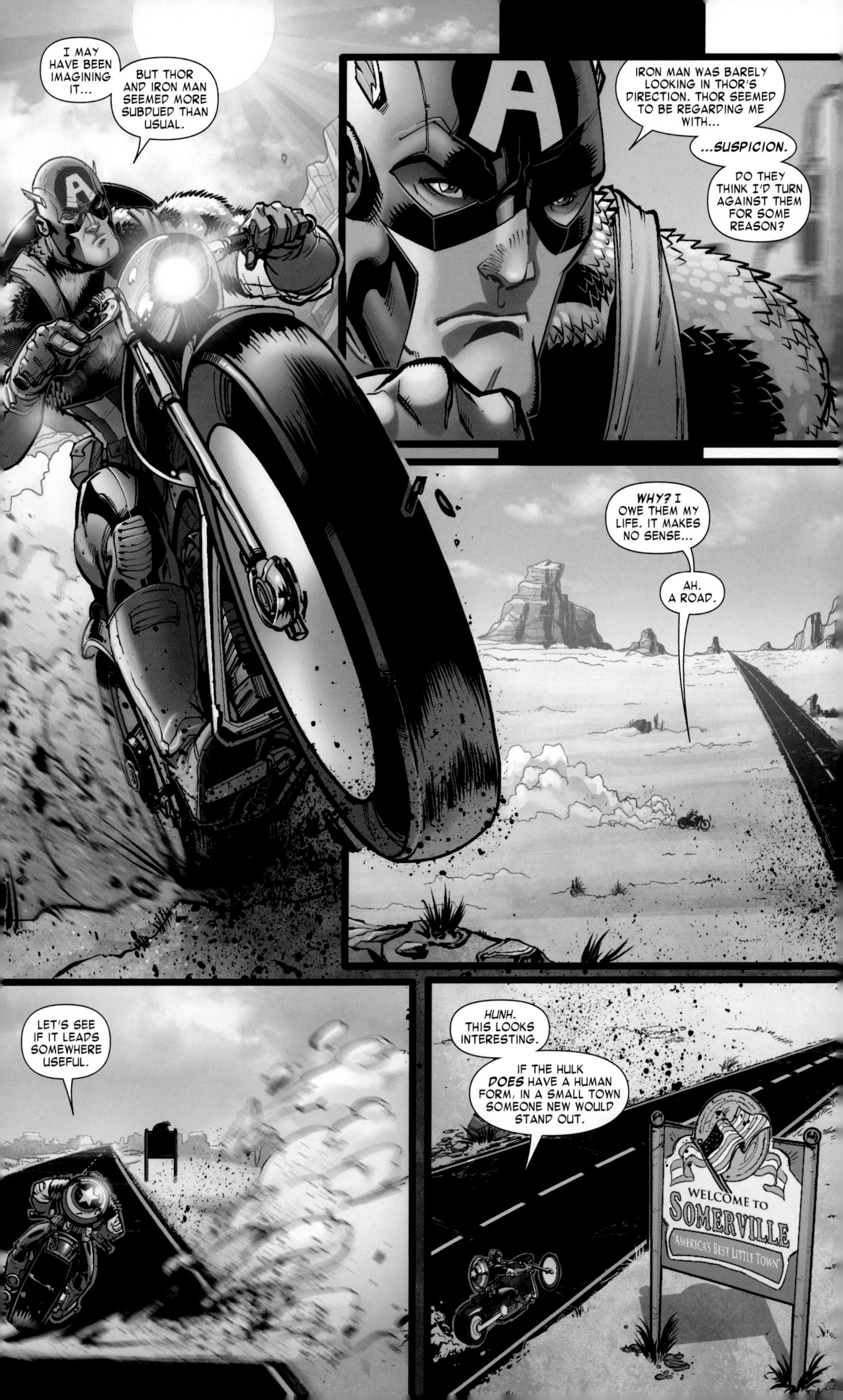

I MAY HAVE BEEN IMAGINING IT...
BUT THOR AND IRON MAN SEEMED MORE SUBDUED THAN USUAL.
IRON MAN WAS BARELY LOOKING IN THOR'S DIRECTION. THOR SEEMED TO BE REGARDING ME WITH...
...SUSPICION.
DO THEY THINK I'D TURN AGAINST THEM FOR SOME REASON?
WHY? I OWE THEM MY LIFE. IT MAKES NO SENSE...
AH. A ROAD.
LET'S SEE IF IT LEADS SOMEWHERE USEFUL.
HUNH. THIS LOOKS INTERESTING.
IF THE HULK DOES HAVE A HUMAN FORM, IN A SMALL TOWN SOMEONE NEW WOULD STAND OUT.
WELCOME TO
SOMERVILLE
AMERICA'S BEST LITTLE TOWN

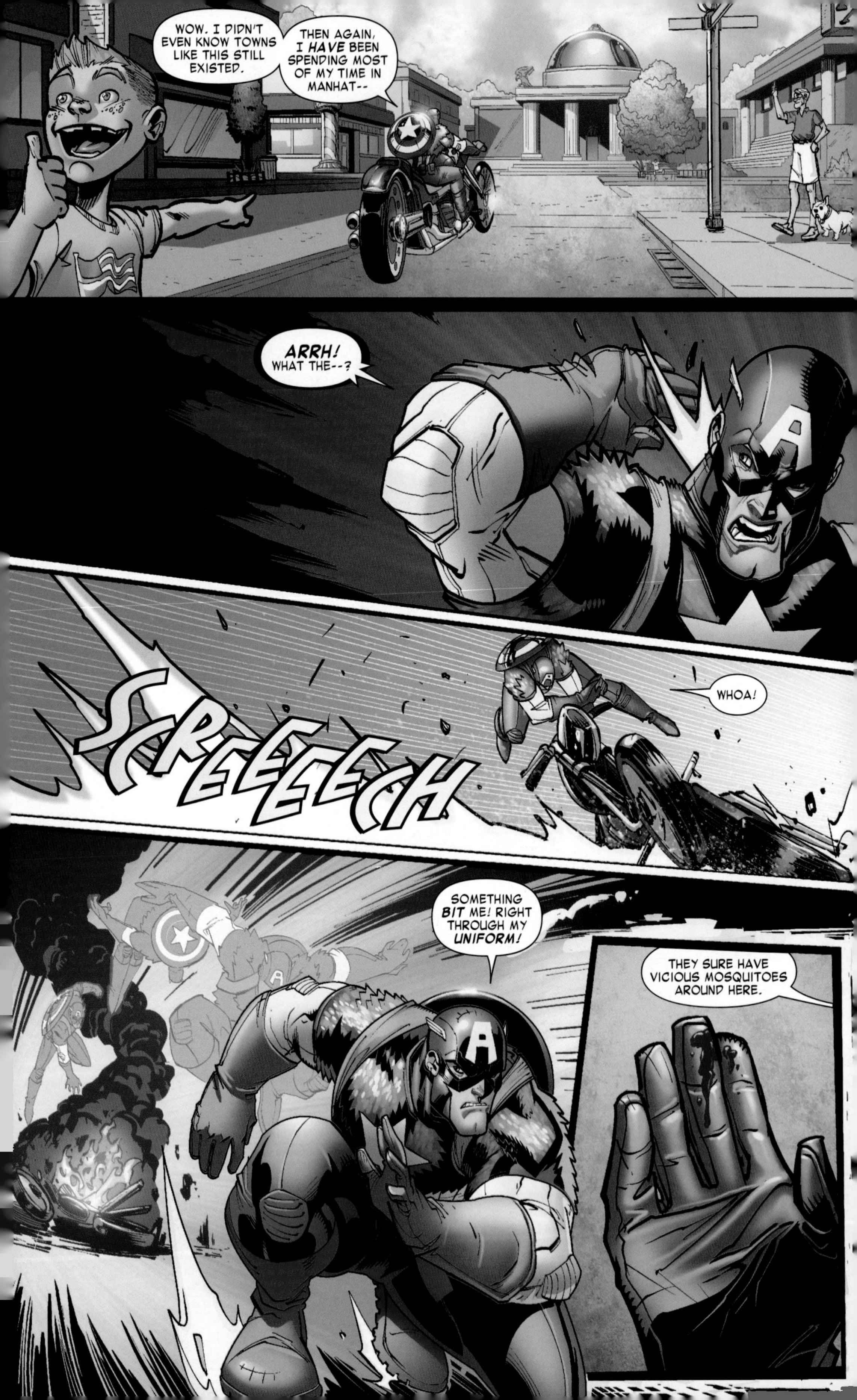
WOW. I DIDN'T EVEN KNOW TOWNS LIKE THIS STILL EXISTED.
THEN AGAIN, I *HAVE* BEEN SPENDING MOST OF MY TIME IN MANHAT--
ARRH! WHAT THE--?
SCREEEECH
WHOA!
SOMETHING ***BIT*** ME! RIGHT THROUGH MY ***UNIFORM!***
THEY SURE HAVE VICIOUS MOSQUITOES AROUND HERE.

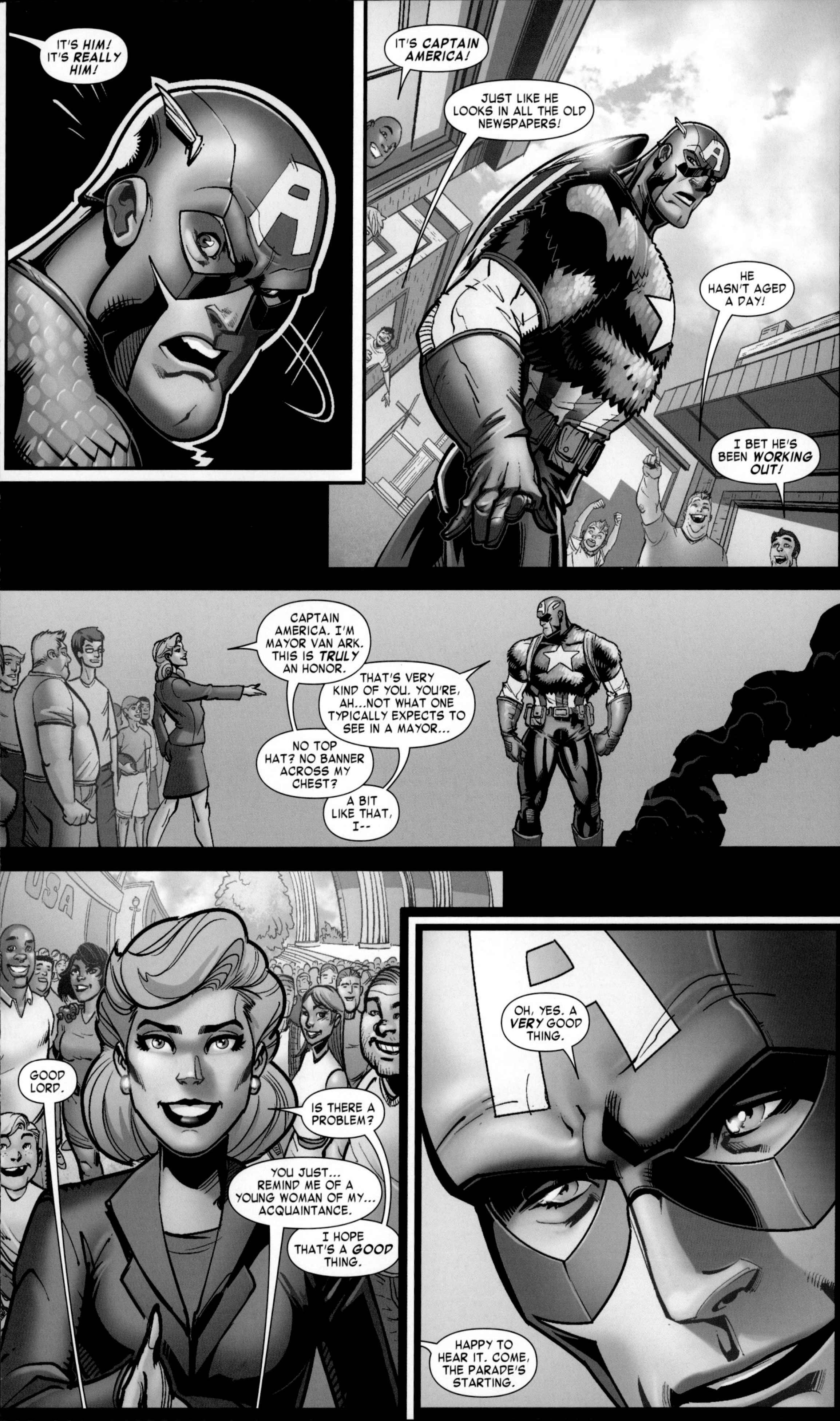
IT'S HIM! IT'S REALLY HIM!
IT'S CAPTAIN AMERICA!
JUST LIKE HE LOOKS IN ALL THE OLD NEWSPAPERS!
HE HASN'T AGED A DAY!
I BET HE'S BEEN WORKING OUT!
CAPTAIN AMERICA. I'M MAYOR VAN ARK. THIS IS TRULY AN HONOR.
THAT'S VERY KIND OF YOU. YOU'RE, AH...NOT WHAT ONE TYPICALLY EXPECTS TO SEE IN A MAYOR...
NO TOP HAT? NO BANNER ACROSS MY CHEST?
A BIT LIKE THAT, I--
GOOD LORD.
IS THERE A PROBLEM?
YOU JUST... REMIND ME OF A YOUNG WOMAN OF MY... ACQUAINTANCE.
I HOPE THAT'S A GOOD THING.
OH, YES. A VERY GOOD THING.
HAPPY TO HEAR IT. COME, THE PARADE'S STARTING.

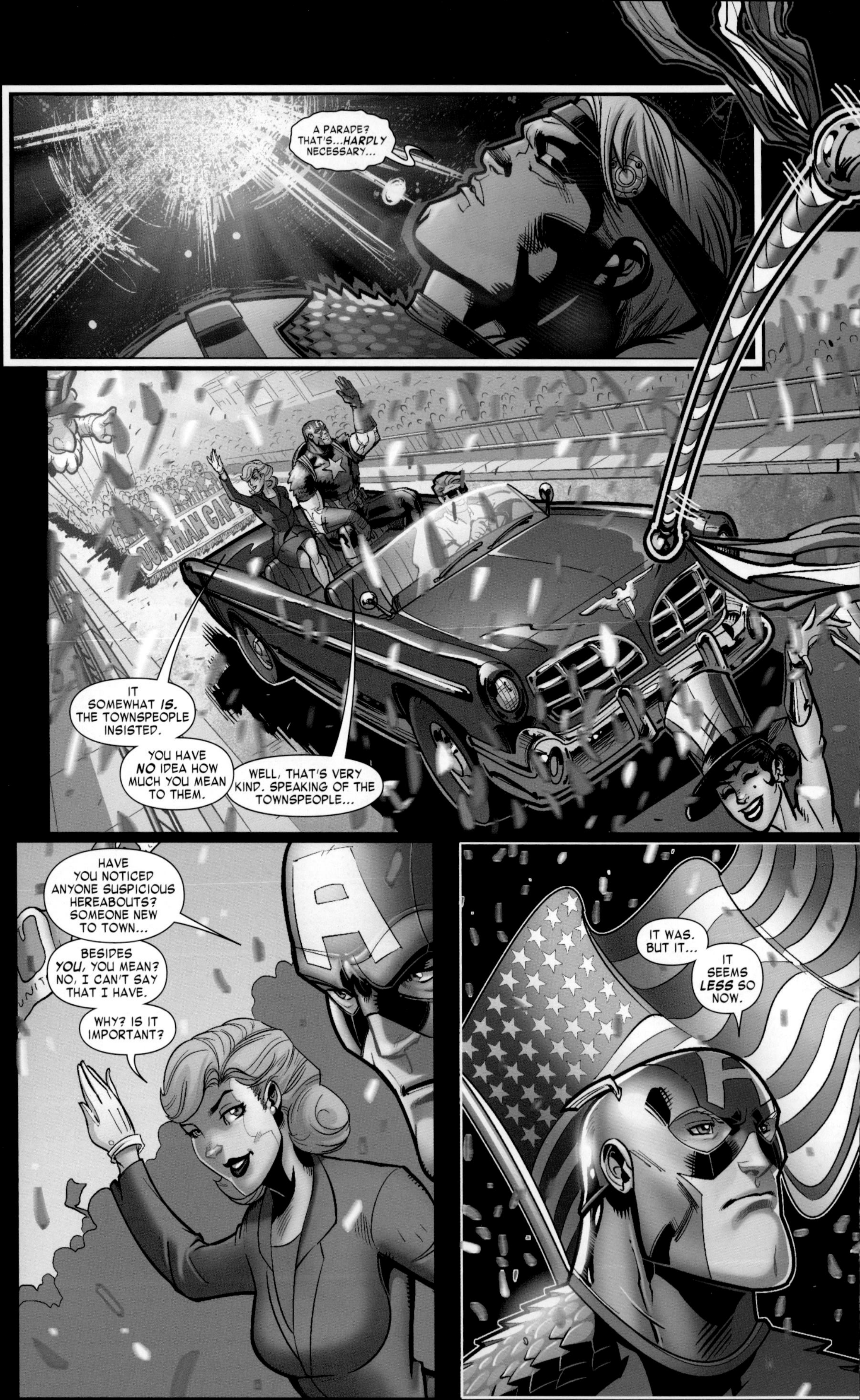
A PARADE? THAT'S...HARDLY NECESSARY...
IT SOMEWHAT IS. THE TOWNSPEOPLE INSISTED.
YOU HAVE NO IDEA HOW MUCH YOU MEAN TO THEM.
WELL, THAT'S VERY KIND. SPEAKING OF THE TOWNSPEOPLE...
HAVE YOU NOTICED ANYONE SUSPICIOUS HEREABOUTS? SOMEONE NEW TO TOWN...
BESIDES YOU, YOU MEAN? NO, I CAN'T SAY THAT I HAVE.
WHY? IS IT IMPORTANT?
IT WAS. BUT IT...
IT SEEMS LESS SO NOW.

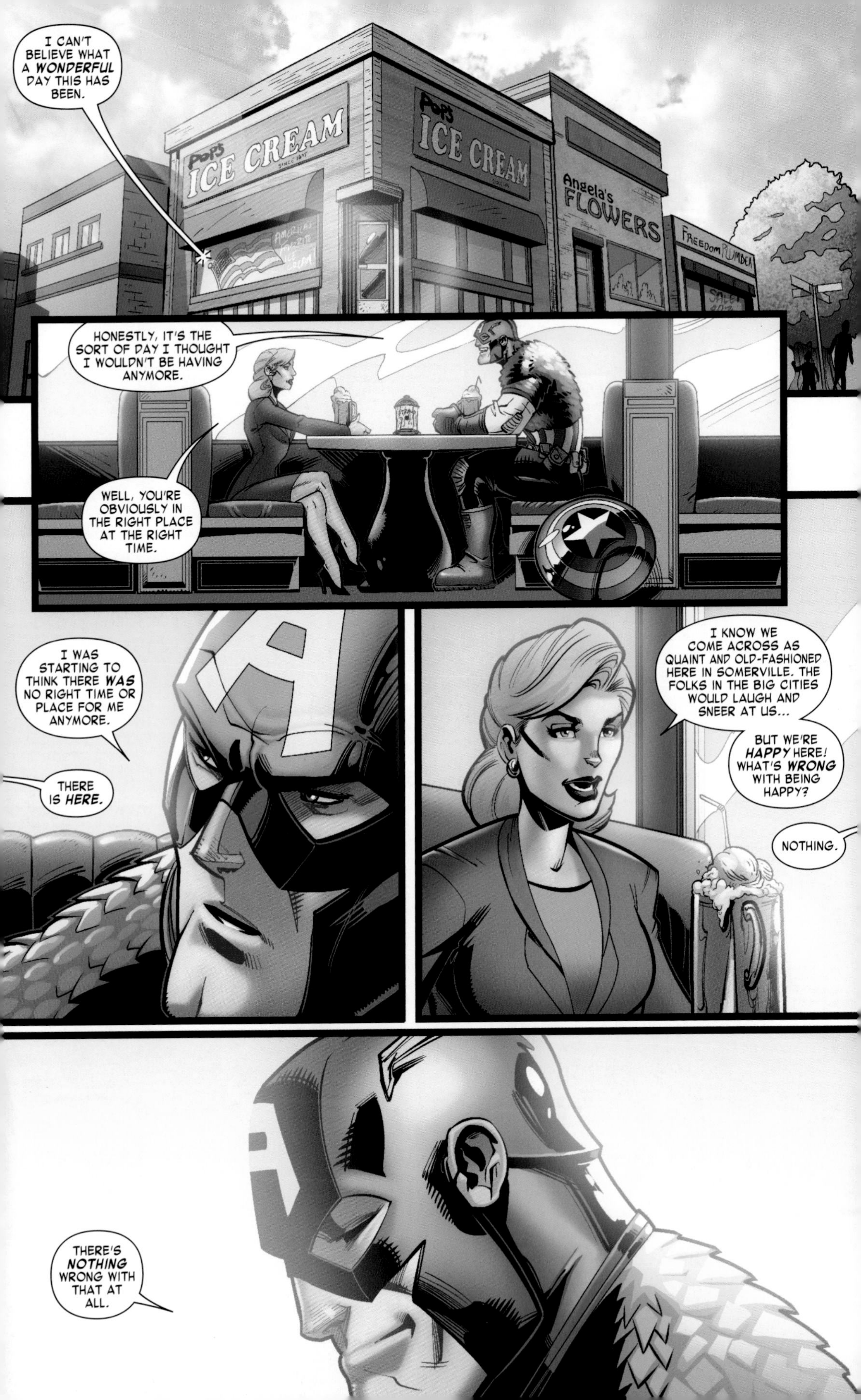
POP'S ICE CREAM
POP'S ICE CREAM
Angela's FLOWERS
FREEDOM PLUMBER
I CAN'T BELIEVE WHAT A WONDERFUL DAY THIS HAS BEEN.
HONESTLY, IT'S THE SORT OF DAY I THOUGHT I WOULDN'T BE HAVING ANYMORE.
WELL, YOU'RE OBVIOUSLY IN THE RIGHT PLACE AT THE RIGHT TIME.
I WAS STARTING TO THINK THERE WAS NO RIGHT TIME OR PLACE FOR ME ANYMORE.
THERE IS HERE.
I KNOW WE COME ACROSS AS QUAINT AND OLD-FASHIONED HERE IN SOMERVILLE. THE FOLKS IN THE BIG CITIES WOULD LAUGH AND SNEER AT US...
BUT WE'RE HAPPY HERE! WHAT'S WRONG WITH BEING HAPPY?
NOTHING.
THERE'S NOTHING WRONG WITH THAT AT ALL.

I KNOW IT'S NOT RIGHT OF ME TO ASK. YOU BELONG TO THE WORLD.

BUT IF YOU WOULD EVER CONSIDER MAKING SOMERVILLE YOUR HOME... IF YOU COULD MAKE THAT JUMP TO HAPPINESS...

JUMP...

YES. A--

JUMP...LIKE THE *HULK*...

I DON'T--?

I WAS... LOOKING FOR THE HULK... WASN'T I?

I DON'T RECALL YOU MENTIONING--

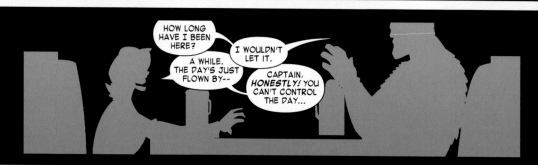

HOW LONG HAVE I BEEN HERE?

A WHILE. THE DAY'S JUST FLOWN BY--

I WOULDN'T LET IT.

CAPTAIN, *HONESTLY!* YOU CAN'T CONTROL THE DAY...

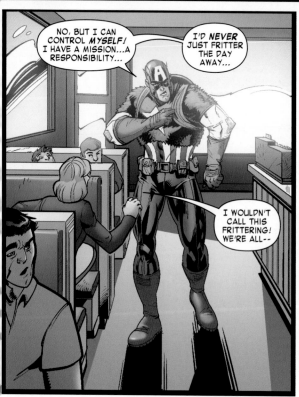

NO, BUT I CAN CONTROL *MYSELF!* I HAVE A MISSION...A RESPONSIBILITY...

I'D *NEVER* JUST FRITTER THE DAY AWAY...

I WOULDN'T CALL THIS FRITTERING! WE'RE ALL--

YOU'RE ALL *WHAT? WHAT* ARE YOU? *WHO* ARE YOU?

YOU'RE HURTING ME!

I'LL DO MORE THAN THA UNLESS YOU--

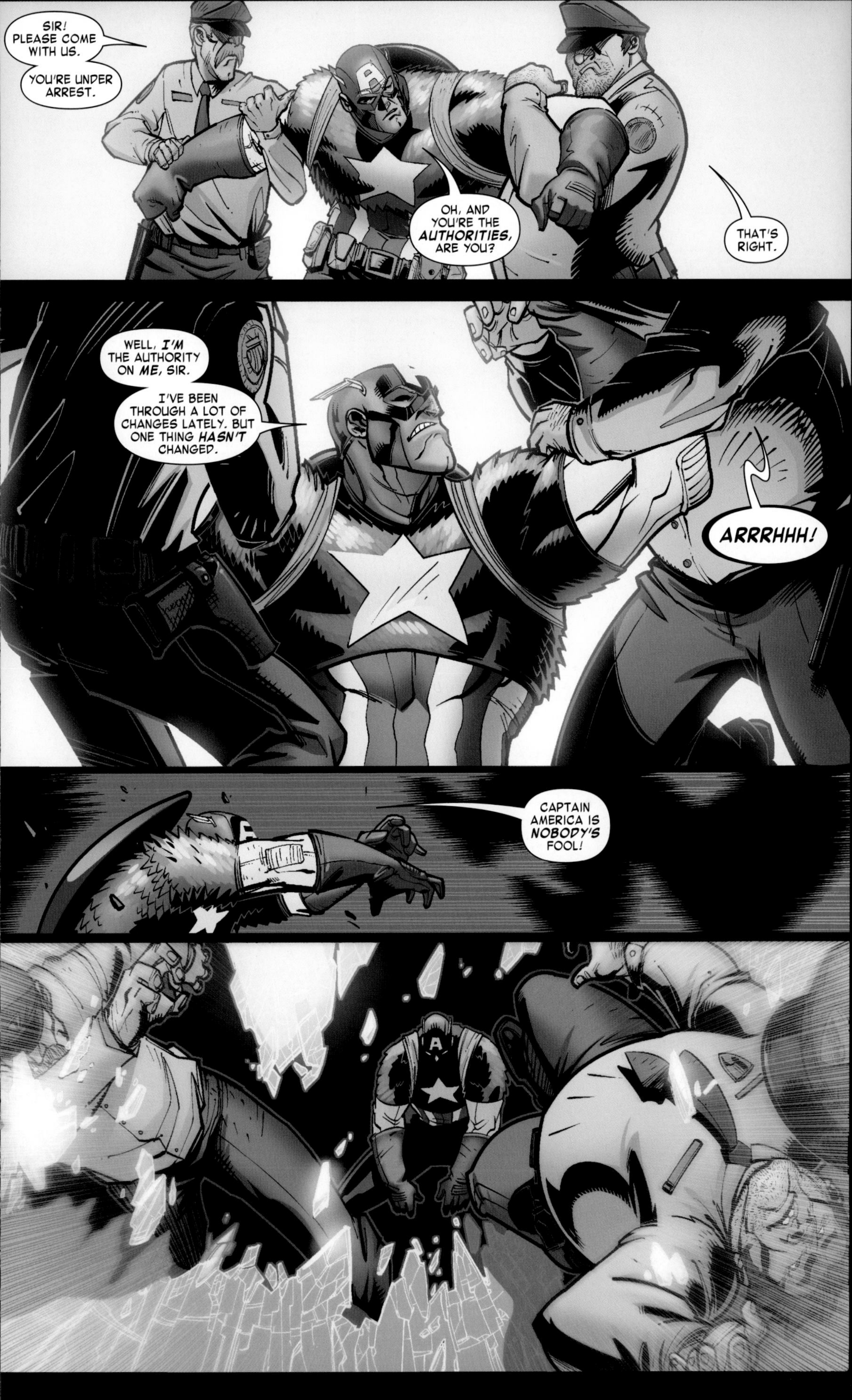
SIR! PLEASE COME WITH US.
YOU'RE UNDER ARREST.
OH, AND YOU'RE THE AUTHORITIES, ARE YOU?
THAT'S RIGHT.
WELL, I'M THE AUTHORITY ON ME, SIR.
I'VE BEEN THROUGH A LOT OF CHANGES LATELY. BUT ONE THING HASN'T CHANGED.
ARRRHHH!
CAPTAIN AMERICA IS NOBODY'S FOOL!

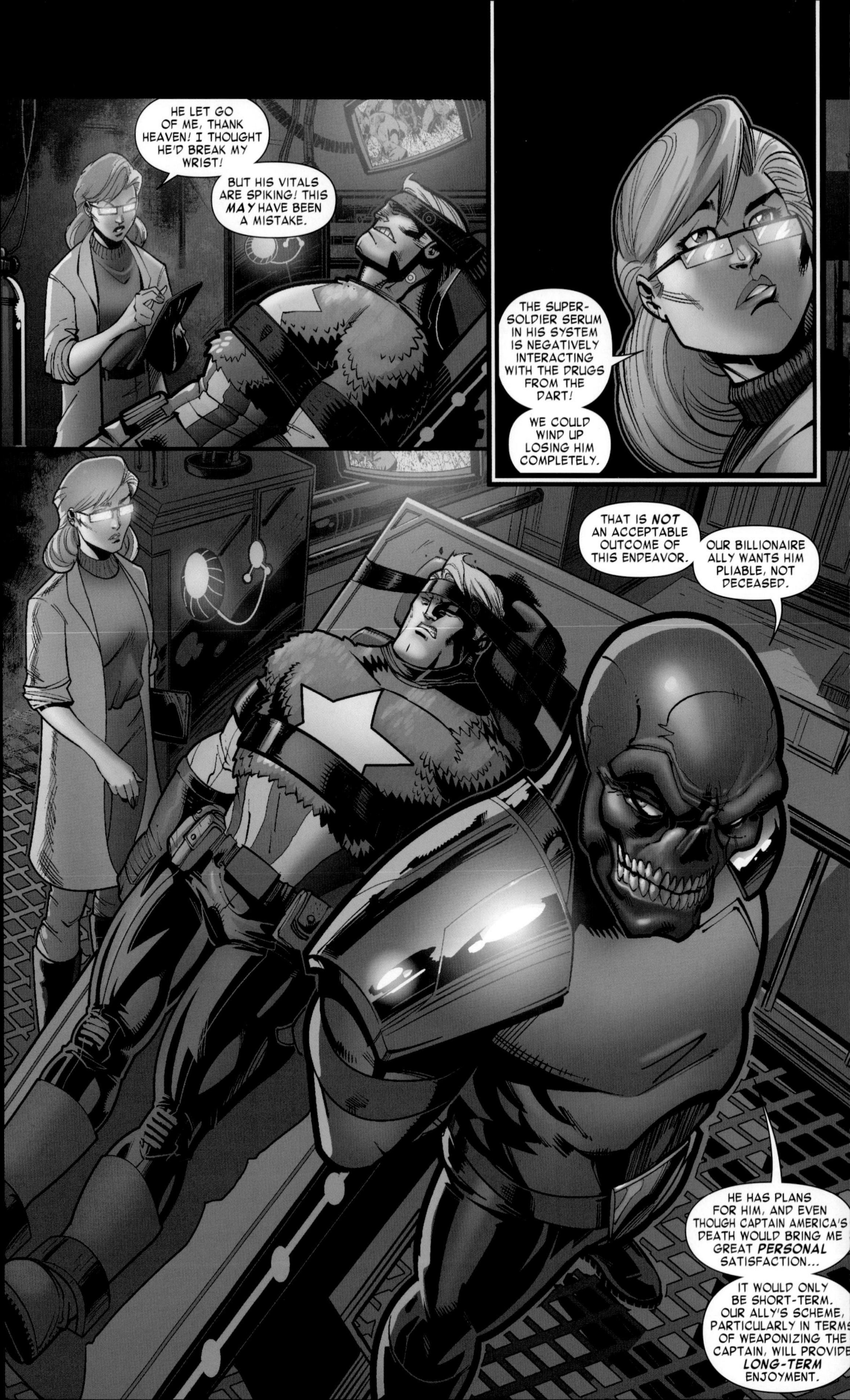
HE LET GO OF ME, THANK HEAVEN! I THOUGHT HE'D BREAK MY WRIST!
BUT HIS VITALS ARE SPIKING! THIS *MAY* HAVE BEEN A MISTAKE.
THE SUPER-SOLDIER SERUM IN HIS SYSTEM IS NEGATIVELY INTERACTING WITH THE DRUGS FROM THE DART!
WE COULD WIND UP LOSING HIM COMPLETELY.
THAT IS *NOT* AN ACCEPTABLE OUTCOME OF THIS ENDEAVOR.
OUR BILLIONAIRE ALLY WANTS HIM PLIABLE, NOT DECEASED.
HE HAS PLANS FOR HIM, AND EVEN THOUGH CAPTAIN AMERICA'S DEATH WOULD BRING ME GREAT *PERSONAL* SATISFACTION...
IT WOULD ONLY BE SHORT-TERM. OUR ALLY'S SCHEME, PARTICULARLY IN TERMS OF WEAPONIZING THE CAPTAIN, WILL PROVIDE *LONG-TERM* ENJOYMENT.

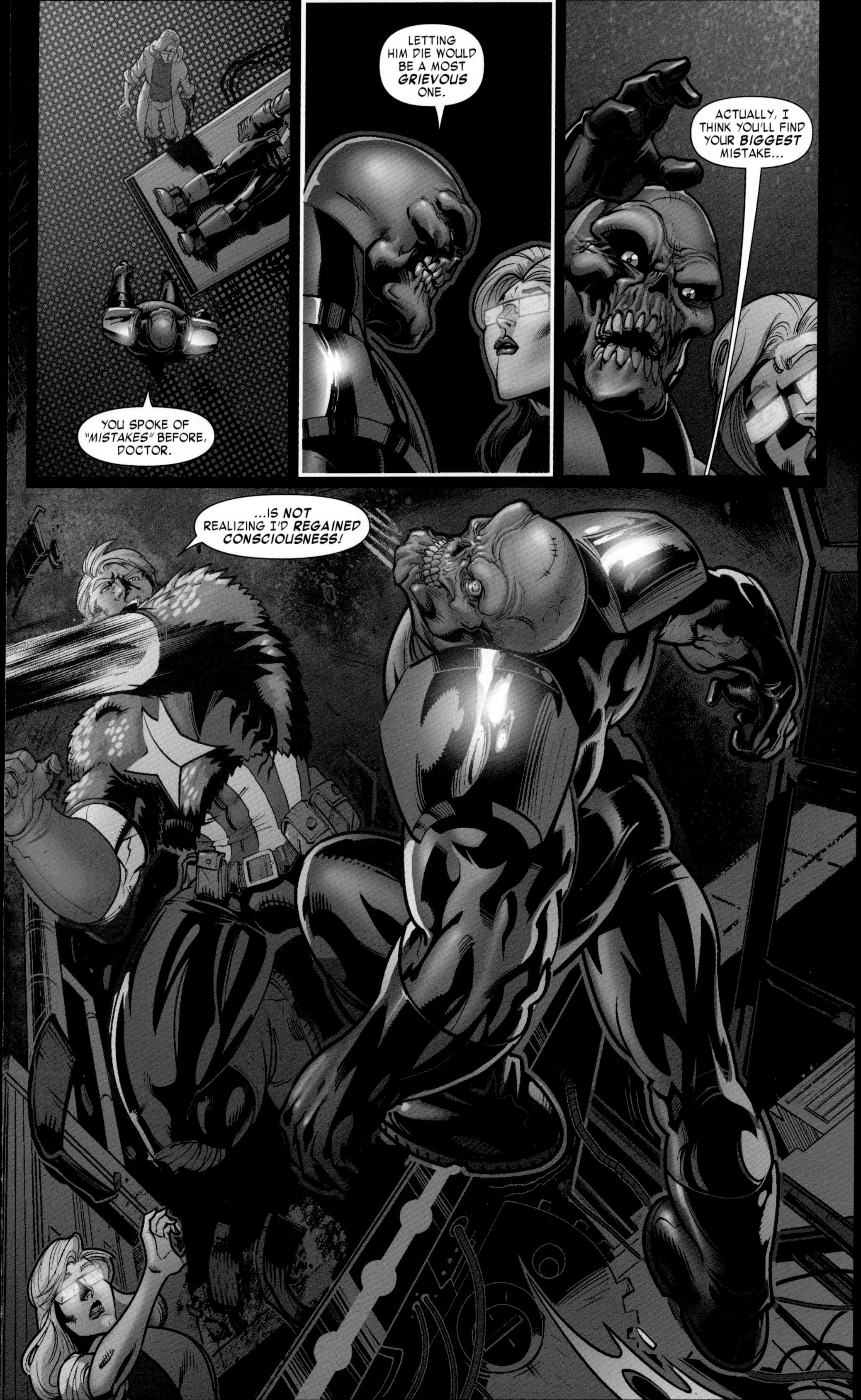
YOU SPOKE OF "MISTAKES" BEFORE, DOCTOR.
LETTING HIM DIE WOULD BE A MOST GRIEVOUS ONE.
ACTUALLY, I THINK YOU'LL FIND YOUR BIGGEST MISTAKE...
...IS NOT REALIZING I'D REGAINED CONSCIOUSNESS!

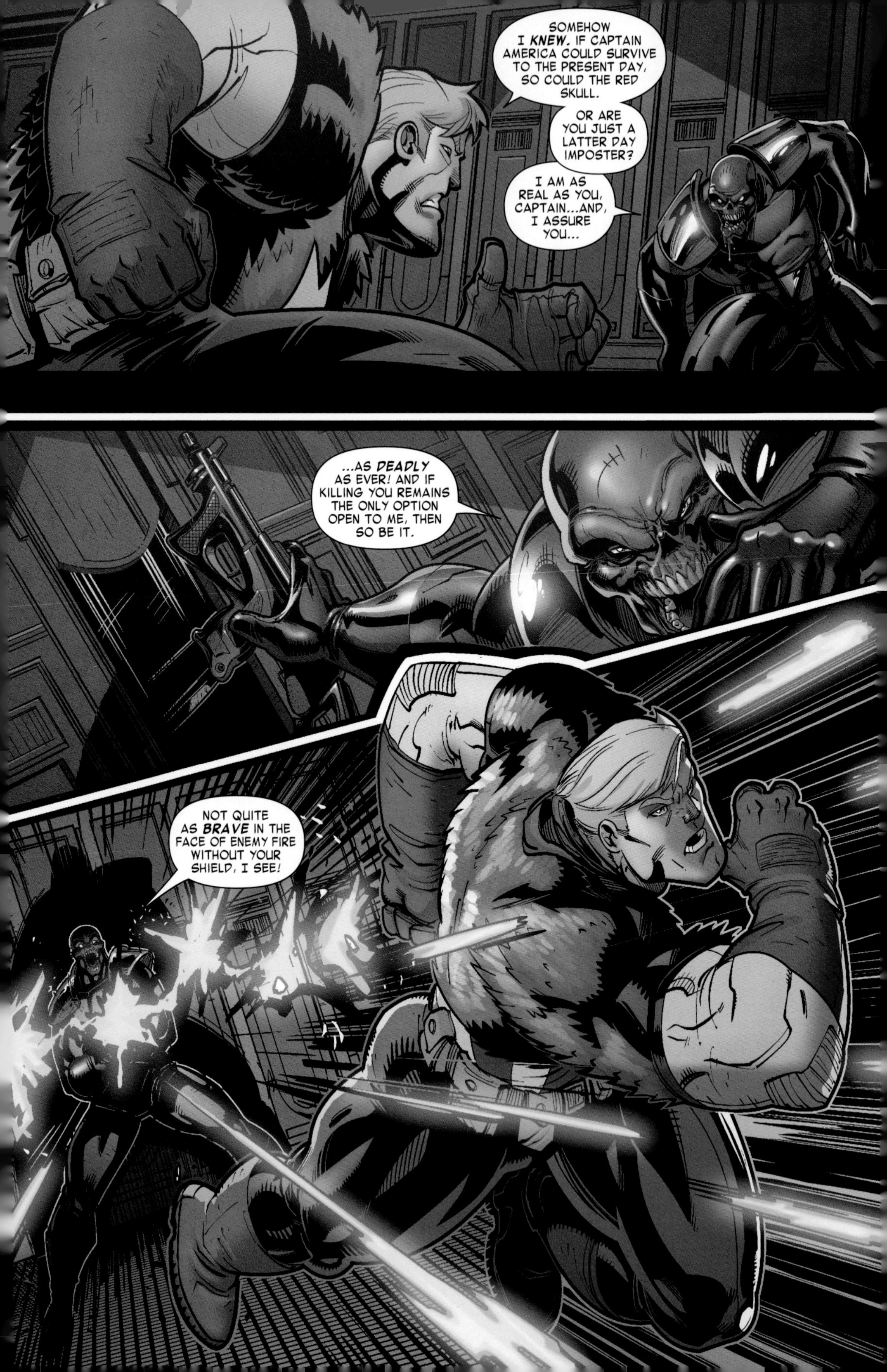
SOMEHOW I KNEW. IF CAPTAIN AMERICA COULD SURVIVE TO THE PRESENT DAY, SO COULD THE RED SKULL.
OR ARE YOU JUST A LATTER DAY IMPOSTER?
I AM AS REAL AS YOU, CAPTAIN...AND, I ASSURE YOU...
...AS DEADLY AS EVER! AND IF KILLING YOU REMAINS THE ONLY OPTION OPEN TO ME, THEN SO BE IT.
NOT QUITE AS BRAVE IN THE FACE OF ENEMY FIRE WITHOUT YOUR SHIELD, I SEE!

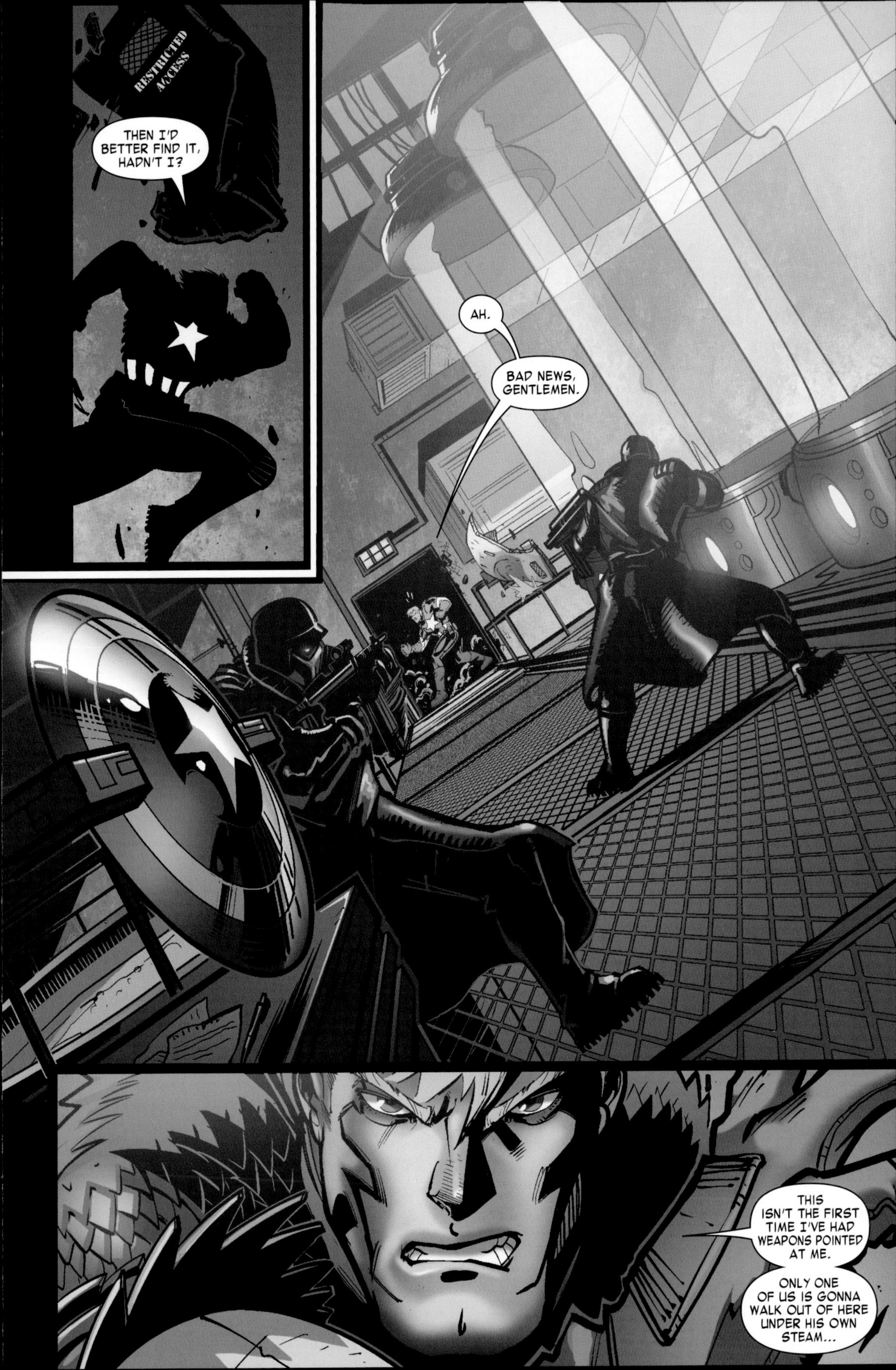
RESTRICTED ACCESS
THEN I'D BETTER FIND IT, HADN'T I?
AH.
BAD NEWS, GENTLEMEN.
THIS ISN'T THE FIRST TIME I'VE HAD WEAPONS POINTED AT ME.
ONLY ONE OF US IS GONNA WALK OUT OF HERE UNDER HIS OWN STEAM...

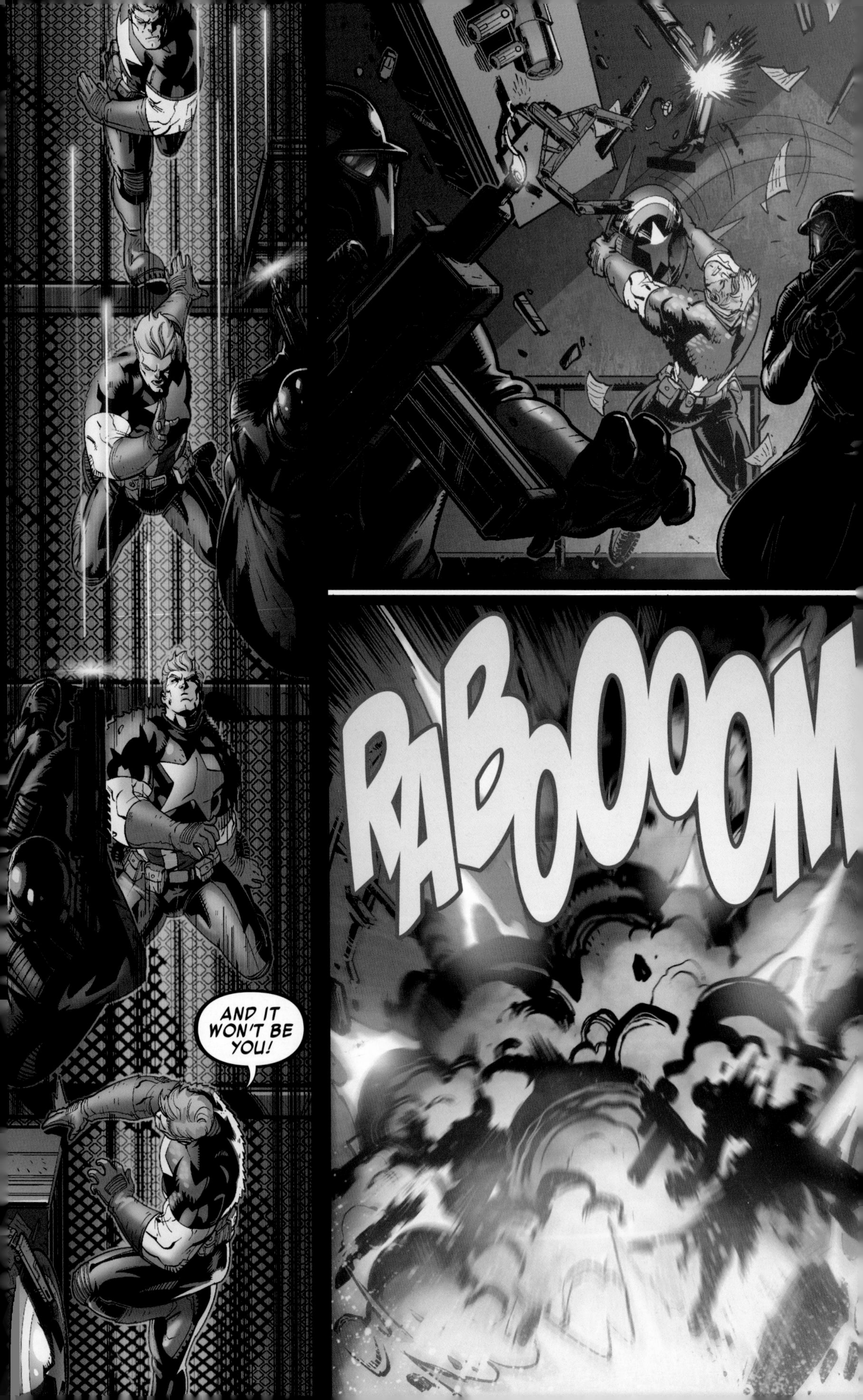
AND IT WON'T BE YOU!
RABOOOOM

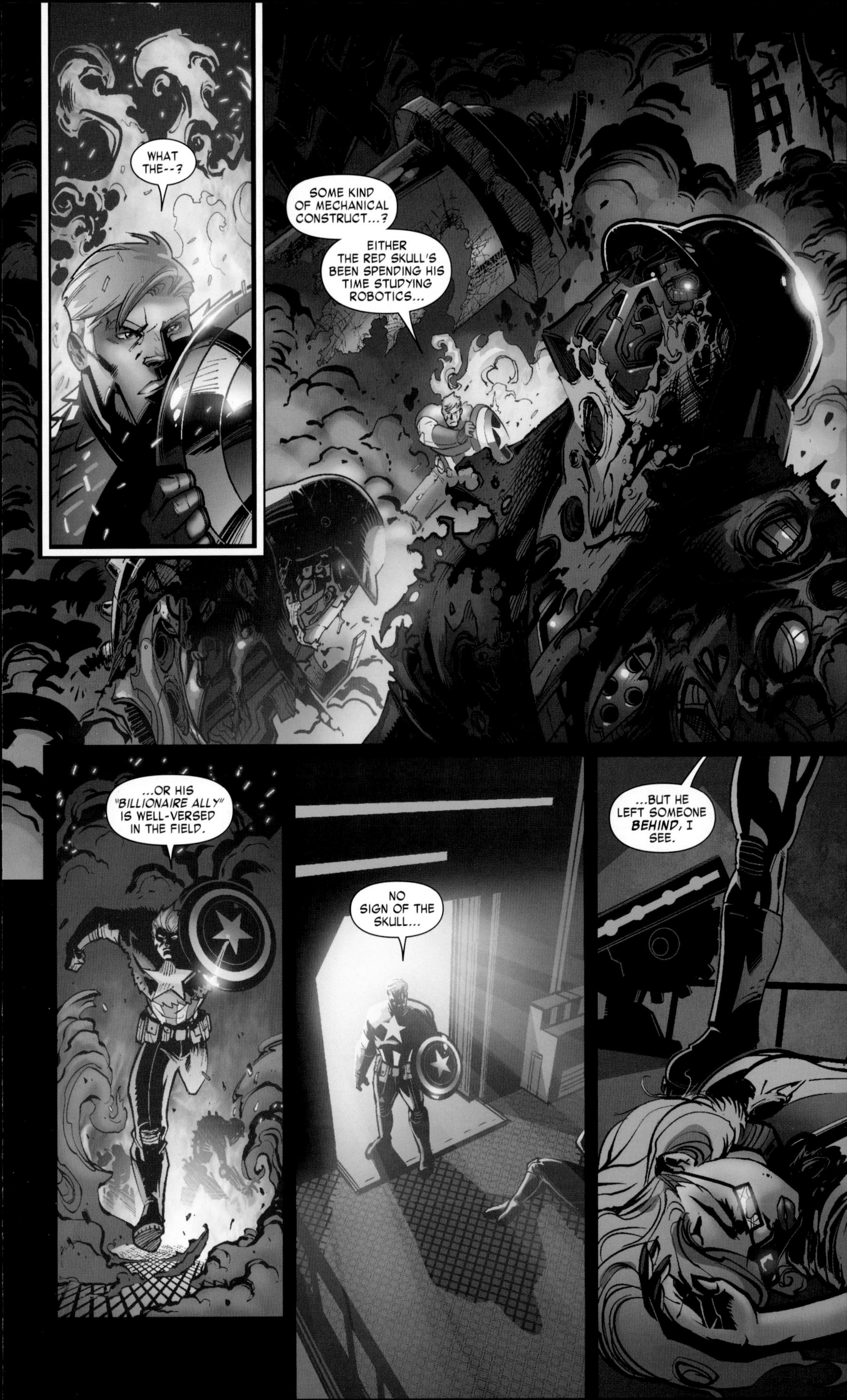
WHAT THE--?
SOME KIND OF MECHANICAL CONSTRUCT...?
EITHER THE RED SKULL'S BEEN SPENDING HIS TIME STUDYING ROBOTICS...
...OR HIS "BILLIONAIRE ALLY" IS WELL-VERSED IN THE FIELD.
NO SIGN OF THE SKULL...
...BUT HE LEFT SOMEONE BEHIND, I SEE.

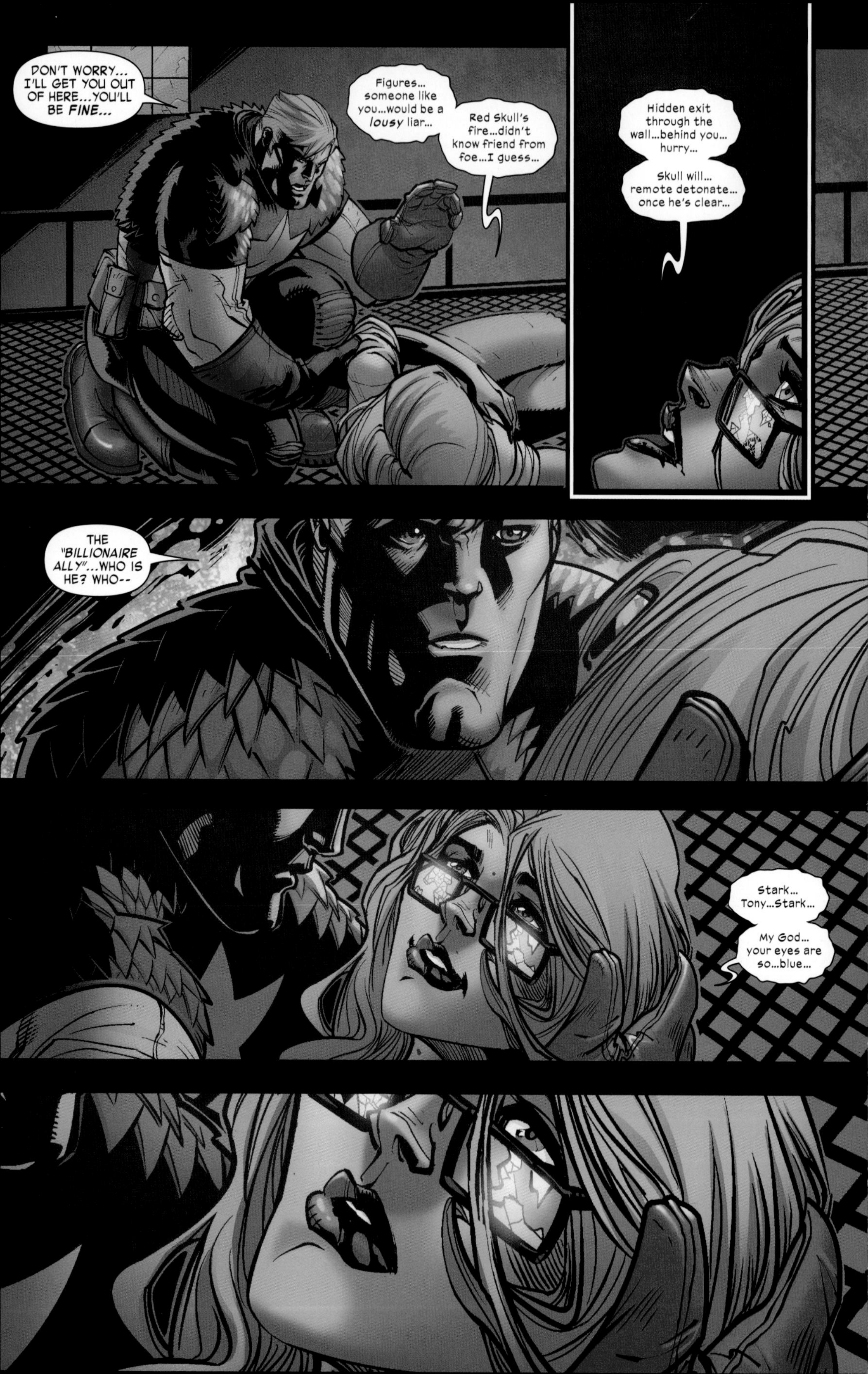
DON'T WORRY... I'LL GET YOU OUT OF HERE...YOU'LL BE FINE...
Figures... someone like you...would be a lousy liar...
Red Skull's fire...didn't know friend from foe...I guess...
Hidden exit through the wall...behind you... hurry...
Skull will... remote detonate... once he's clear...
THE "BILLIONAIRE ALLY"...WHO IS HE? WHO--
Stark... Tony...Stark...
My God... your eyes are so...blue...

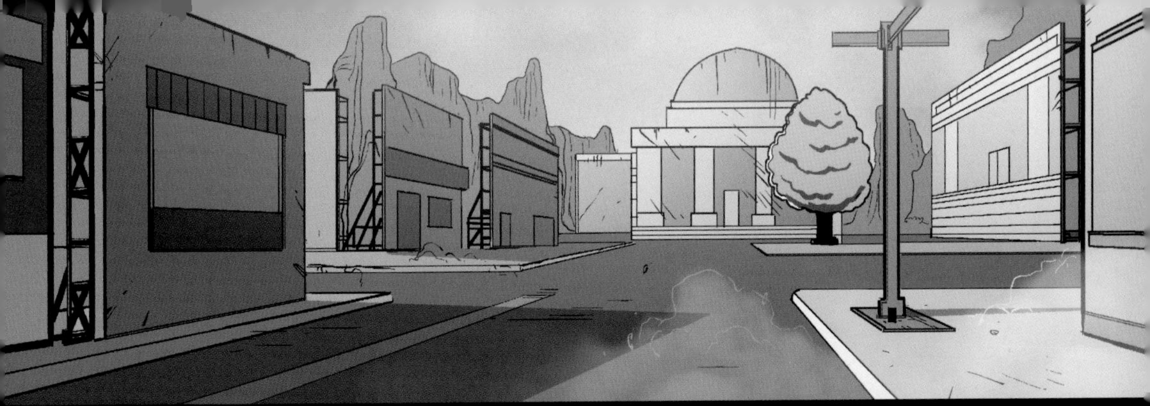

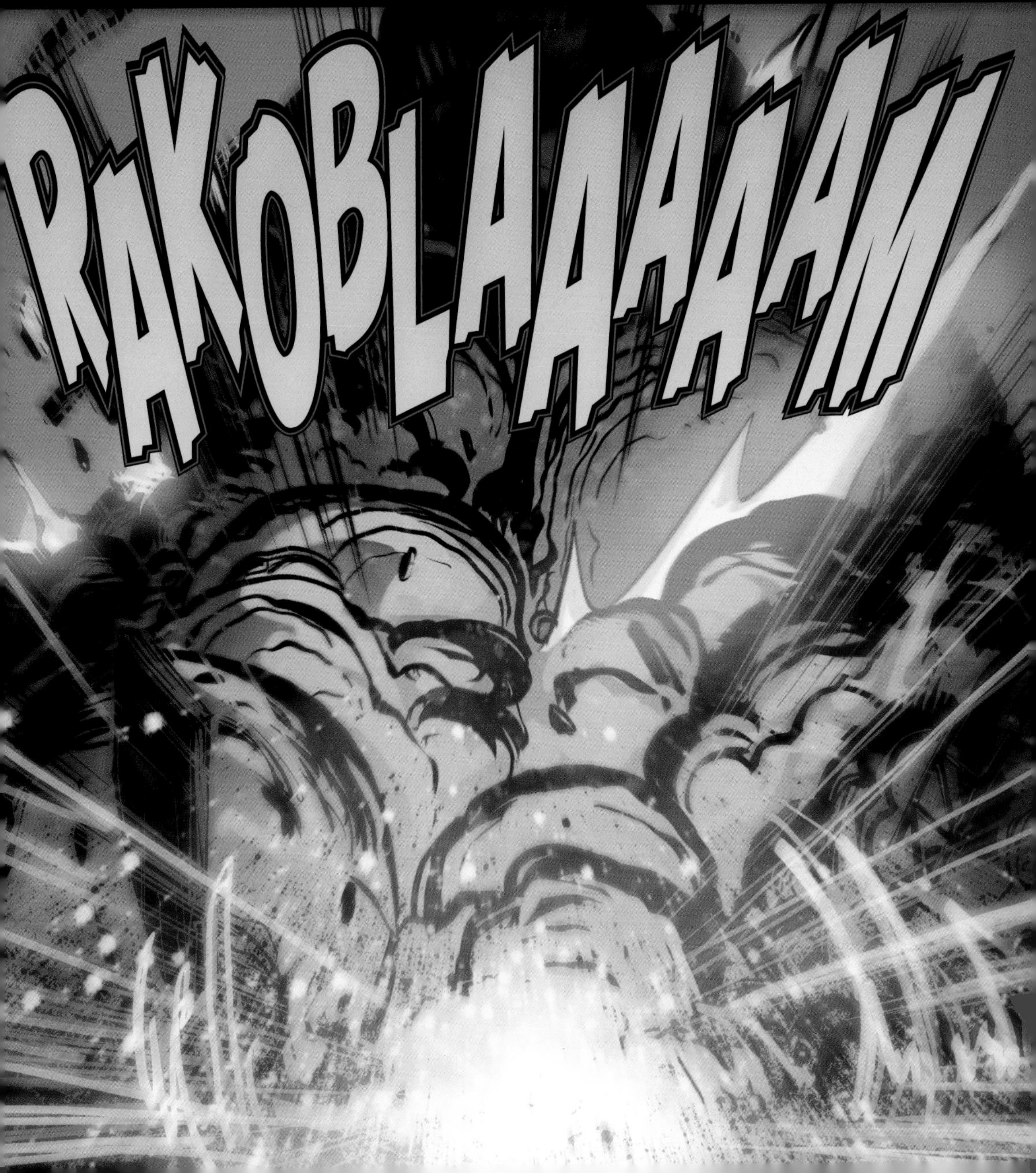
RAKOBLAAAAAM

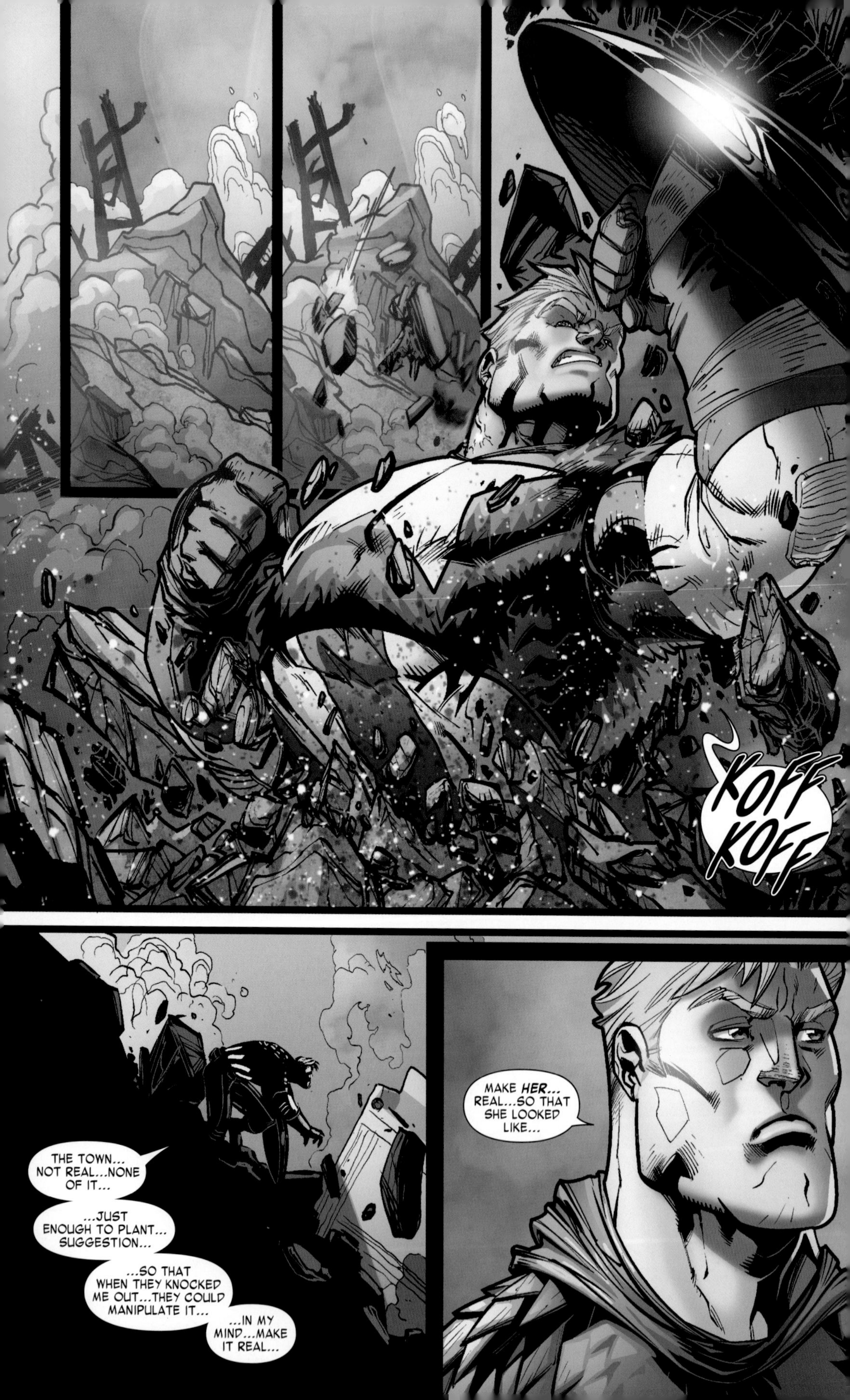
KOFF KOFF
THE TOWN... NOT REAL...NONE OF IT...
...JUST ENOUGH TO PLANT... SUGGESTION...
...SO THAT WHEN THEY KNOCKED ME OUT...THEY COULD MANIPULATE IT...
...IN MY MIND...MAKE IT REAL...
MAKE HER... REAL...SO THAT SHE LOOKED LIKE...

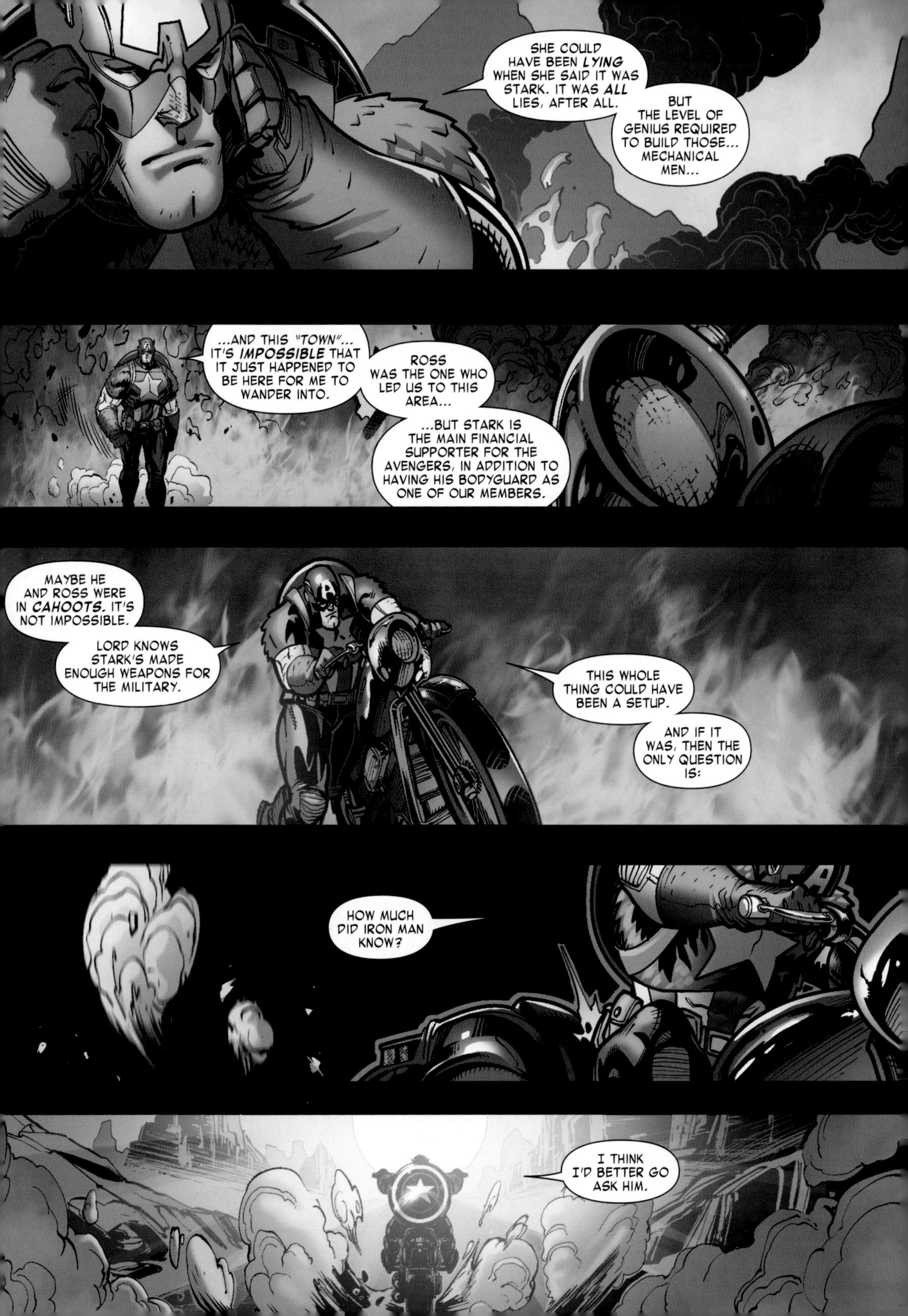
SHE COULD HAVE BEEN LYING WHEN SHE SAID IT WAS STARK. IT WAS ALL LIES, AFTER ALL.
BUT THE LEVEL OF GENIUS REQUIRED TO BUILD THOSE... MECHANICAL MEN...
...AND THIS "TOWN"... IT'S IMPOSSIBLE THAT IT JUST HAPPENED TO BE HERE FOR ME TO WANDER INTO.
ROSS WAS THE ONE WHO LED US TO THIS AREA...
...BUT STARK IS THE MAIN FINANCIAL SUPPORTER FOR THE AVENGERS, IN ADDITION TO HAVING HIS BODYGUARD AS ONE OF OUR MEMBERS.
MAYBE HE AND ROSS WERE IN CAHOOTS. IT'S NOT IMPOSSIBLE.
LORD KNOWS STARK'S MADE ENOUGH WEAPONS FOR THE MILITARY.
THIS WHOLE THING COULD HAVE BEEN A SETUP.
AND IF IT WAS, THEN THE ONLY QUESTION IS:
HOW MUCH DID IRON MAN KNOW?
I THINK I'D BETTER GO ASK HIM.

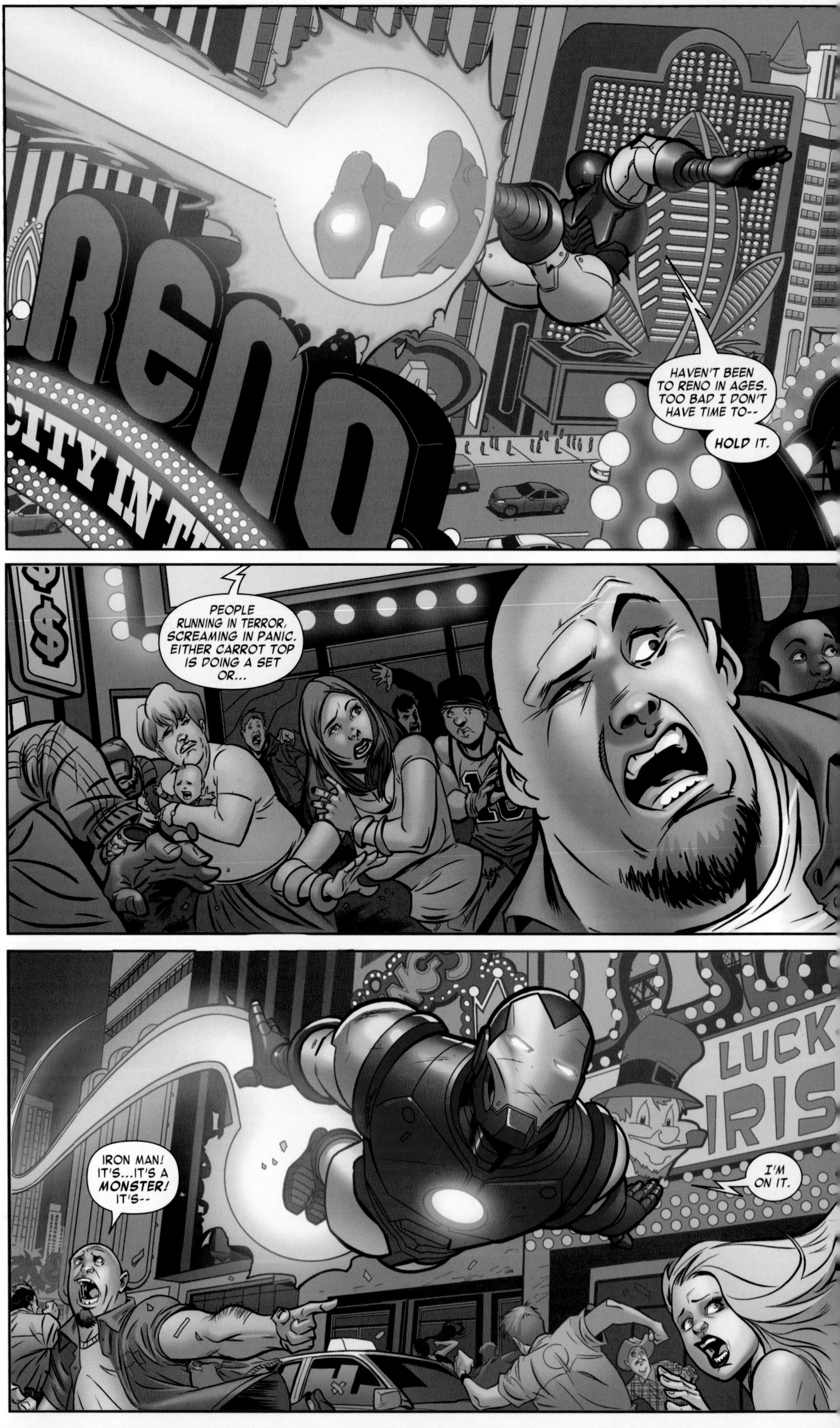
RENO
CITY IN TH
HAVEN'T BEEN TO RENO IN AGES. TOO BAD I DON'T HAVE TIME TO--
HOLD IT.
PEOPLE RUNNING IN TERROR, SCREAMING IN PANIC. EITHER CARROT TOP IS DOING A SET OR...
LUCK
IRIS
IRON MAN! IT'S...IT'S A MONSTER! IT'S--
I'M ON IT.

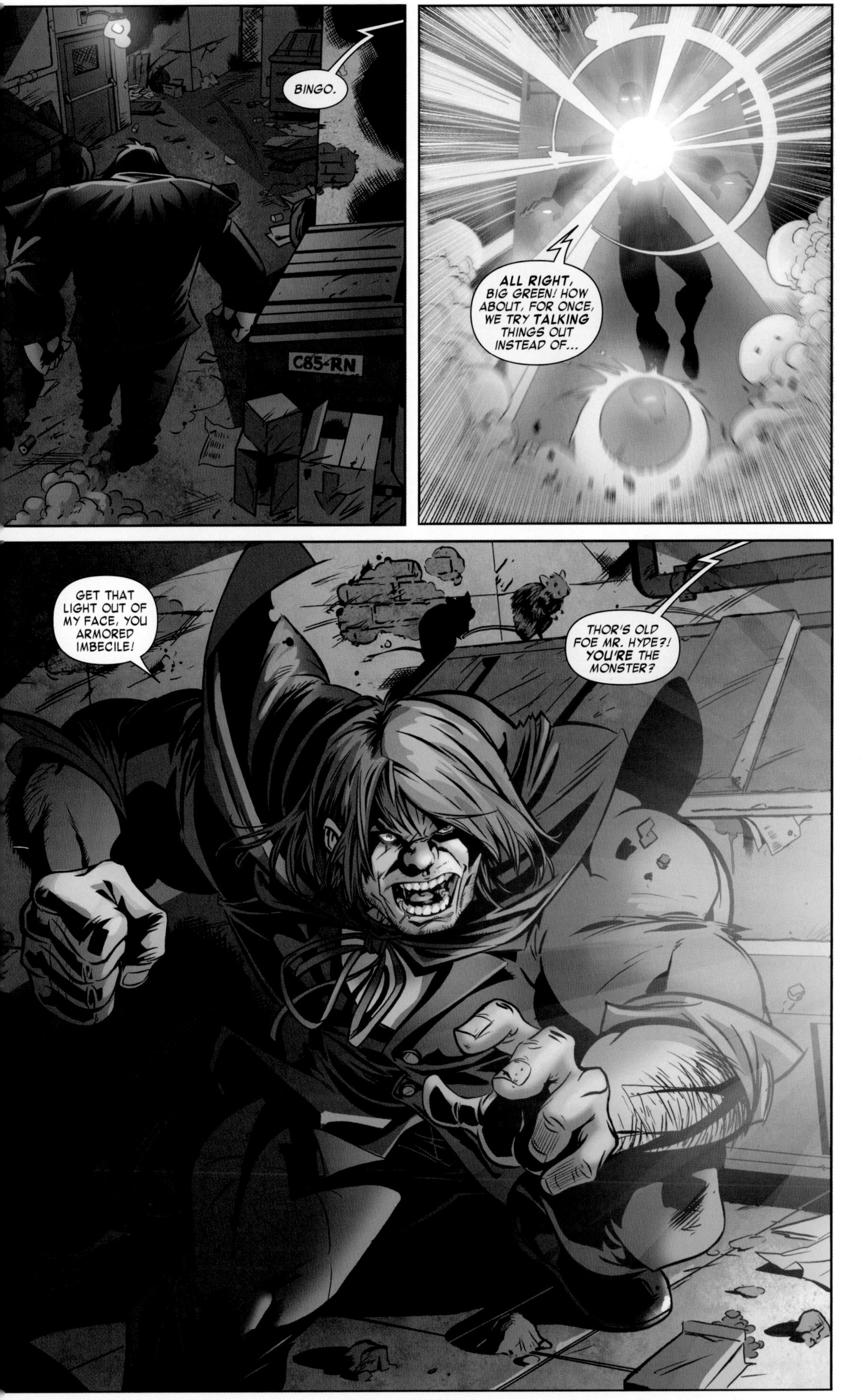
BINGO.
ALL RIGHT, BIG GREEN! HOW ABOUT, FOR ONCE, WE TRY TALKING THINGS OUT INSTEAD OF...
C85-RN
GET THAT LIGHT OUT OF MY FACE, YOU ARMORED IMBECILE!
THOR'S OLD FOE MR. HYDE?! YOU'RE THE MONSTER?

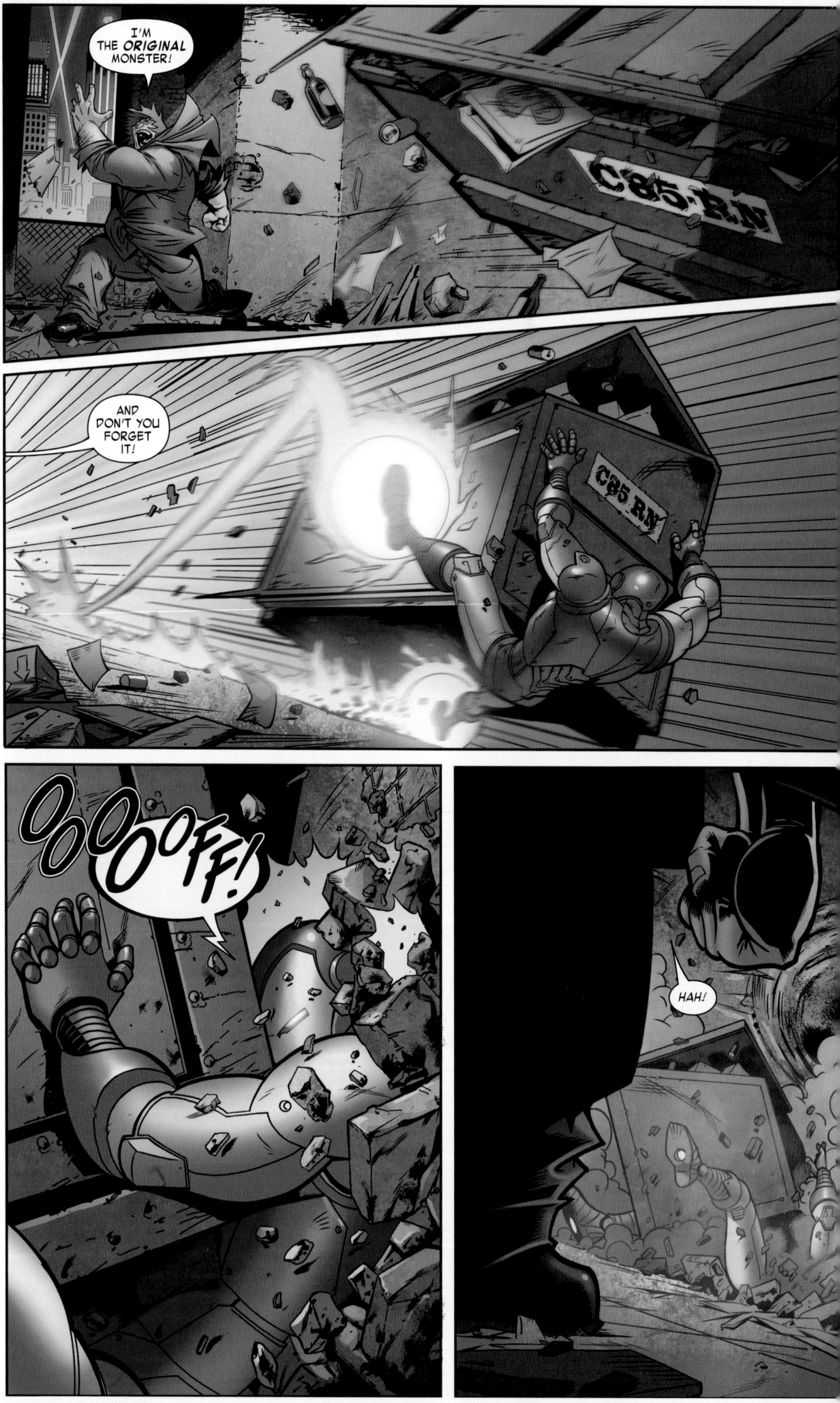
I'M THE *ORIGINAL* MONSTER!
C85 R.N
AND DON'T YOU FORGET IT!
C85 RN
OOOOOFF!
HAH!

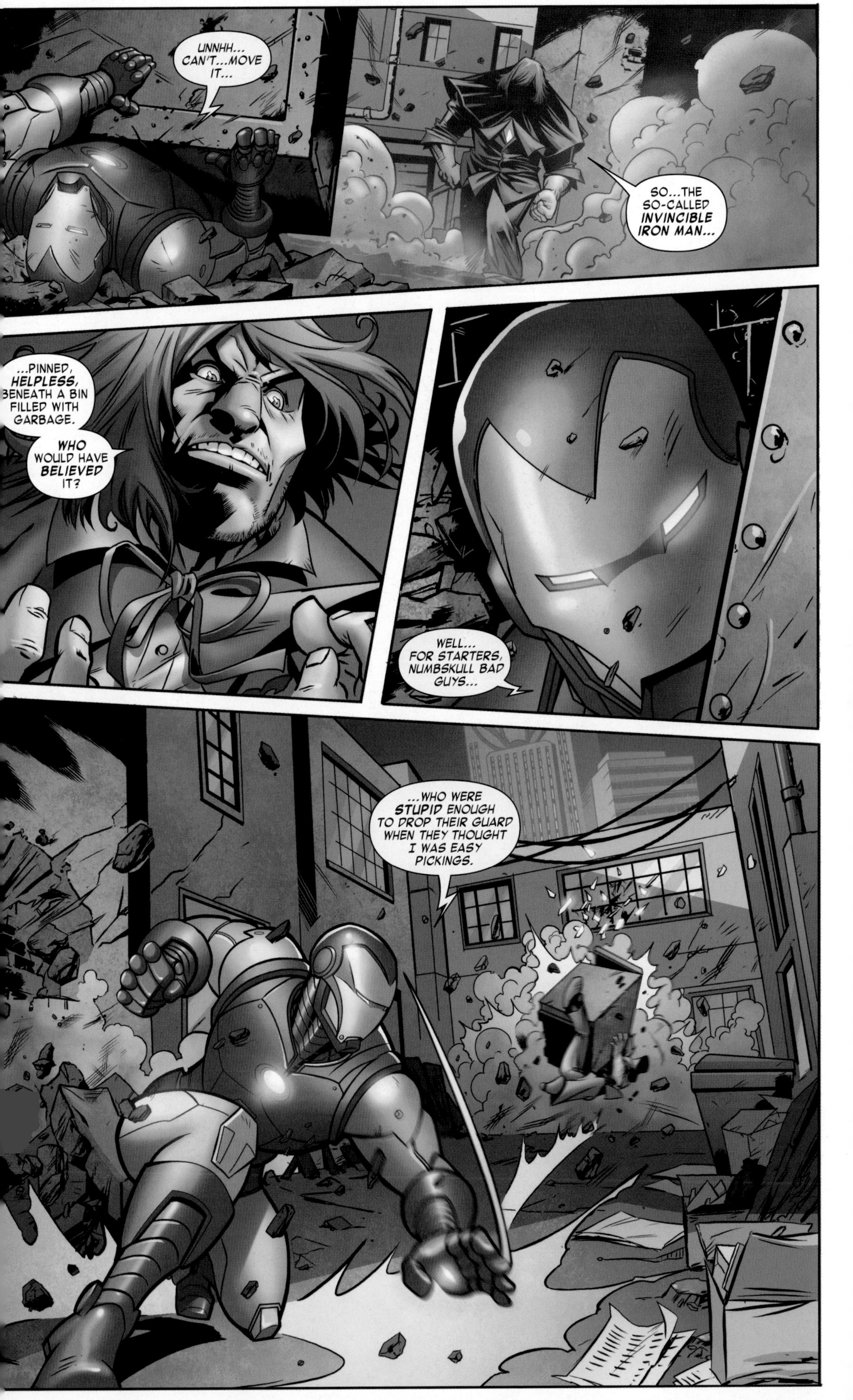
UNNHH... CAN'T...MOVE IT...
SO...THE SO-CALLED INVINCIBLE IRON MAN...
...PINNED, HELPLESS, BENEATH A BIN FILLED WITH GARBAGE.
WHO WOULD HAVE BELIEVED IT?
WELL... FOR STARTERS, NUMBSKULL BAD GUYS...
...WHO WERE STUPID ENOUGH TO DROP THEIR GUARD WHEN THEY THOUGHT I WAS EASY PICKINGS.

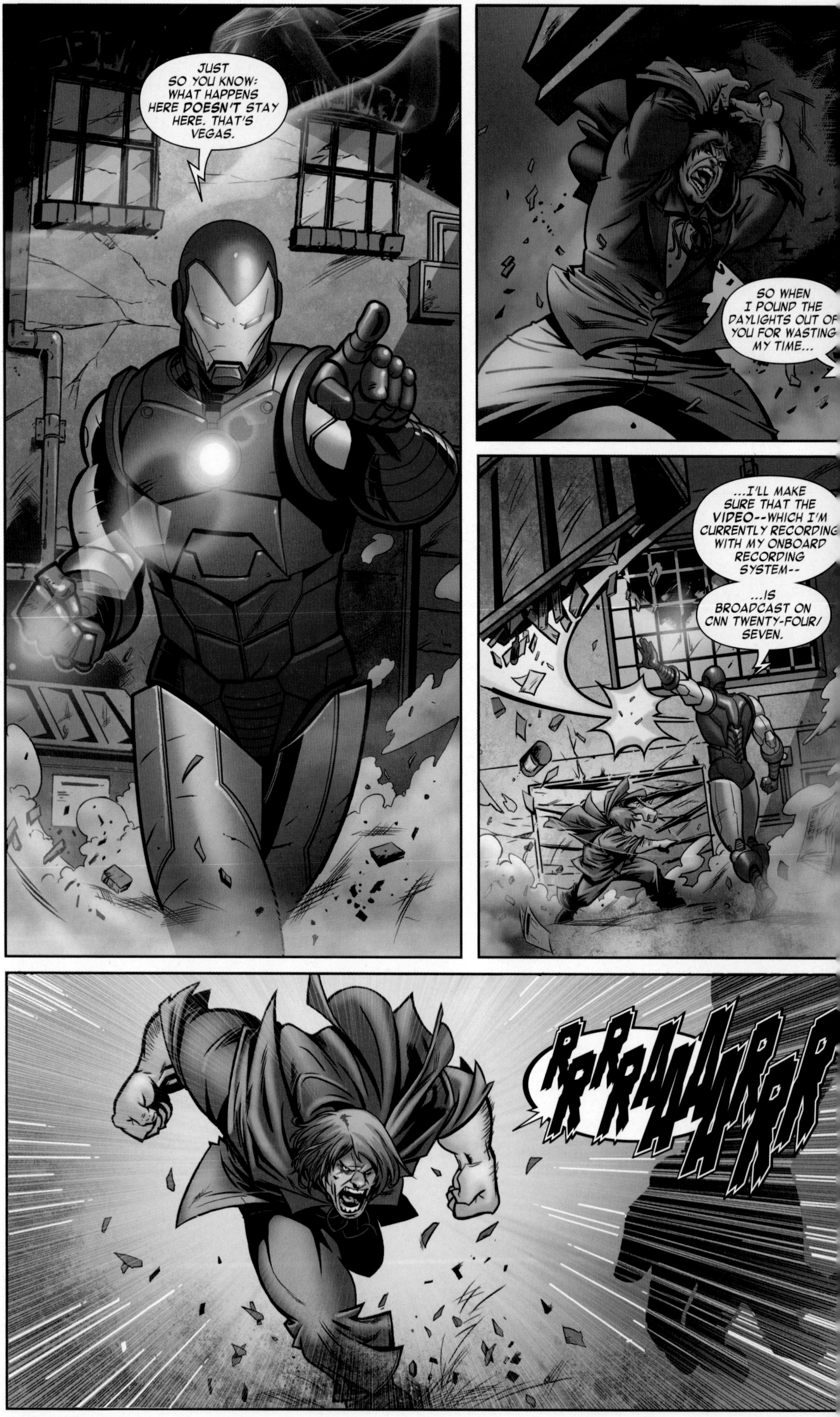
JUST SO YOU KNOW: WHAT HAPPENS HERE DOESN'T STAY HERE. THAT'S VEGAS.
SO WHEN I POUND THE DAYLIGHTS OUT OF YOU FOR WASTING MY TIME...
...I'LL MAKE SURE THAT THE VIDEO--WHICH I'M CURRENTLY RECORDING WITH MY ONBOARD RECORDING SYSTEM--
...IS BROADCAST ON CNN TWENTY-FOUR/SEVEN.
RRRRAAAARRRR

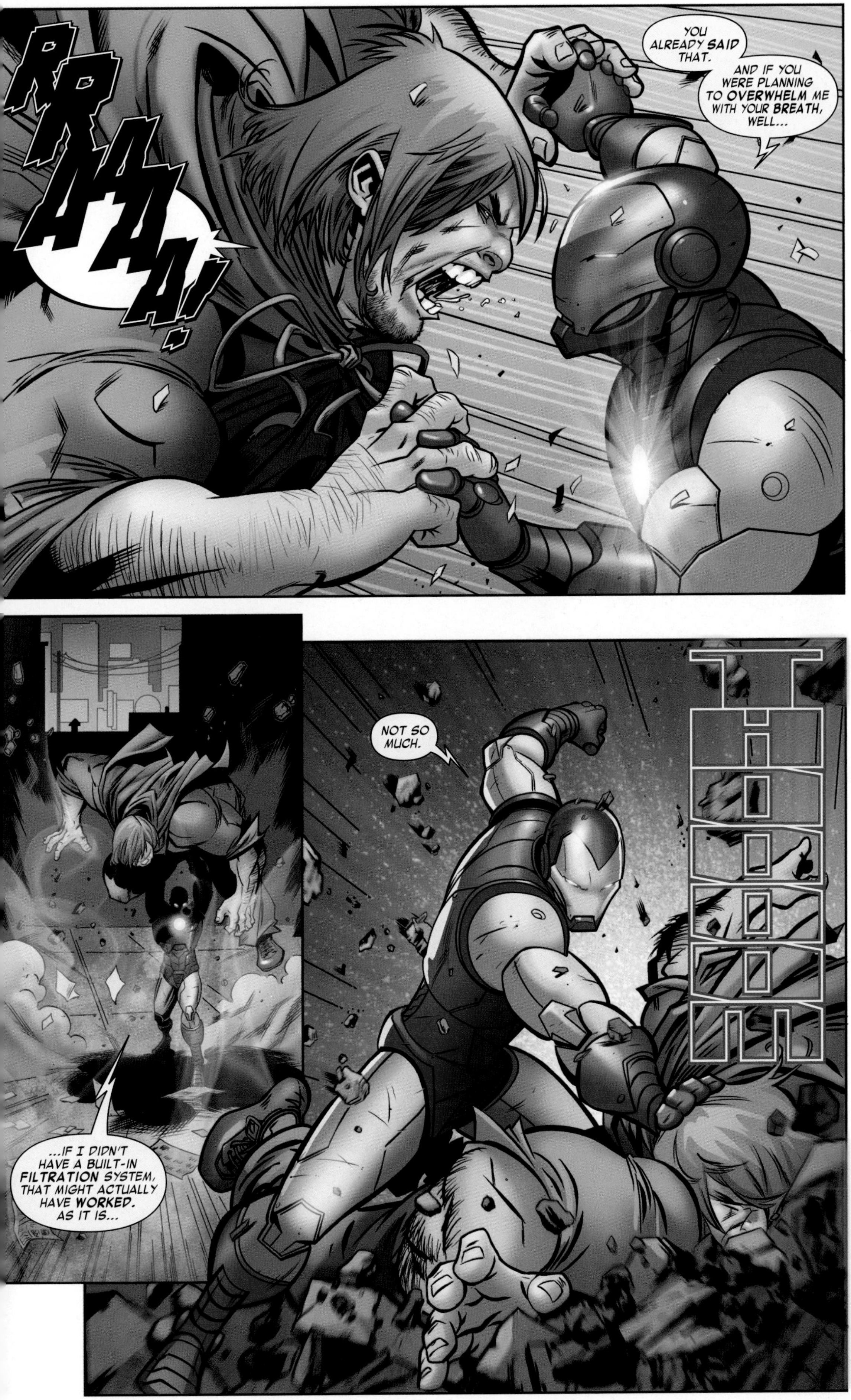
RRAAAA!
YOU ALREADY SAID THAT.
AND IF YOU WERE PLANNING TO OVERWHELM ME WITH YOUR BREATH, WELL...
...IF I DIDN'T HAVE A BUILT-IN FILTRATION SYSTEM, THAT MIGHT ACTUALLY HAVE WORKED. AS IT IS...
NOT SO MUCH.
THOOOOM

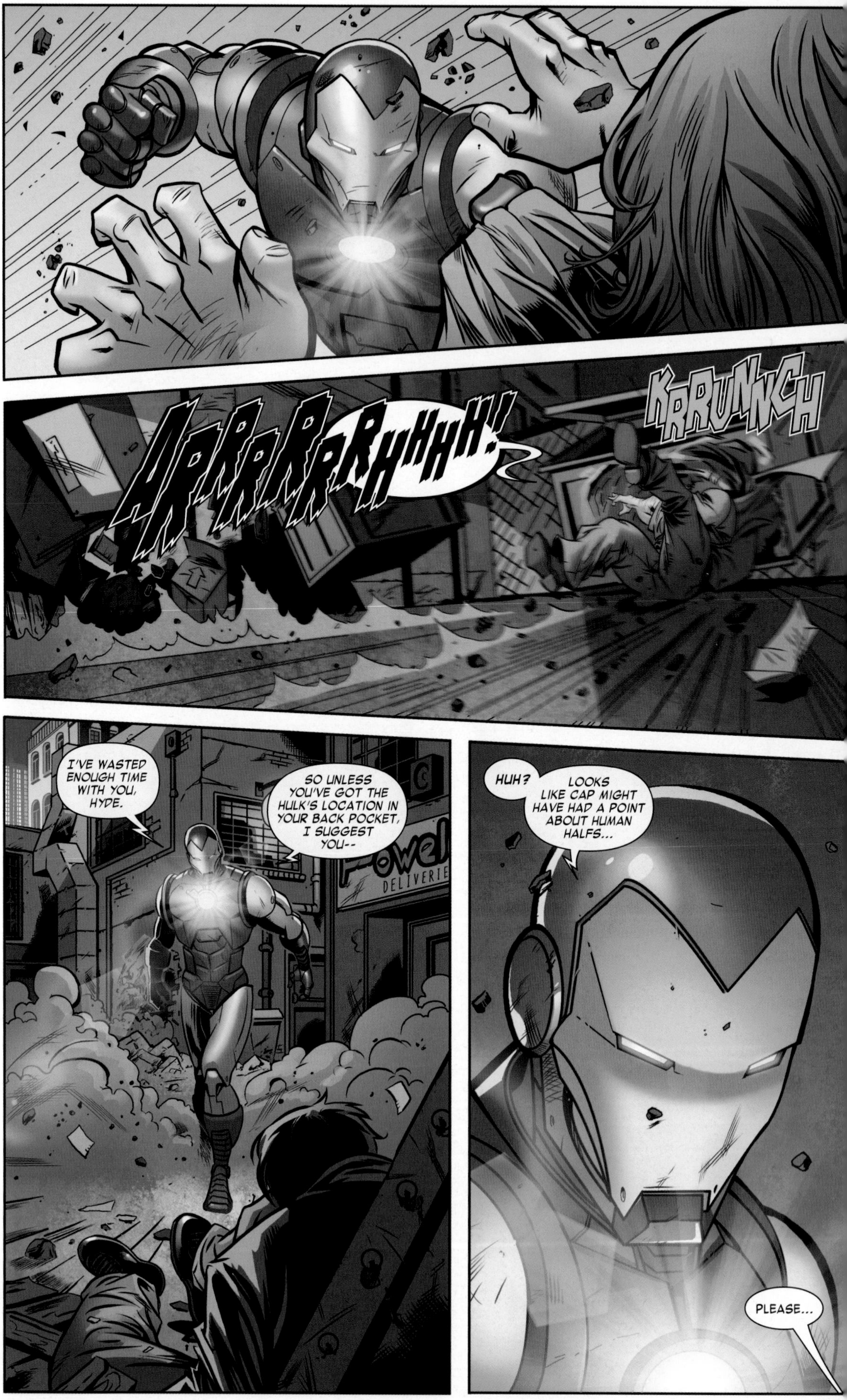
ARRRRRRRHHHH!!
KRRUNNCH
I'VE WASTED ENOUGH TIME WITH YOU, HYDE.
SO UNLESS YOU'VE GOT THE HULK'S LOCATION IN YOUR BACK POCKET, I SUGGEST YOU--
DELIVERIE
HUH?
LOOKS LIKE CAP MIGHT HAVE HAD A POINT ABOUT HUMAN HALFS...
PLEASE...

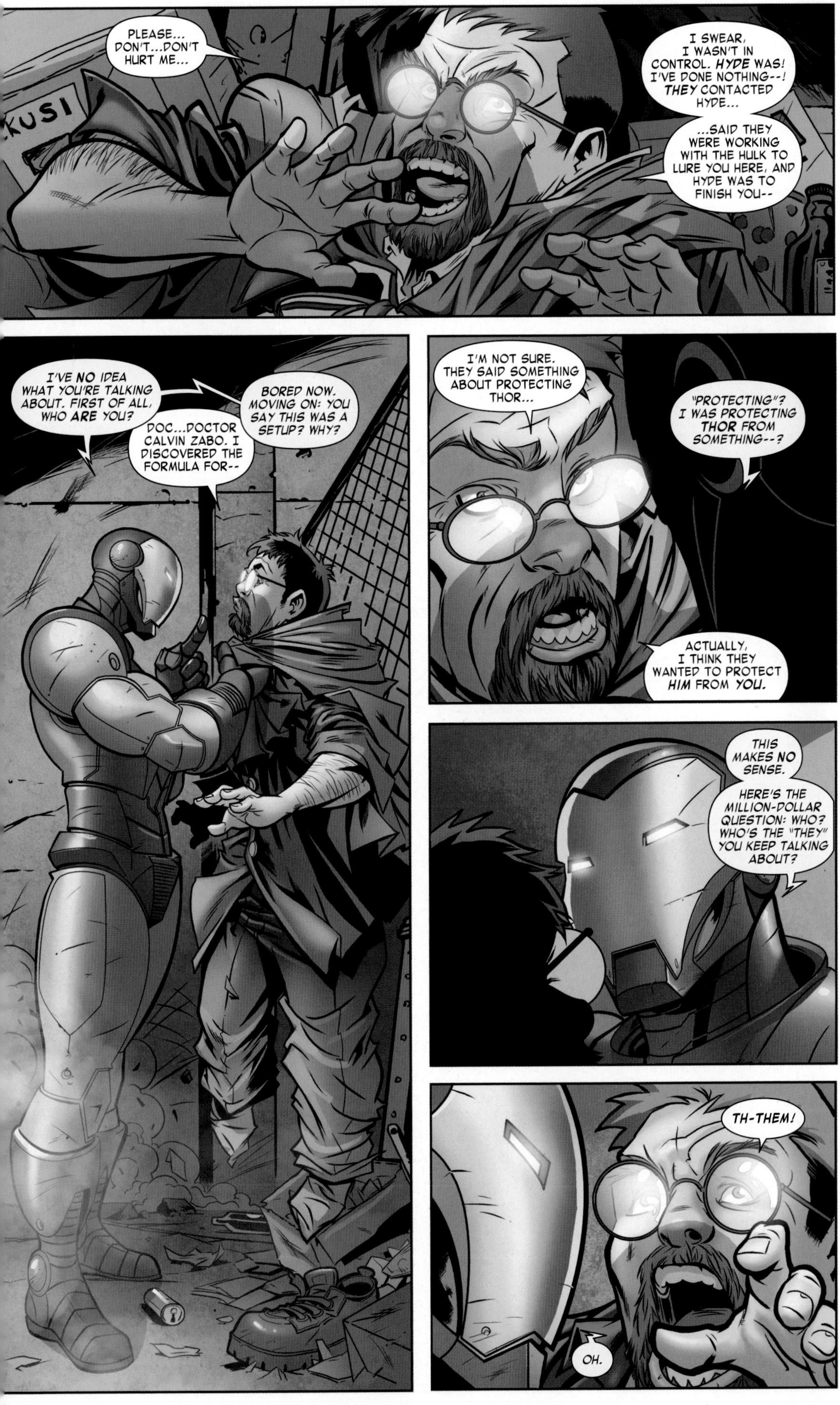

PLEASE... DON'T...DON'T HURT ME...
I SWEAR, I WASN'T IN CONTROL. HYDE WAS! I'VE DONE NOTHING--! THEY CONTACTED HYDE...
...SAID THEY WERE WORKING WITH THE HULK TO LURE YOU HERE, AND HYDE WAS TO FINISH YOU--
I'VE NO IDEA WHAT YOU'RE TALKING ABOUT. FIRST OF ALL, WHO ARE YOU?
DOC...DOCTOR CALVIN ZABO. I DISCOVERED THE FORMULA FOR--
BORED NOW. MOVING ON: YOU SAY THIS WAS A SETUP? WHY?
I'M NOT SURE. THEY SAID SOMETHING ABOUT PROTECTING THOR...
"PROTECTING"? I WAS PROTECTING THOR FROM SOMETHING--?
ACTUALLY, I THINK THEY WANTED TO PROTECT HIM FROM YOU.
THIS MAKES NO SENSE.
HERE'S THE MILLION-DOLLAR QUESTION: WHO? WHO'S THE "THEY" YOU KEEP TALKING ABOUT?
TH-THEM!
OH.

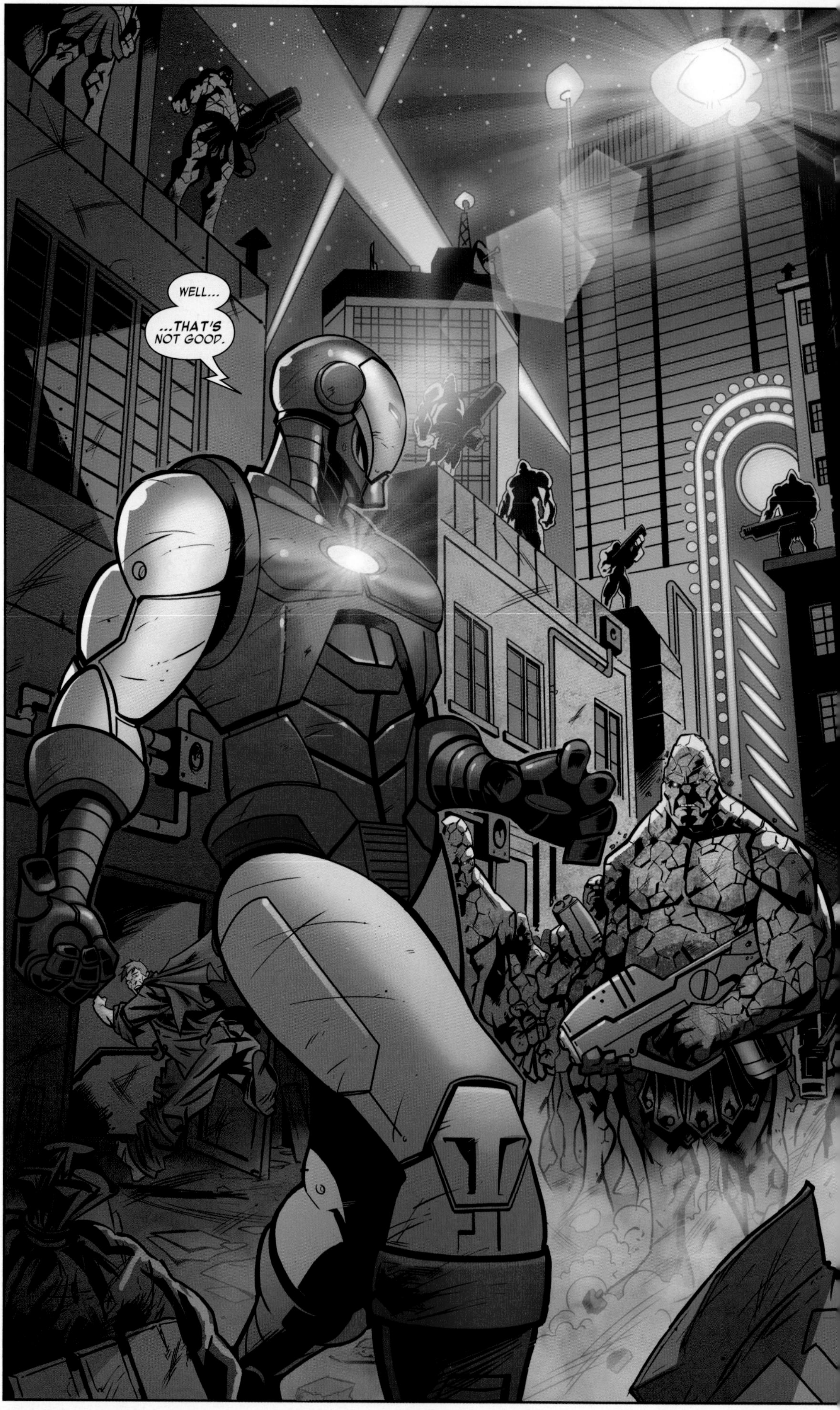
WELL...
...THAT'S NOT GOOD.

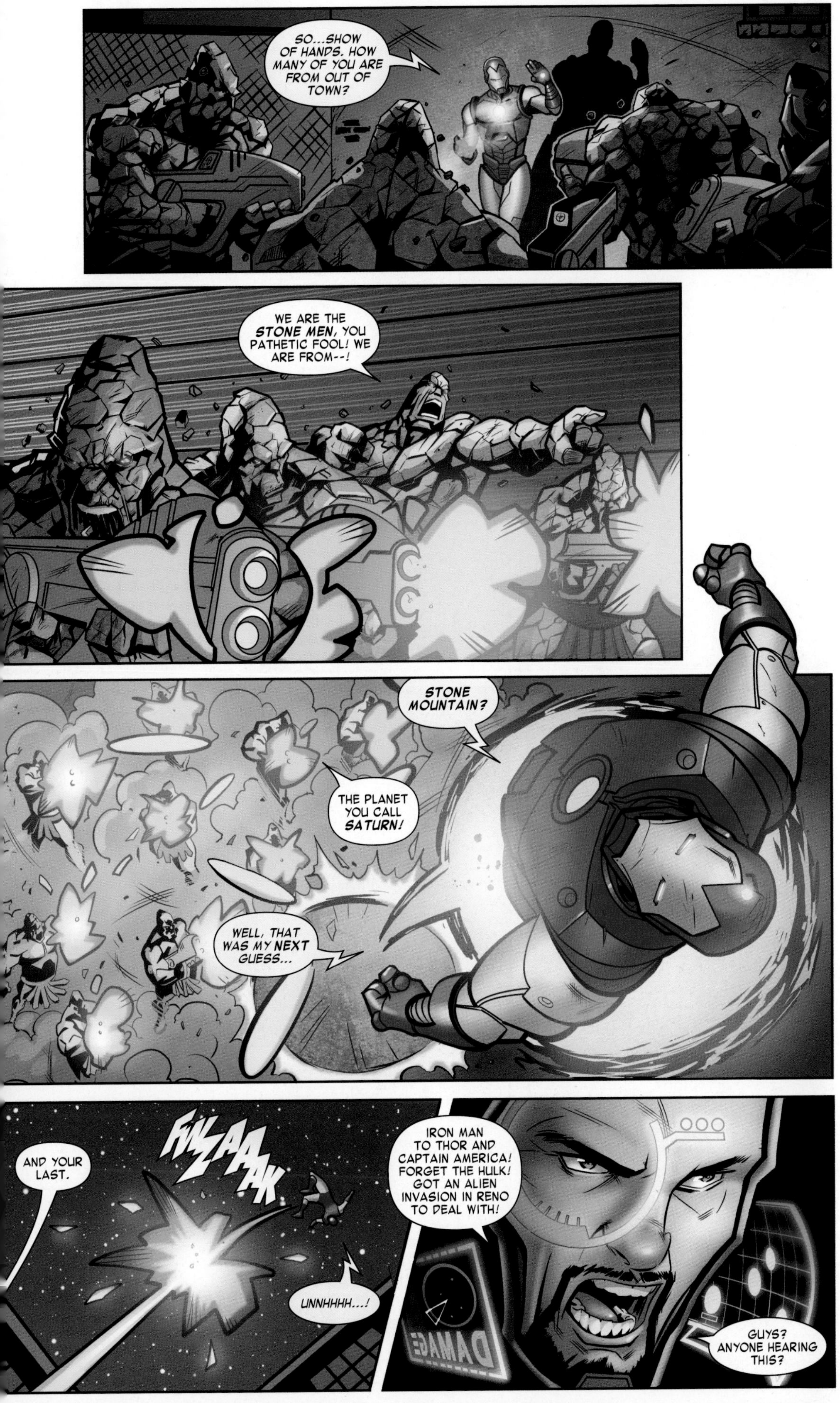
SO...SHOW OF HANDS. HOW MANY OF YOU ARE FROM OUT OF TOWN?
WE ARE THE STONE MEN, YOU PATHETIC FOOL! WE ARE FROM--!
STONE MOUNTAIN?
THE PLANET YOU CALL SATURN!
WELL, THAT WAS MY NEXT GUESS...
AND YOUR LAST.
FWZAAAK
UNNHHHH...!
IRON MAN TO THOR AND CAPTAIN AMERICA! FORGET THE HULK! GOT AN ALIEN INVASION IN RENO TO DEAL WITH!
GUYS? ANYONE HEARING THIS?

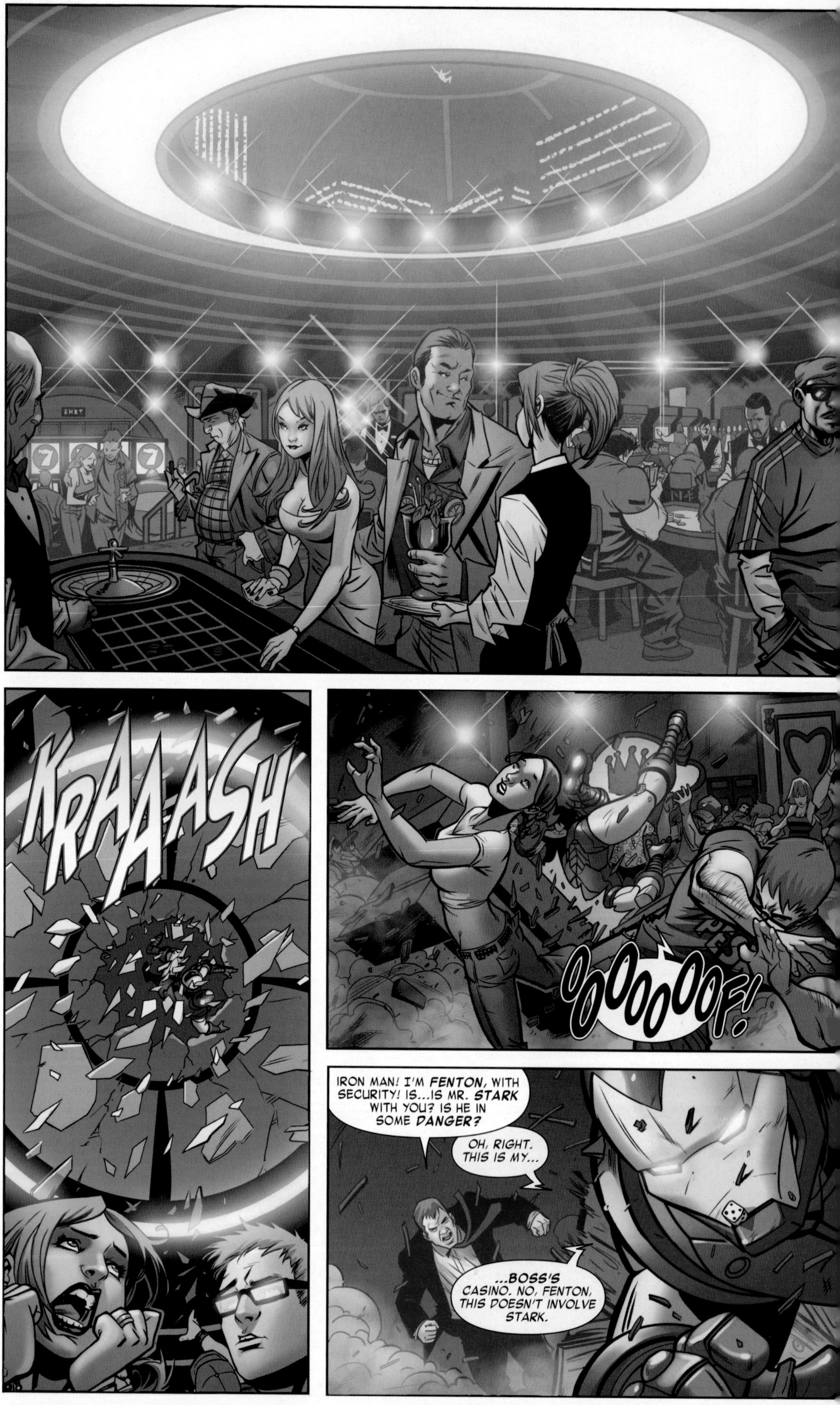
KRAAASH
OOOOOOF!
IRON MAN! I'M FENTON, WITH SECURITY! IS...IS MR. STARK WITH YOU? IS HE IN SOME DANGER?
OH, RIGHT. THIS IS MY...
...BOSS'S CASINO. NO, FENTON, THIS DOESN'T INVOLVE STARK.

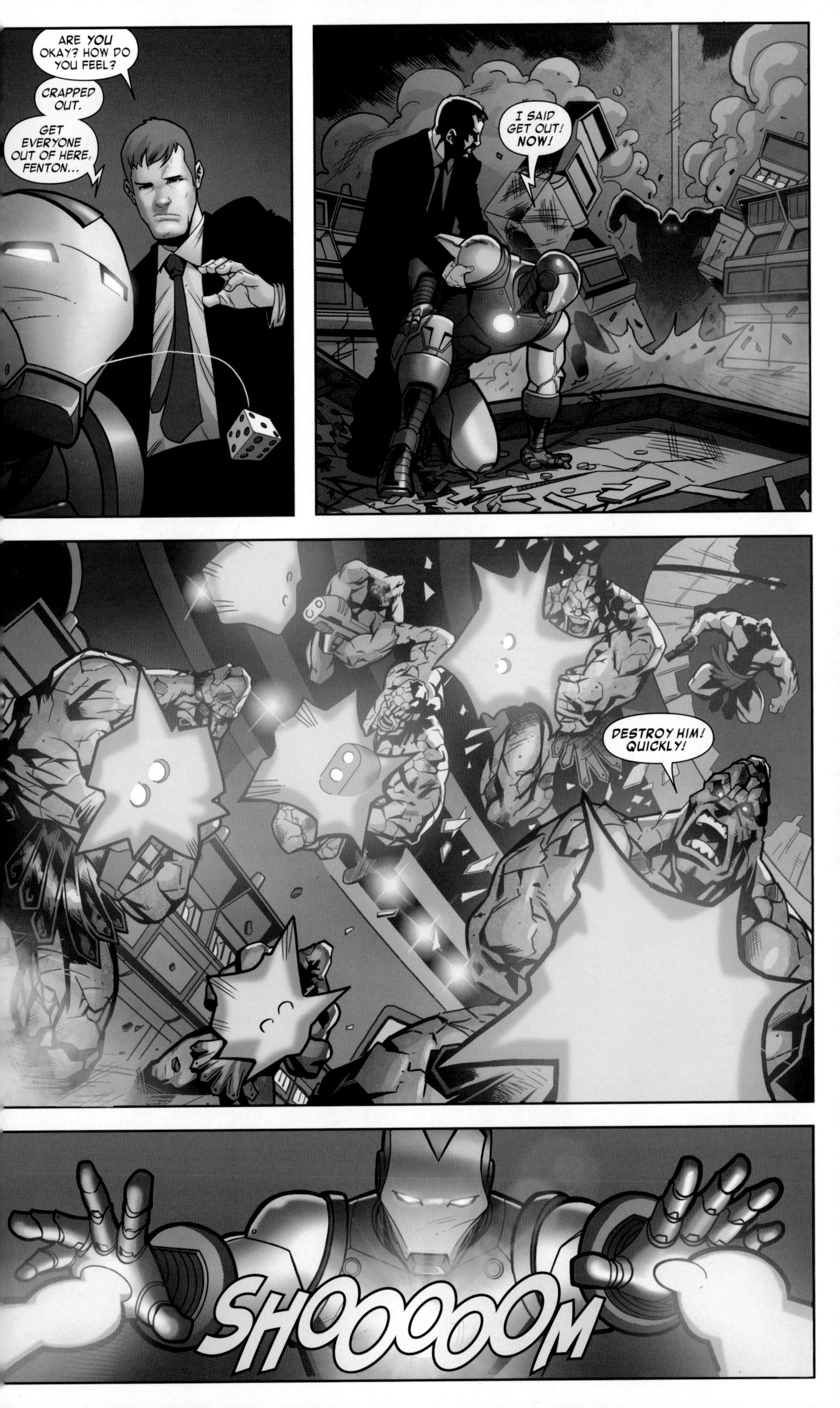
ARE YOU OKAY? HOW DO YOU FEEL?
CRAPPED OUT.
GET EVERYONE OUT OF HERE, FENTON...
I SAID GET OUT! NOW!
DESTROY HIM! QUICKLY!
SHOOOOOOM

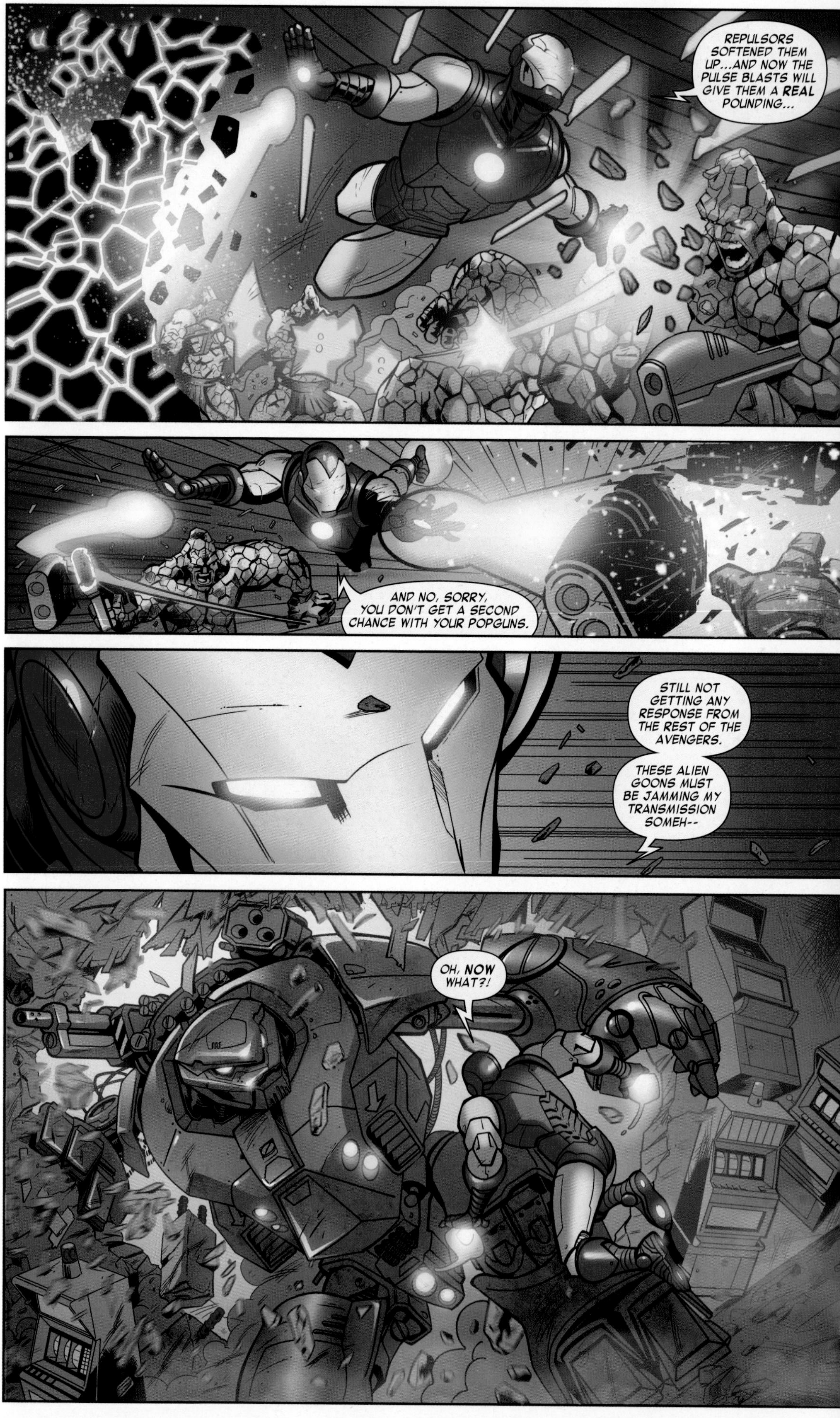
REPULSORS SOFTENED THEM UP...AND NOW THE PULSE BLASTS WILL GIVE THEM A REAL POUNDING...
AND NO, SORRY, YOU DON'T GET A SECOND CHANCE WITH YOUR POPGUNS.
STILL NOT GETTING ANY RESPONSE FROM THE REST OF THE AVENGERS.
THESE ALIEN GOONS MUST BE JAMMING MY TRANSMISSION SOMEH--
OH, NOW WHAT?!

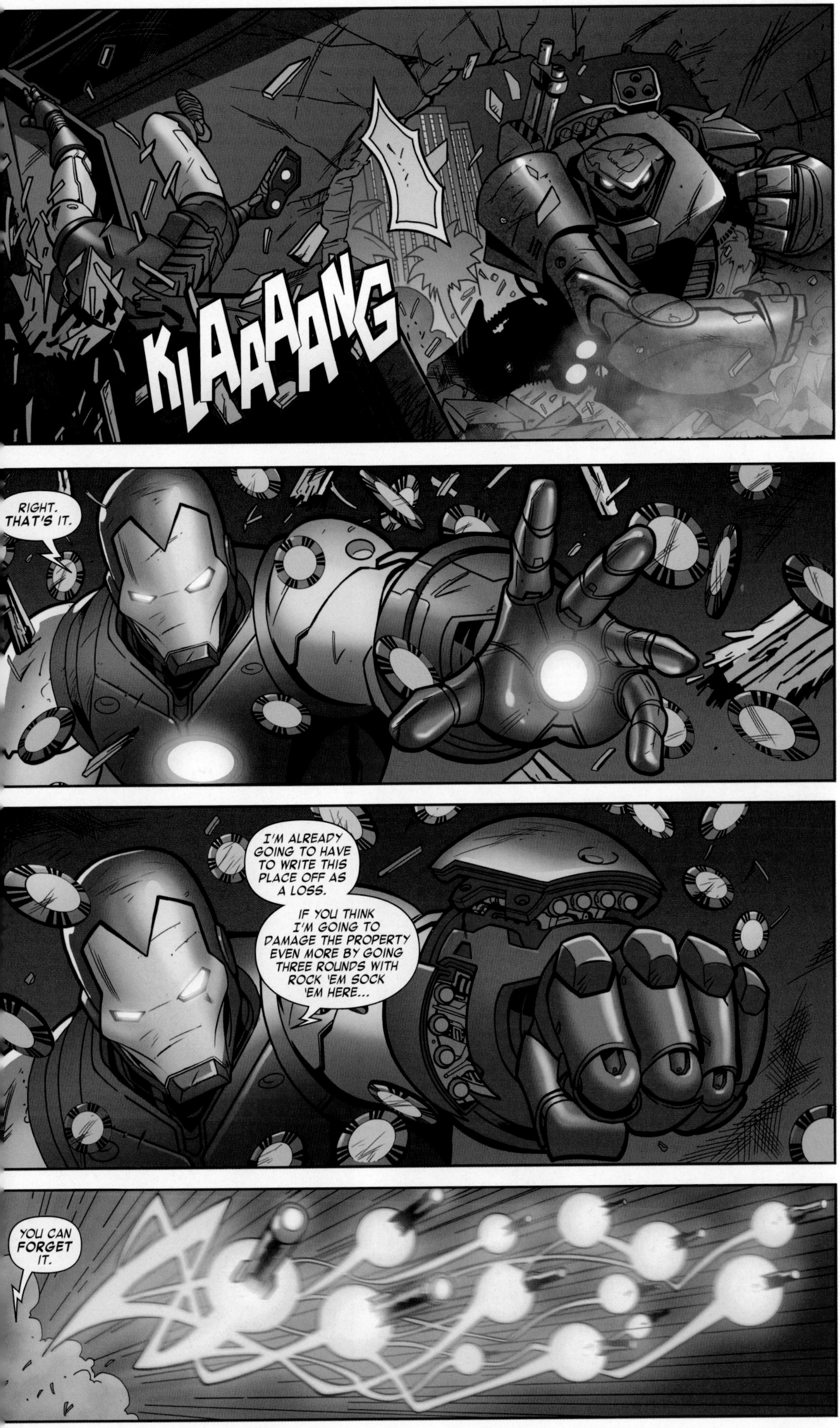
KLAAAANG
RIGHT. THAT'S IT.
I'M ALREADY GOING TO HAVE TO WRITE THIS PLACE OFF AS A LOSS.
IF YOU THINK I'M GOING TO DAMAGE THE PROPERTY EVEN MORE BY GOING THREE ROUNDS WITH ROCK 'EM SOCK 'EM HERE...
YOU CAN FORGET IT.

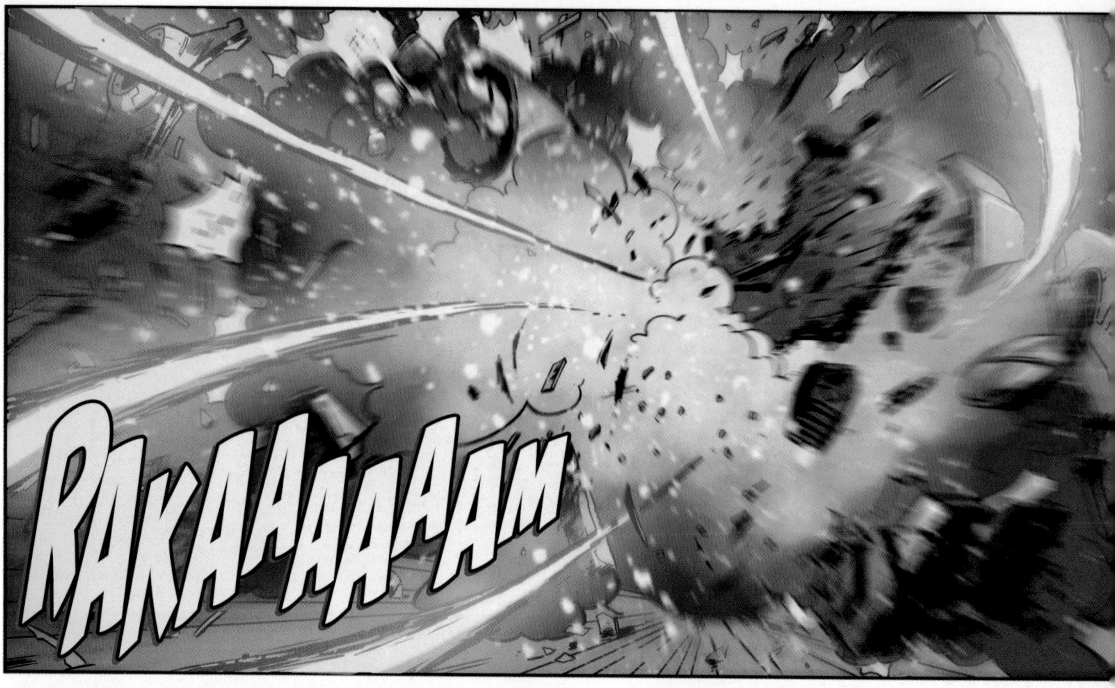
RAKAAAAAAAM

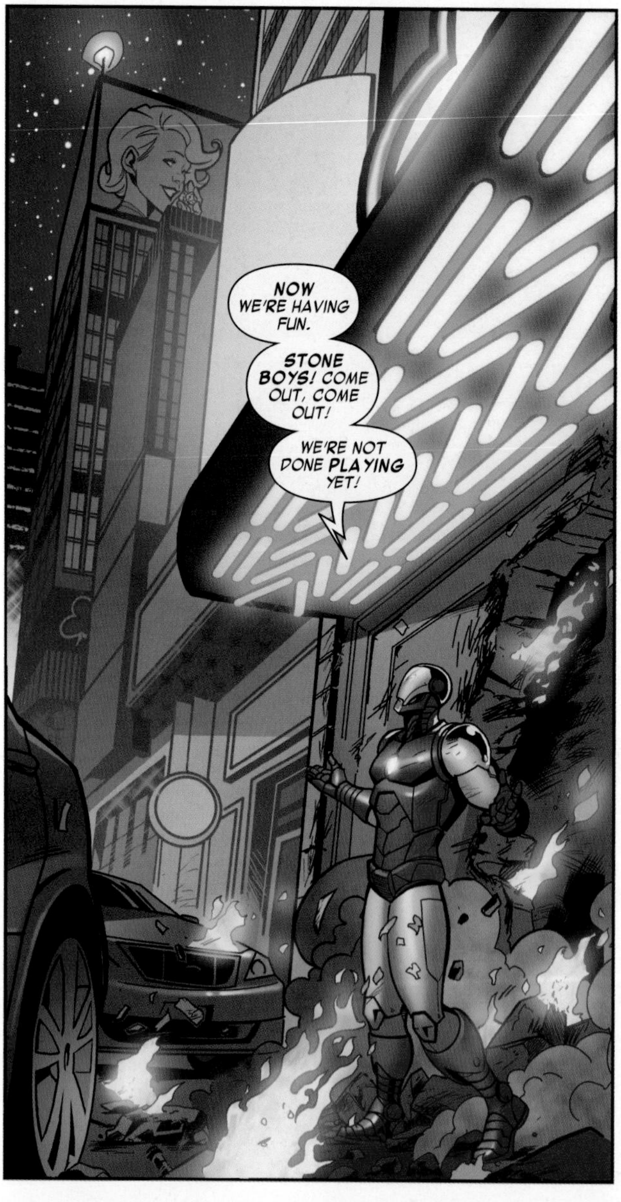
NOW WE'RE HAVING FUN.
STONE BOYS! COME OUT, COME OUT!
WE'RE NOT DONE PLAYING YET!

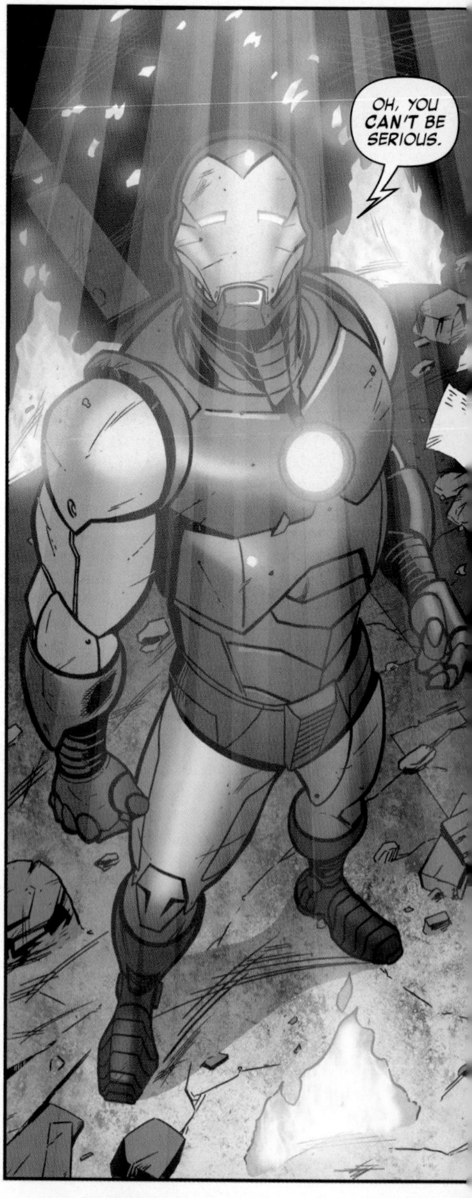
OH, YOU CAN'T BE SERIOUS.

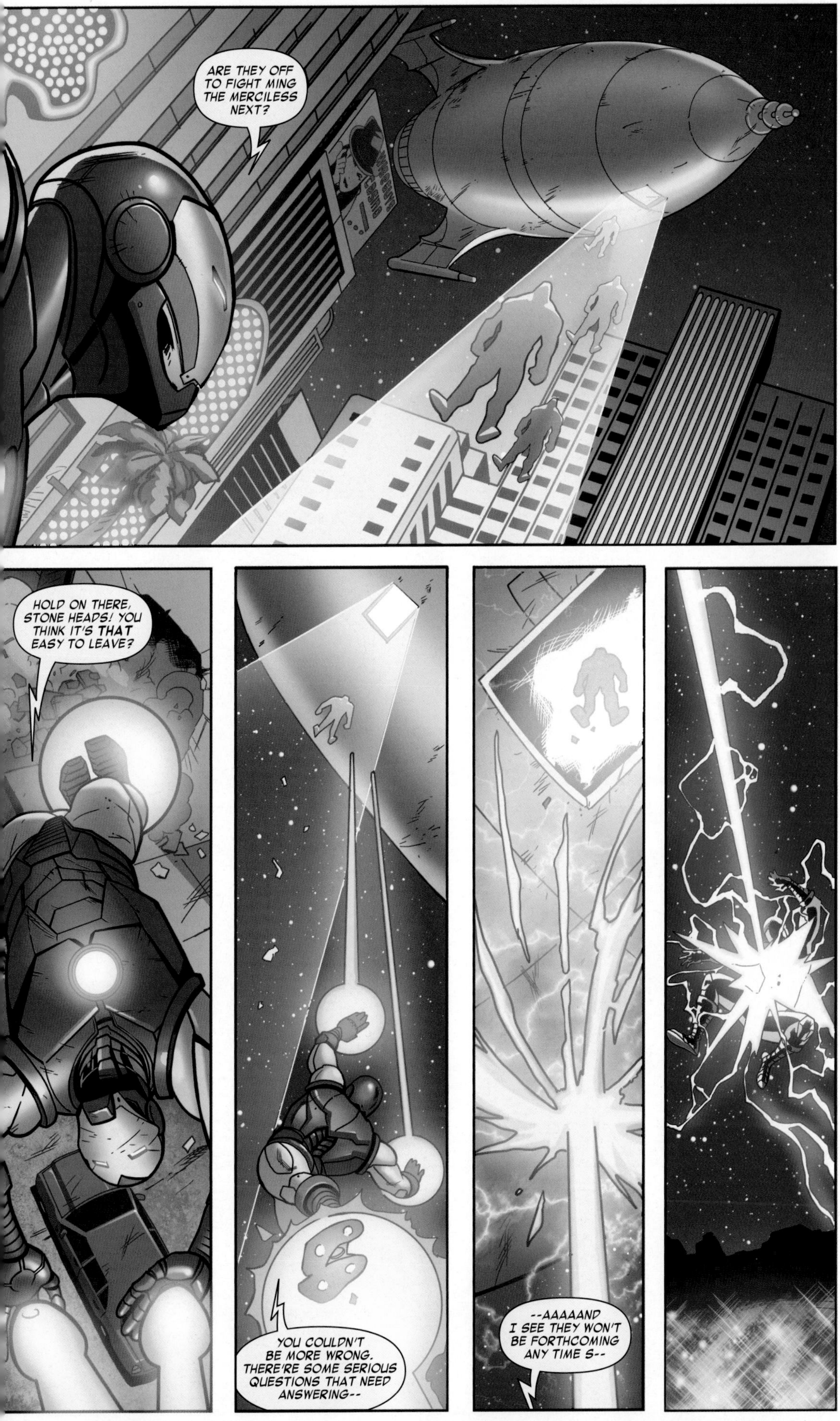
ARE THEY OFF TO FIGHT MING THE MERCILESS NEXT?
HOLD ON THERE, STONE HEADS! YOU THINK IT'S **THAT** EASY TO LEAVE?
YOU COULDN'T BE MORE WRONG. THERE'RE SOME SERIOUS QUESTIONS THAT NEED ANSWERING--
--AAAAAND I SEE THEY WON'T BE FORTHCOMING ANY TIME S--

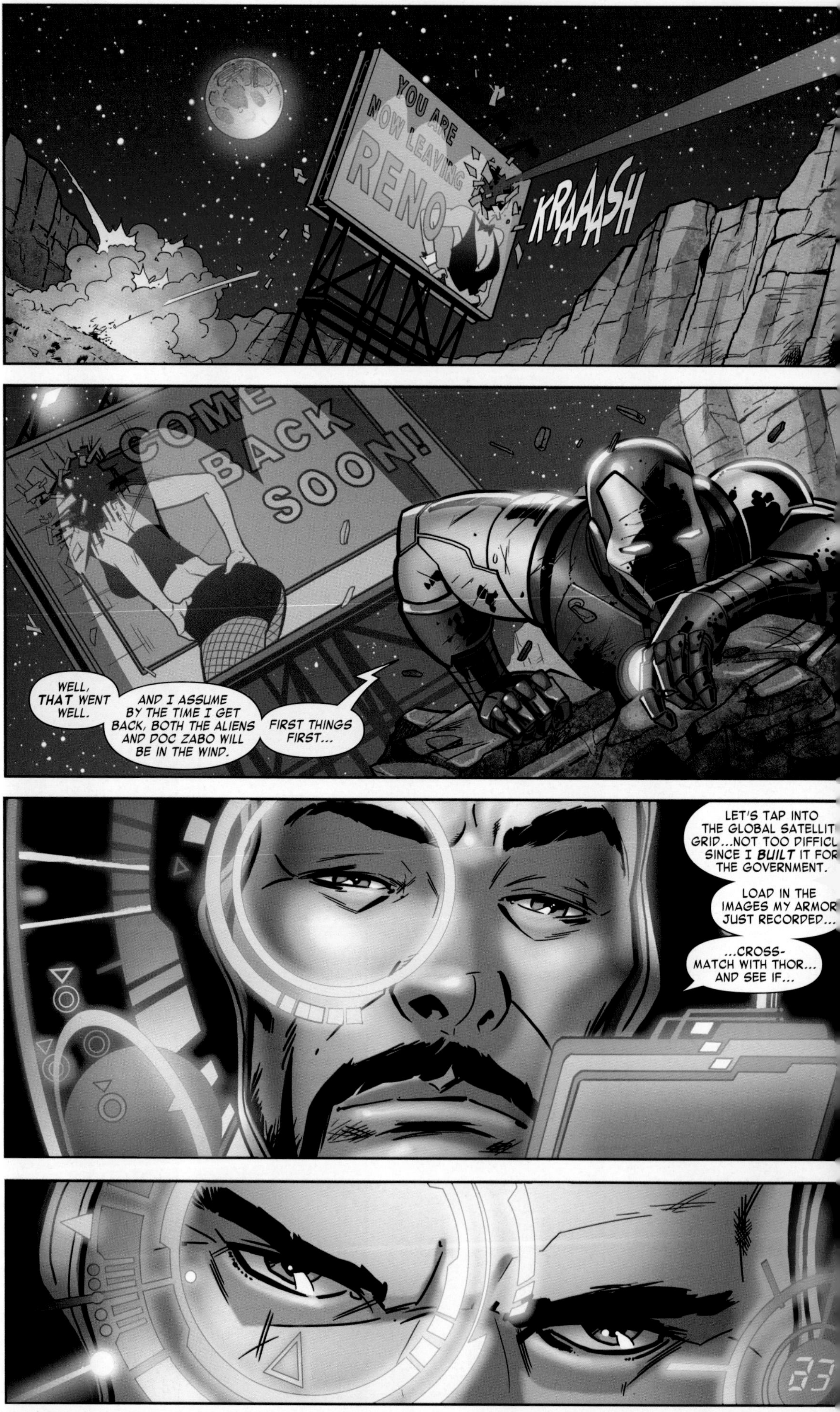
YOU ARE NOW LEAVING RENO
KRAAASH
COME BACK SOON!
WELL, THAT WENT WELL.
AND I ASSUME BY THE TIME I GET BACK, BOTH THE ALIENS AND DOC ZABO WILL BE IN THE WIND.
FIRST THINGS FIRST...
LET'S TAP INTO THE GLOBAL SATELLIT GRID...NOT TOO DIFFICL SINCE I BUILT IT FOR THE GOVERNMENT.
LOAD IN THE IMAGES MY ARMOR JUST RECORDED...
...CROSS-MATCH WITH THOR... AND SEE IF...

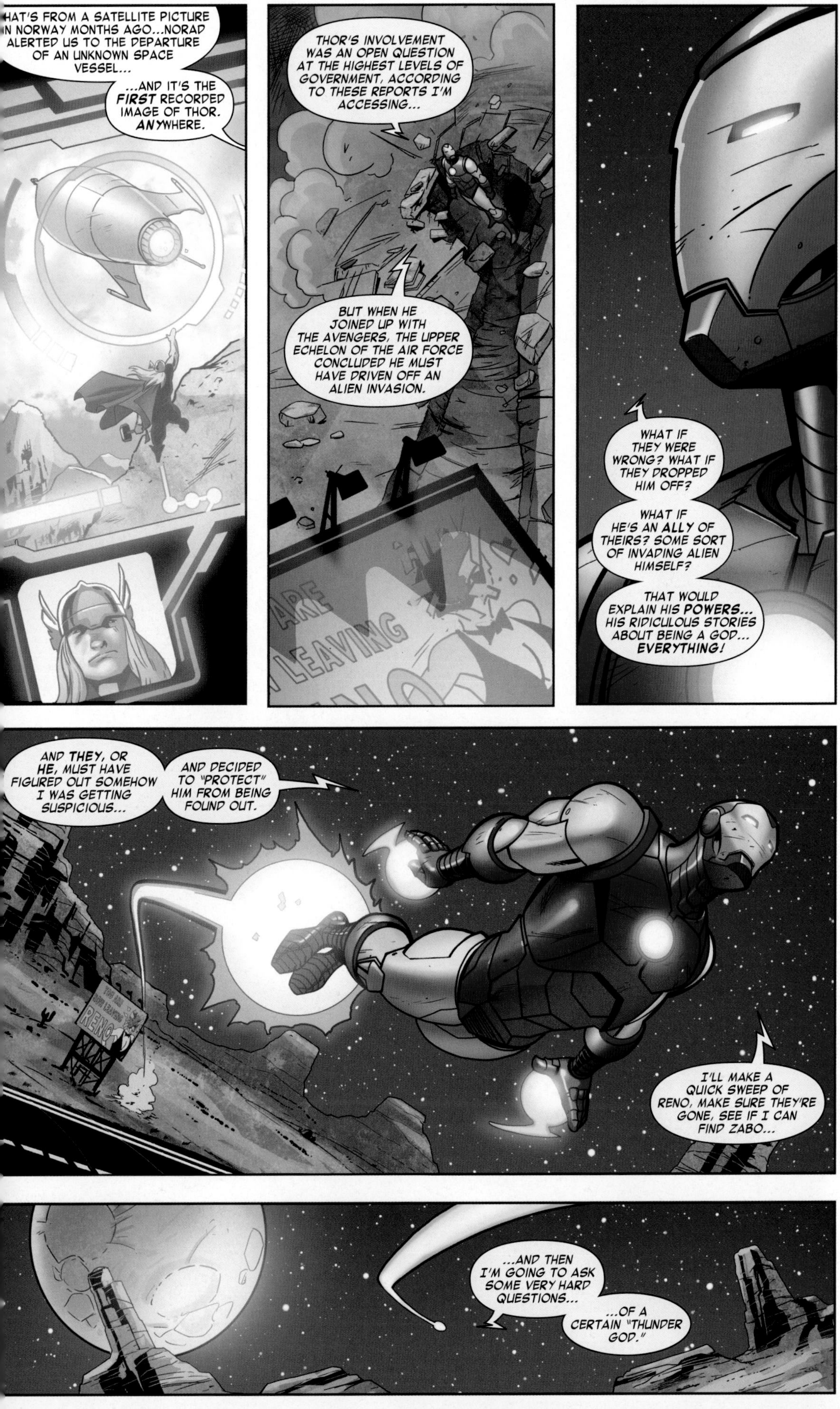
HAT'S FROM A SATELLITE PICTURE N NORWAY MONTHS AGO...NORAD ALERTED US TO THE DEPARTURE OF AN UNKNOWN SPACE VESSEL...
...AND IT'S THE FIRST RECORDED IMAGE OF THOR. ANYWHERE.
THOR'S INVOLVEMENT WAS AN OPEN QUESTION AT THE HIGHEST LEVELS OF GOVERNMENT, ACCORDING TO THESE REPORTS I'M ACCESSING...
BUT WHEN HE JOINED UP WITH THE AVENGERS, THE UPPER ECHELON OF THE AIR FORCE CONCLUDED HE MUST HAVE DRIVEN OFF AN ALIEN INVASION.
WHAT IF THEY WERE WRONG? WHAT IF THEY DROPPED HIM OFF?
WHAT IF HE'S AN ALLY OF THEIRS? SOME SORT OF INVADING ALIEN HIMSELF?
THAT WOULD EXPLAIN HIS POWERS... HIS RIDICULOUS STORIES ABOUT BEING A GOD... EVERYTHING!
AND THEY, OR HE, MUST HAVE FIGURED OUT SOMEHOW I WAS GETTING SUSPICIOUS...
AND DECIDED TO "PROTECT" HIM FROM BEING FOUND OUT.
RENO
I'LL MAKE A QUICK SWEEP OF RENO, MAKE SURE THEY'RE GONE, SEE IF I CAN FIND ZABO...
...AND THEN I'M GOING TO ASK SOME VERY HARD QUESTIONS...
...OF A CERTAIN "THUNDER GOD."

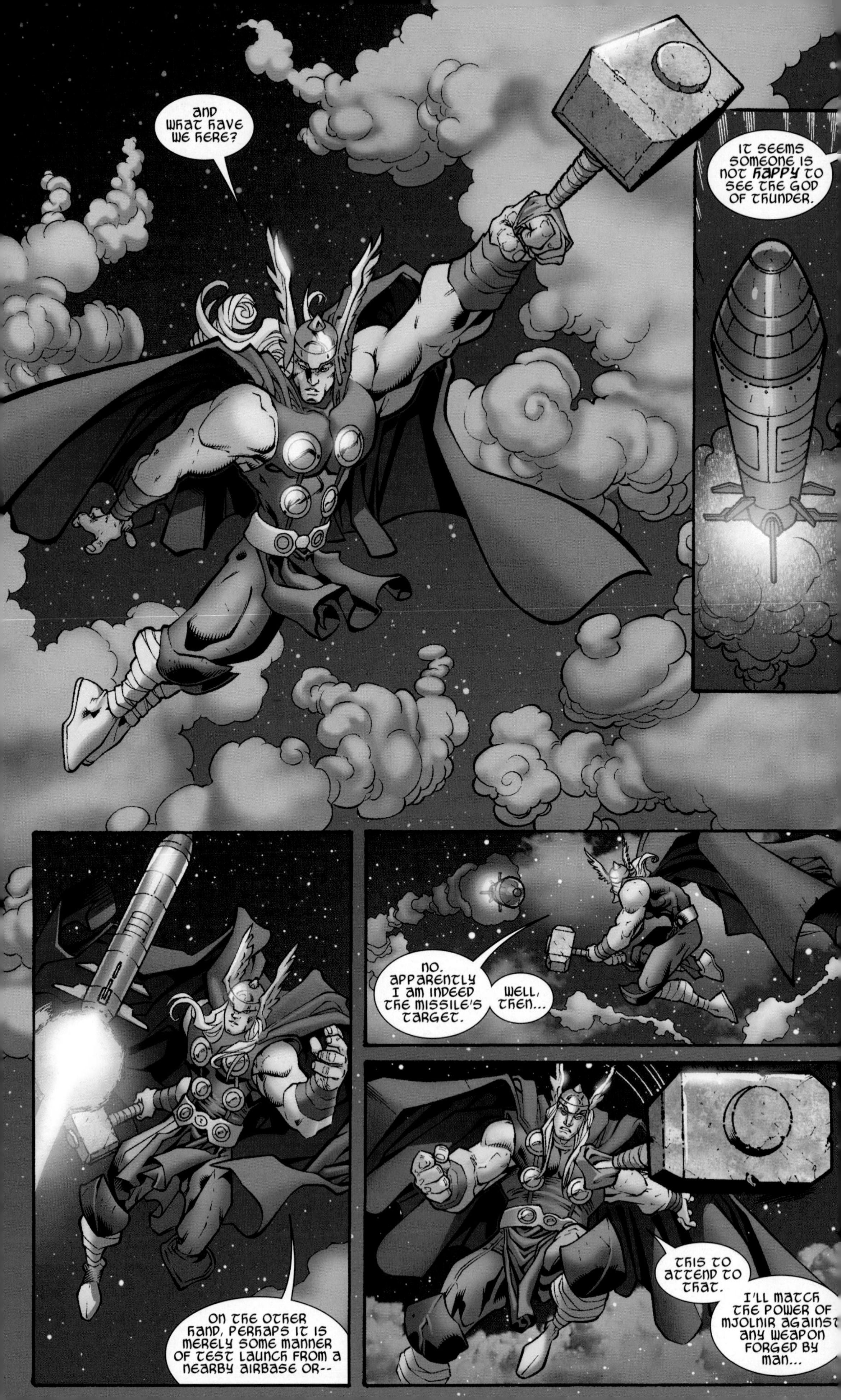

AND WHAT HAVE WE HERE?
IT SEEMS SOMEONE IS NOT HAPPY TO SEE THE GOD OF THUNDER.
ON THE OTHER HAND, PERHAPS IT IS MERELY SOME MANNER OF TEST LAUNCH FROM A NEARBY AIRBASE OR--
NO. APPARENTLY I AM INDEED THE MISSILE'S TARGET.
WELL, THEN...
I'LL MATCH THE POWER OF MJOLNIR AGAINST ANY WEAPON FORGED BY MAN...
THIS TO ATTEND TO THAT.

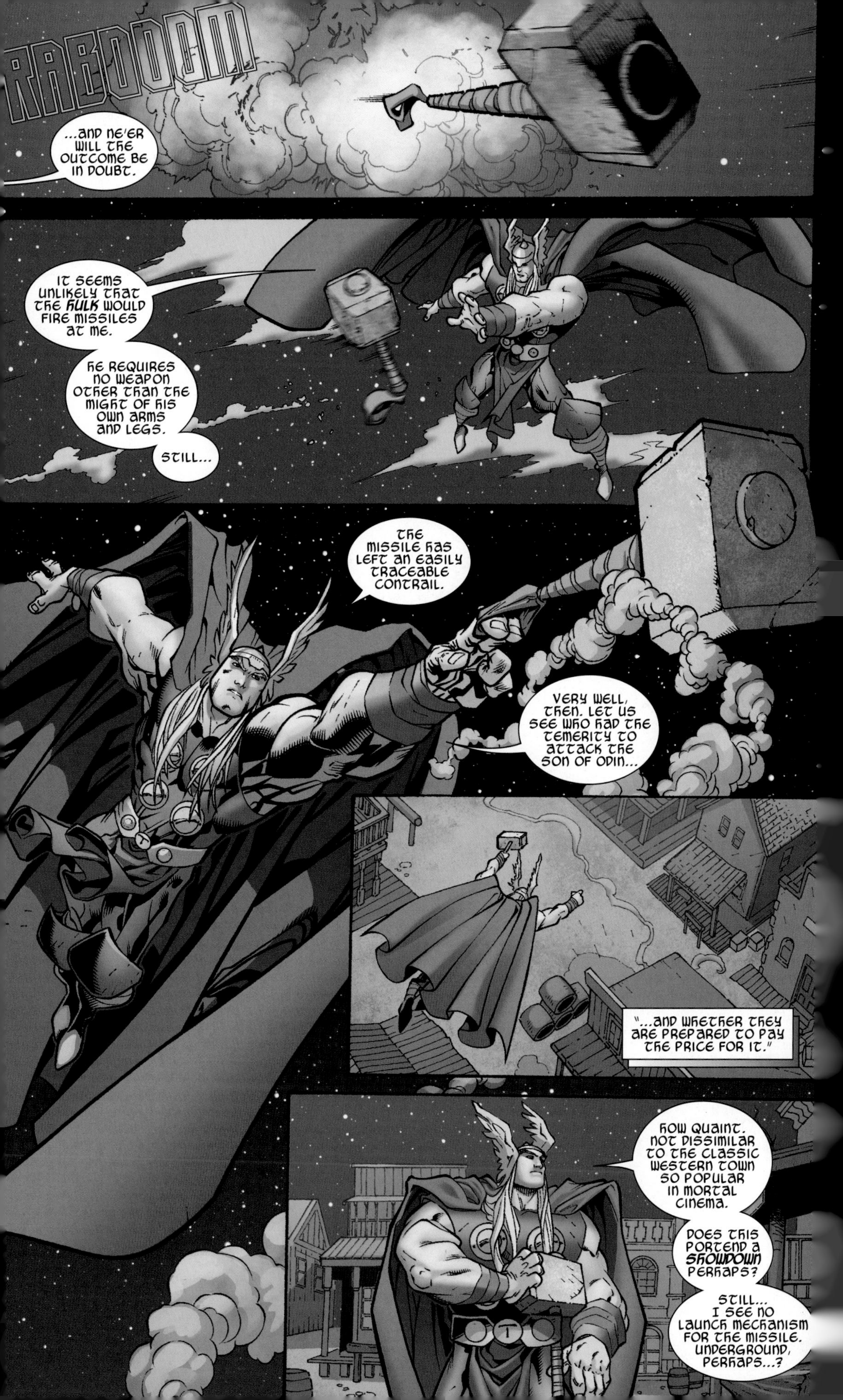
RABOOOM
...AND NE'ER WILL THE OUTCOME BE IN DOUBT.
IT SEEMS UNLIKELY THAT THE HULK WOULD FIRE MISSILES AT ME.
HE REQUIRES NO WEAPON OTHER THAN THE MIGHT OF HIS OWN ARMS AND LEGS.
STILL...
THE MISSILE HAS LEFT AN EASILY TRACEABLE CONTRAIL.
VERY WELL, THEN. LET US SEE WHO HAD THE TEMERITY TO ATTACK THE SON OF ODIN...
"...AND WHETHER THEY ARE PREPARED TO PAY THE PRICE FOR IT."
HOW QUAINT. NOT DISSIMILAR TO THE CLASSIC WESTERN TOWN SO POPULAR IN MORTAL CINEMA.
DOES THIS PORTEND A SHOWDOWN PERHAPS?
STILL... I SEE NO LAUNCH MECHANISM FOR THE MISSILE. UNDERGROUND, PERHAPS...?

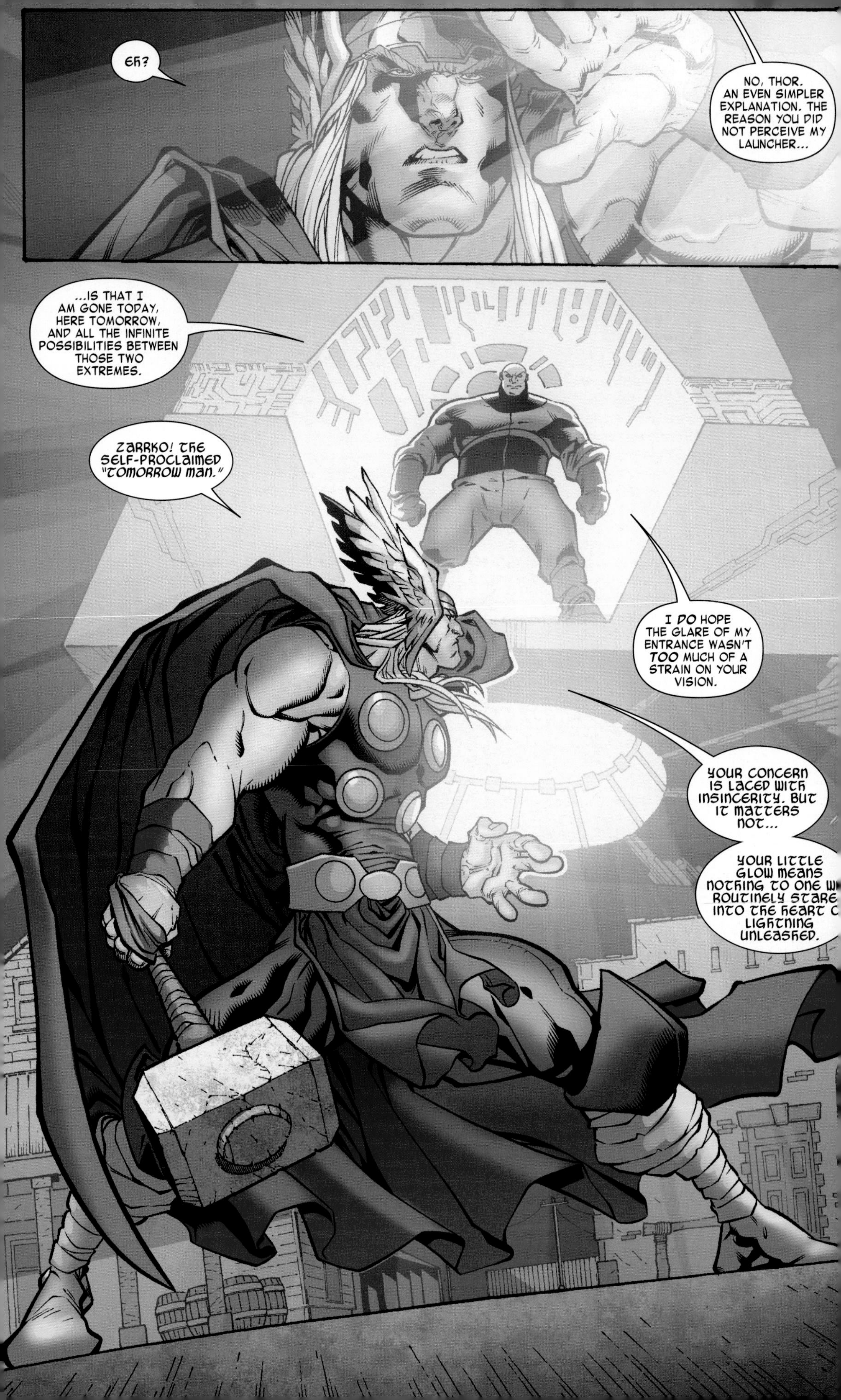
EH?
NO, THOR. AN EVEN SIMPLER EXPLANATION. THE REASON YOU DID NOT PERCEIVE MY LAUNCHER...
...IS THAT I AM GONE TODAY, HERE TOMORROW, AND ALL THE INFINITE POSSIBILITIES BETWEEN THOSE TWO EXTREMES.
ZARRKO! THE SELF-PROCLAIMED "TOMORROW MAN."
I DO HOPE THE GLARE OF MY ENTRANCE WASN'T TOO MUCH OF A STRAIN ON YOUR VISION.
YOUR CONCERN IS LACED WITH INSINCERITY. BUT IT MATTERS NOT...
YOUR LITTLE GLOW MEANS NOTHING TO ONE W ROUTINELY STARE INTO THE HEART C LIGHTNING UNLEASHED.

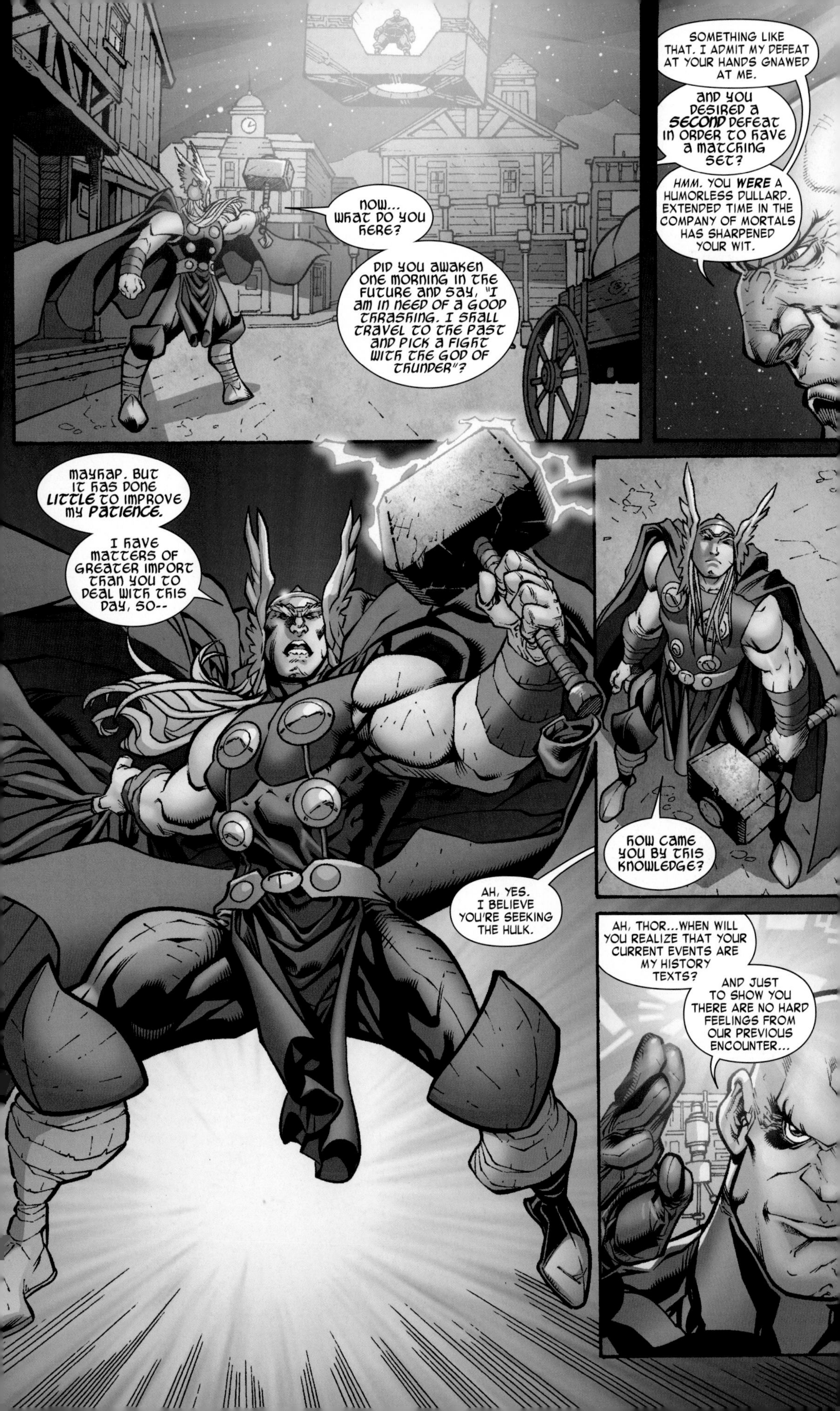
NOW... WHAT DO YOU HERE?
DID YOU AWAKEN ONE MORNING IN THE FUTURE AND SAY, "I AM IN NEED OF A GOOD THRASHING. I SHALL TRAVEL TO THE PAST AND PICK A FIGHT WITH THE GOD OF THUNDER"?
SOMETHING LIKE THAT. I ADMIT MY DEFEAT AT YOUR HANDS GNAWED AT ME.
AND YOU DESIRED A SECOND DEFEAT IN ORDER TO HAVE A MATCHING SET?
HMM. YOU WERE A HUMORLESS DULLARD. EXTENDED TIME IN THE COMPANY OF MORTALS HAS SHARPENED YOUR WIT.
MAYHAP. BUT IT HAS DONE LITTLE TO IMPROVE MY PATIENCE.
I HAVE MATTERS OF GREATER IMPORT THAN YOU TO DEAL WITH THIS DAY, SO--
AH, YES. I BELIEVE YOU'RE SEEKING THE HULK.
HOW CAME YOU BY THIS KNOWLEDGE?
AH, THOR...WHEN WILL YOU REALIZE THAT YOUR CURRENT EVENTS ARE MY HISTORY TEXTS?
AND JUST TO SHOW YOU THERE ARE NO HARD FEELINGS FROM OUR PREVIOUS ENCOUNTER...

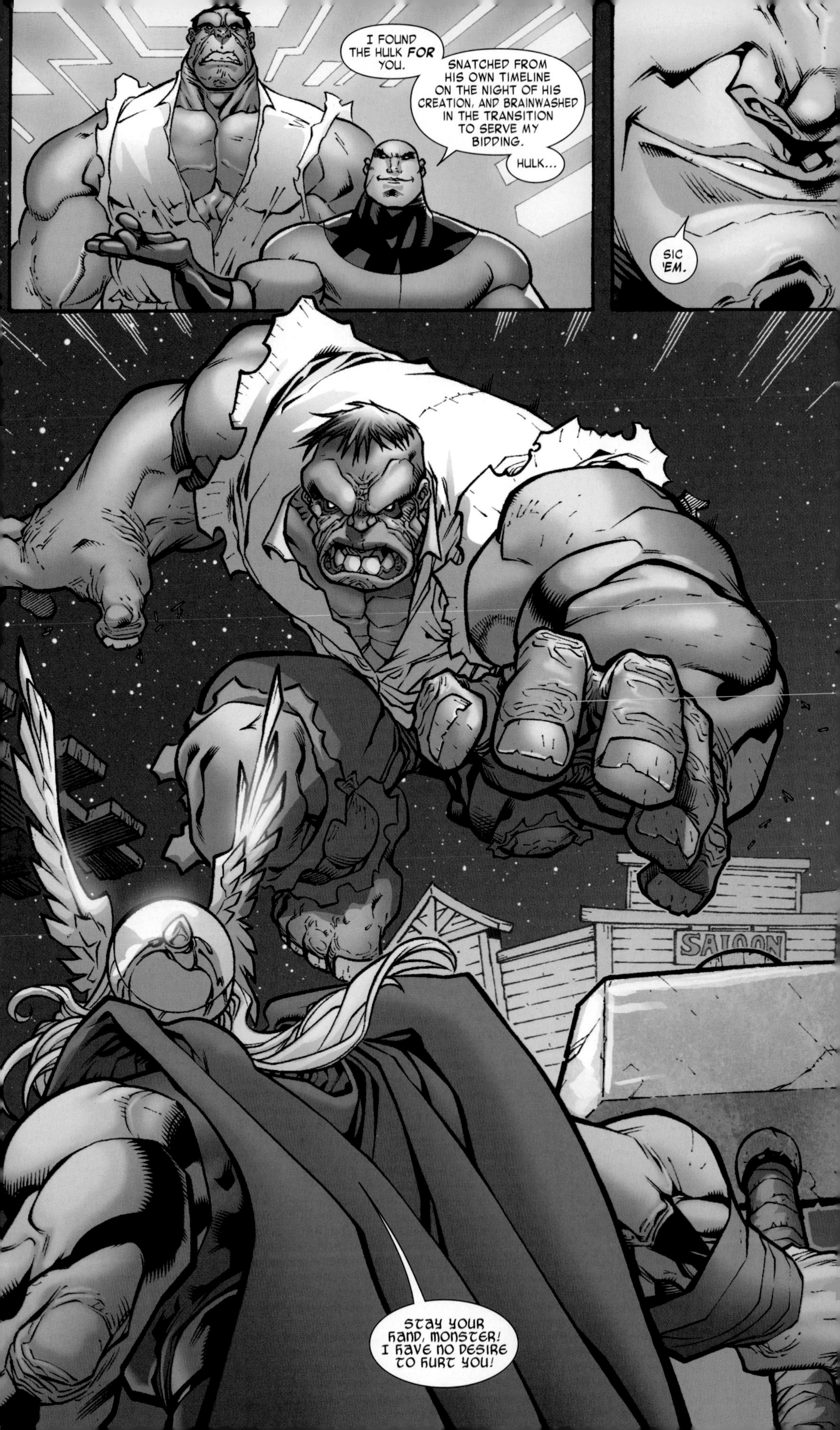
I FOUND THE HULK FOR YOU.
SNATCHED FROM HIS OWN TIMELINE ON THE NIGHT OF HIS CREATION, AND BRAINWASHED IN THE TRANSITION TO SERVE MY BIDDING.
HULK...
SIC 'EM.
SALOON
STAY YOUR HAND, MONSTER! I HAVE NO DESIRE TO HURT YOU!

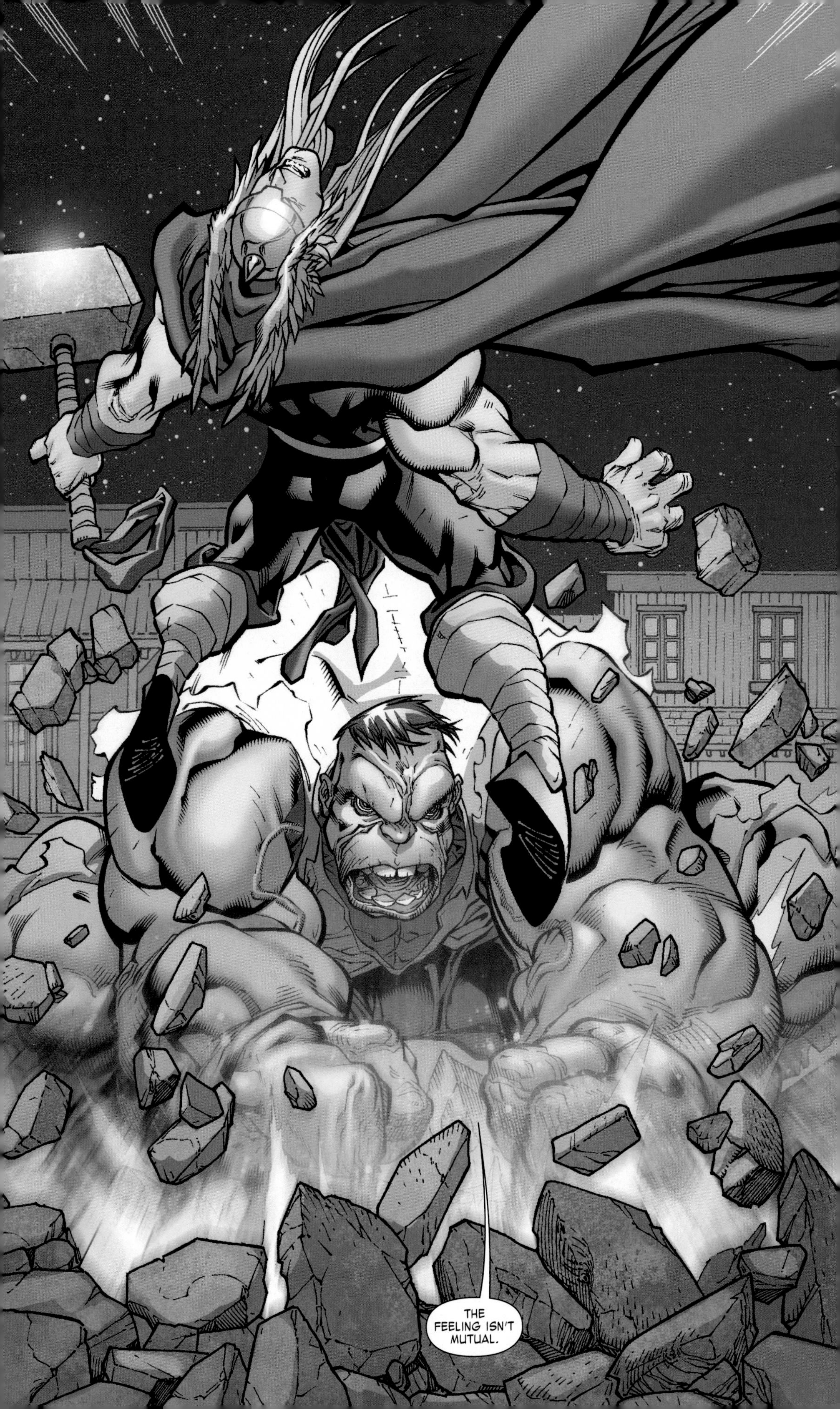
THE FEELING ISN'T MUTUAL.

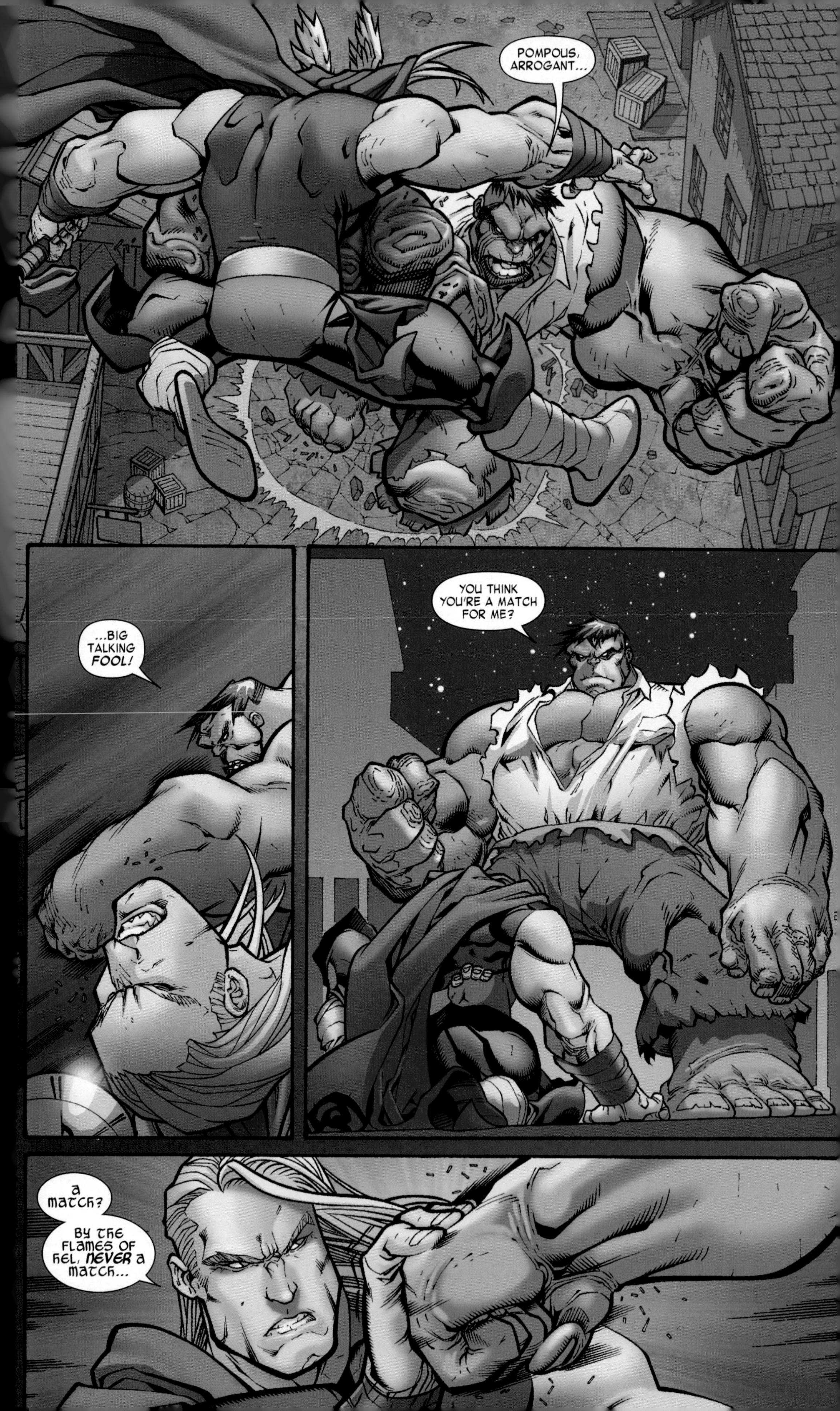
POMPOUS, ARROGANT...
...BIG TALKING FOOL!
YOU THINK YOU'RE A MATCH FOR ME?
A MATCH?
BY THE FLAMES OF HEL, NEVER A MATCH...

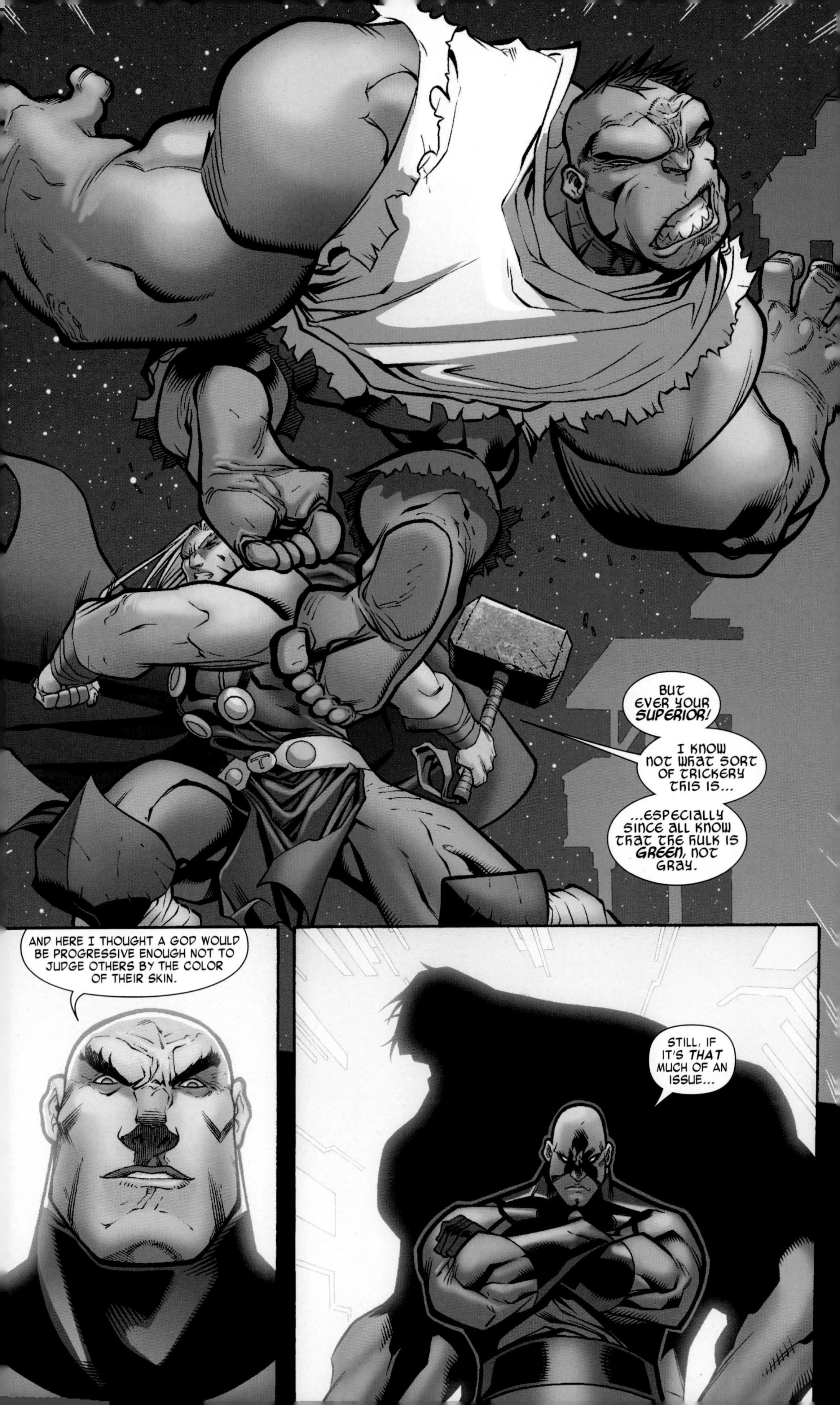
BUT EVER YOUR SUPERIOR!
I KNOW NOT WHAT SORT OF TRICKERY THIS IS...
...ESPECIALLY SINCE ALL KNOW THAT THE HULK IS GREEN, NOT GRAY.
AND HERE I THOUGHT A GOD WOULD BE PROGRESSIVE ENOUGH NOT TO JUDGE OTHERS BY THE COLOR OF THEIR SKIN.
STILL, IF IT'S THAT MUCH OF AN ISSUE...

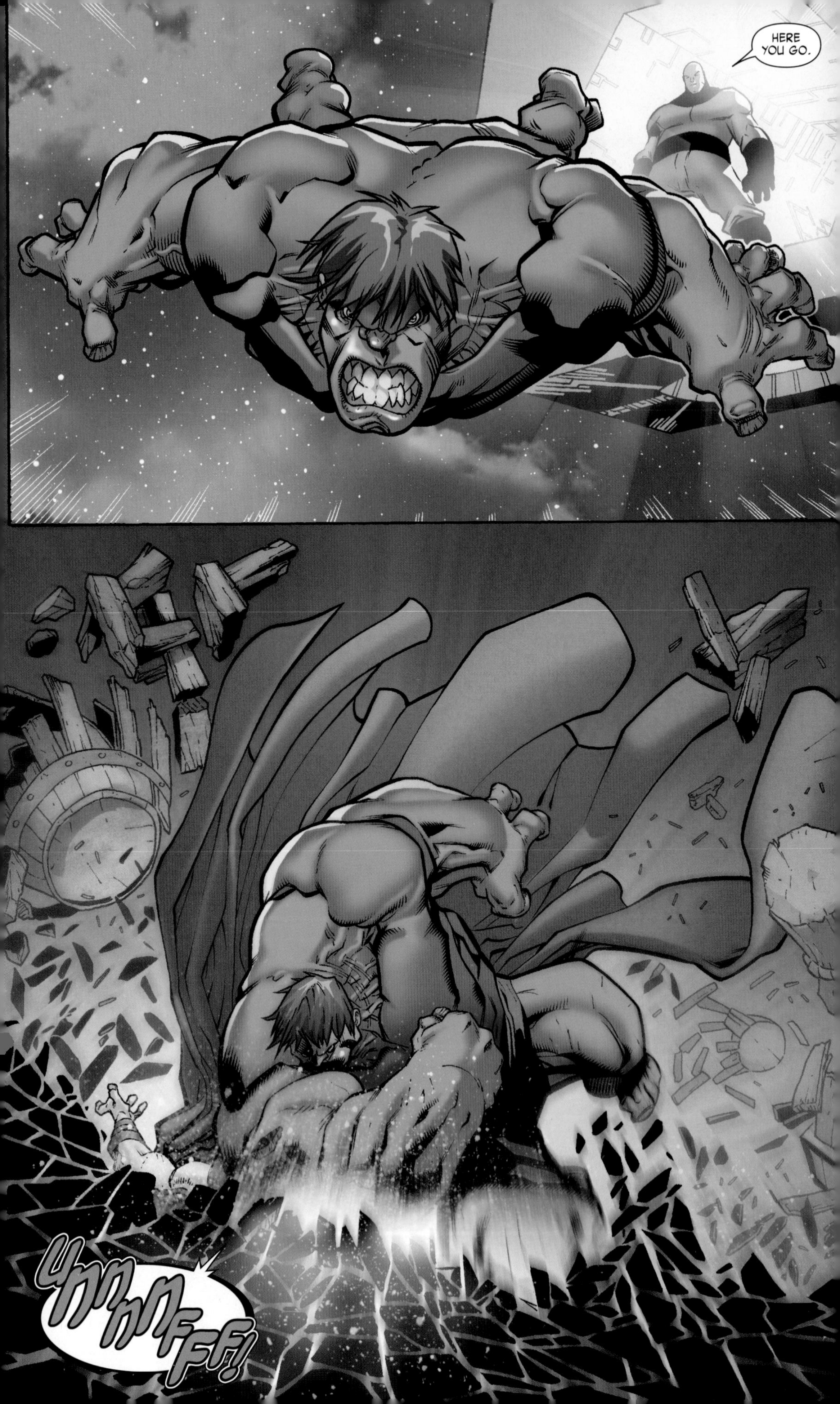
HERE YOU GO.
UNNNNFFF!

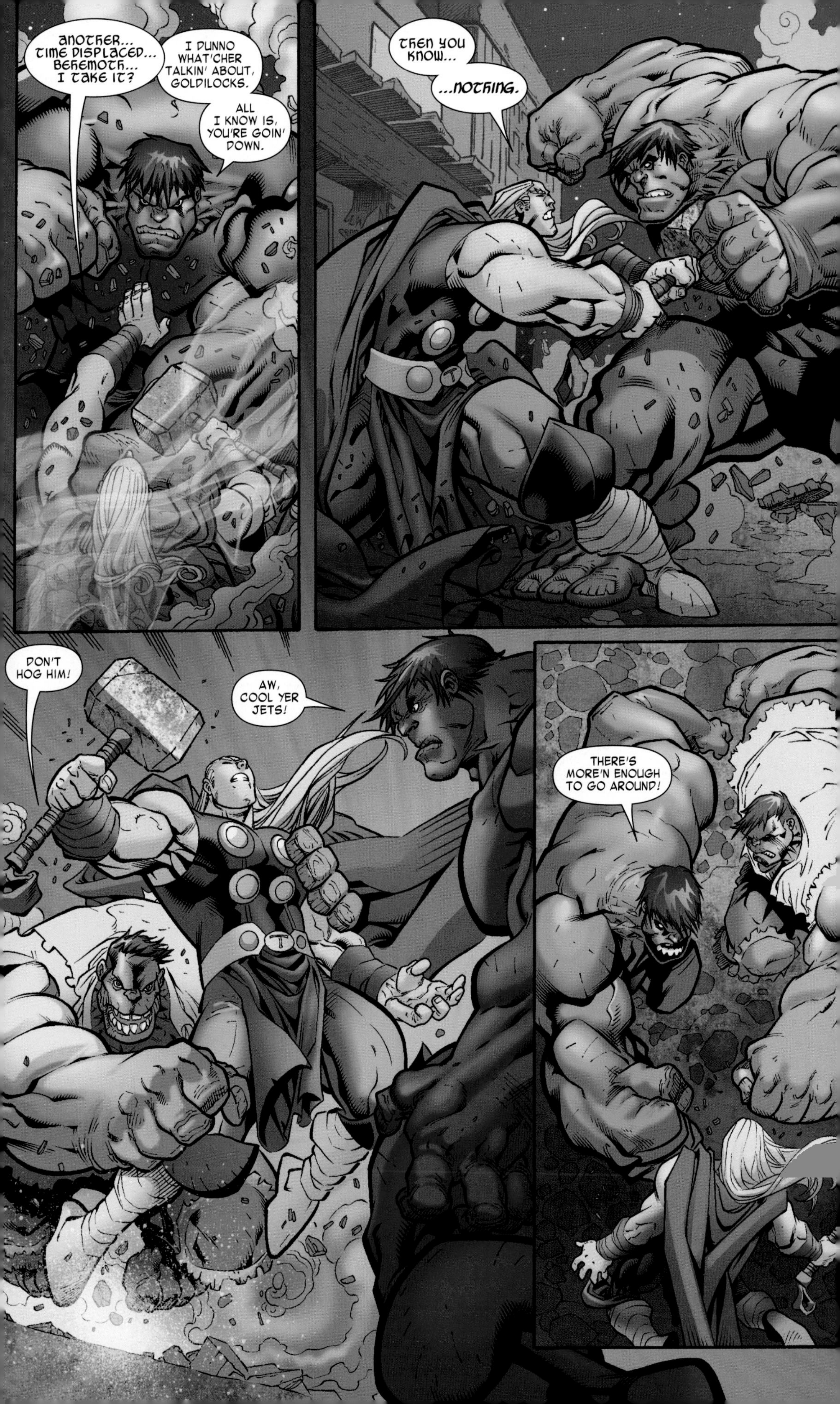
ANOTHER... TIME DISPLACED... BEHEMOTH... I TAKE IT?
I DUNNO WHAT'CHER TALKIN' ABOUT, GOLDILOCKS.
ALL I KNOW IS, YOU'RE GOIN' DOWN.
THEN YOU KNOW...
...NOTHING.
DON'T HOG HIM!
AW, COOL YER JETS!
THERE'S MORE'N ENOUGH TO GO AROUND!

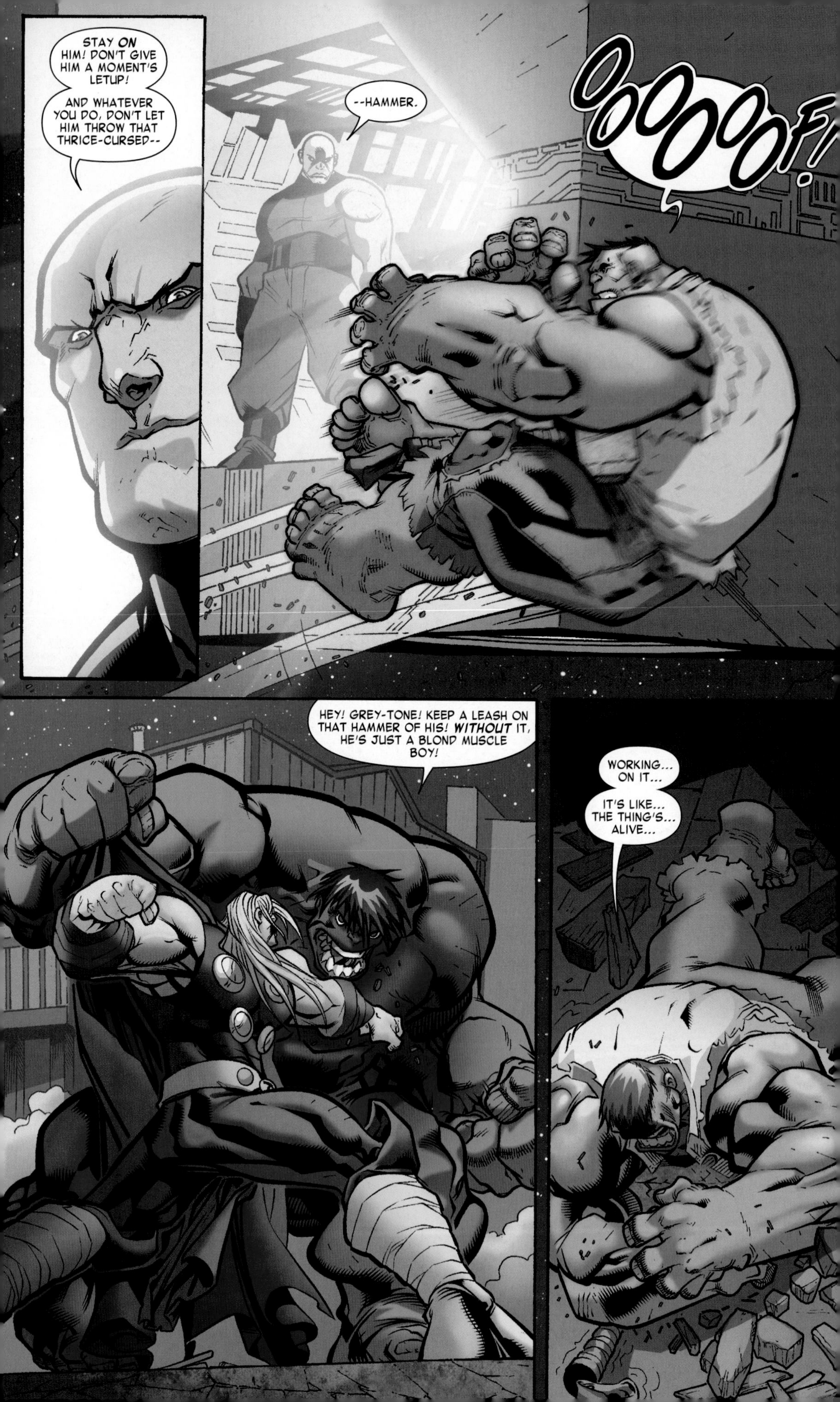
STAY ON HIM! DON'T GIVE HIM A MOMENT'S LETUP!
AND WHATEVER YOU DO, DON'T LET HIM THROW THAT THRICE-CURSED--
--HAMMER.
OOOOOOF!
HEY! GREY-TONE! KEEP A LEASH ON THAT HAMMER OF HIS! WITHOUT IT, HE'S JUST A BLOND MUSCLE BOY!
WORKING... ON IT...
IT'S LIKE... THE THING'S... ALIVE...

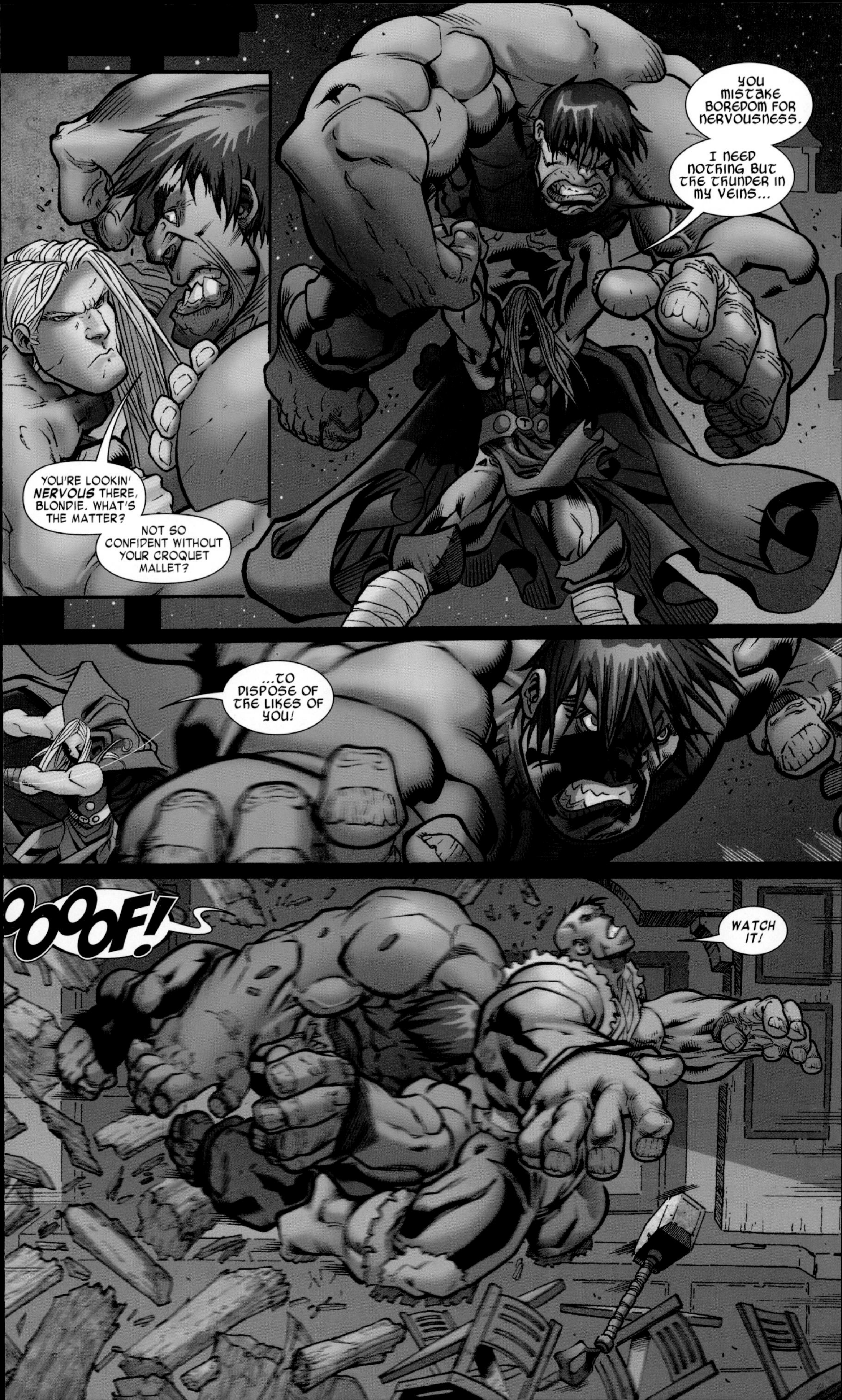
YOU'RE LOOKIN' NERVOUS THERE, BLONDIE. WHAT'S THE MATTER?
NOT SO CONFIDENT WITHOUT YOUR CROQUET MALLET?
YOU MISTAKE BOREDOM FOR NERVOUSNESS.
I NEED NOTHING BUT THE THUNDER IN MY VEINS...
...TO DISPOSE OF THE LIKES OF YOU!
OOOOF!
WATCH IT!

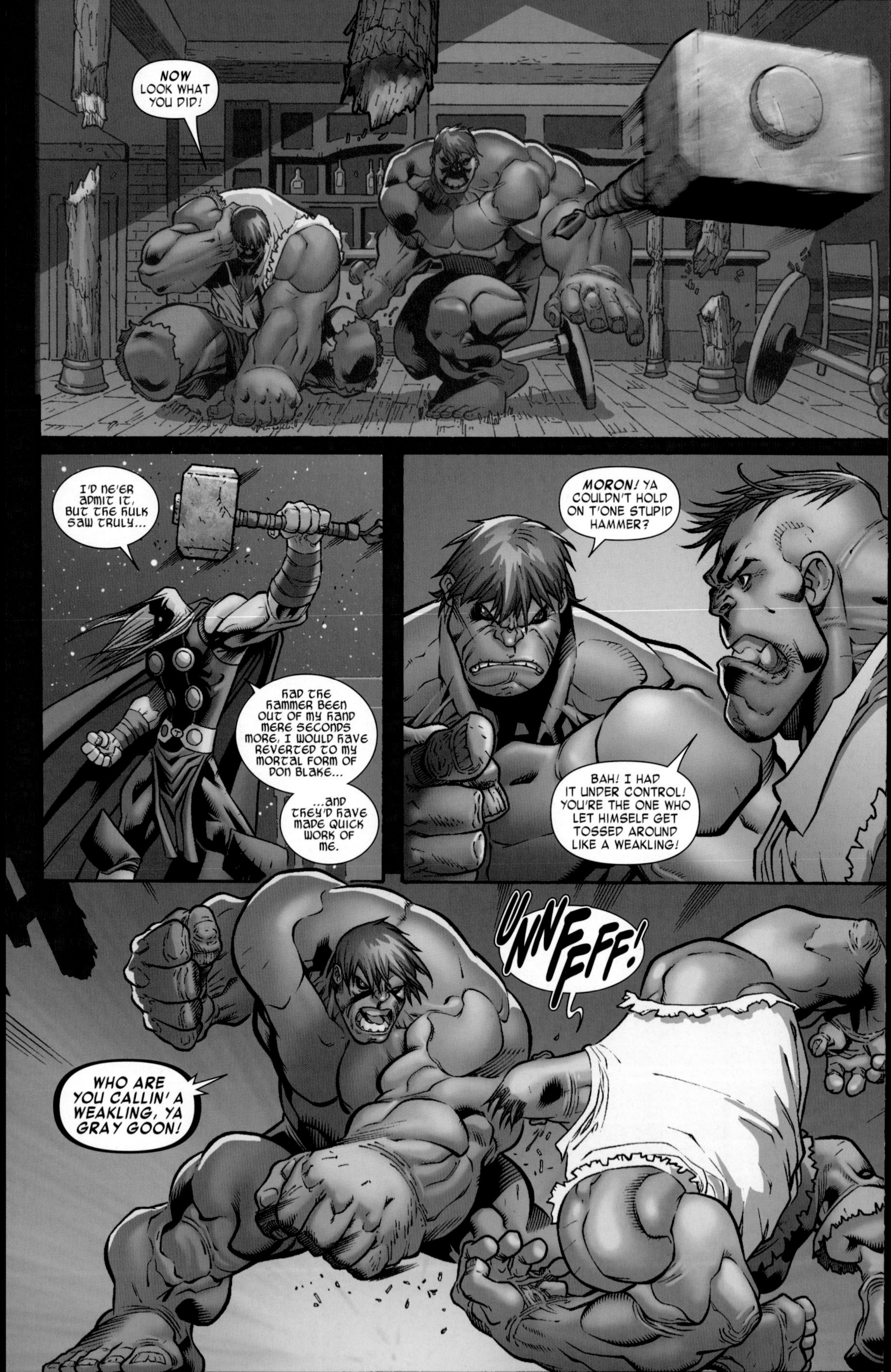
NOW LOOK WHAT YOU DID!
I'D NE'ER ADMIT IT, BUT THE HULK SAW TRULY...
HAD THE HAMMER BEEN OUT OF MY HAND MERE SECONDS MORE, I WOULD HAVE REVERTED TO MY MORTAL FORM OF DON BLAKE...
...AND THEY'D HAVE MADE QUICK WORK OF ME.
MORON! YA COULDN'T HOLD ON T'ONE STUPID HAMMER?
BAH! I HAD IT UNDER CONTROL! YOU'RE THE ONE WHO LET HIMSELF GET TOSSED AROUND LIKE A WEAKLING!
UNNFFFF!
WHO ARE YOU CALLIN' A WEAKLING, YA GRAY GOON!

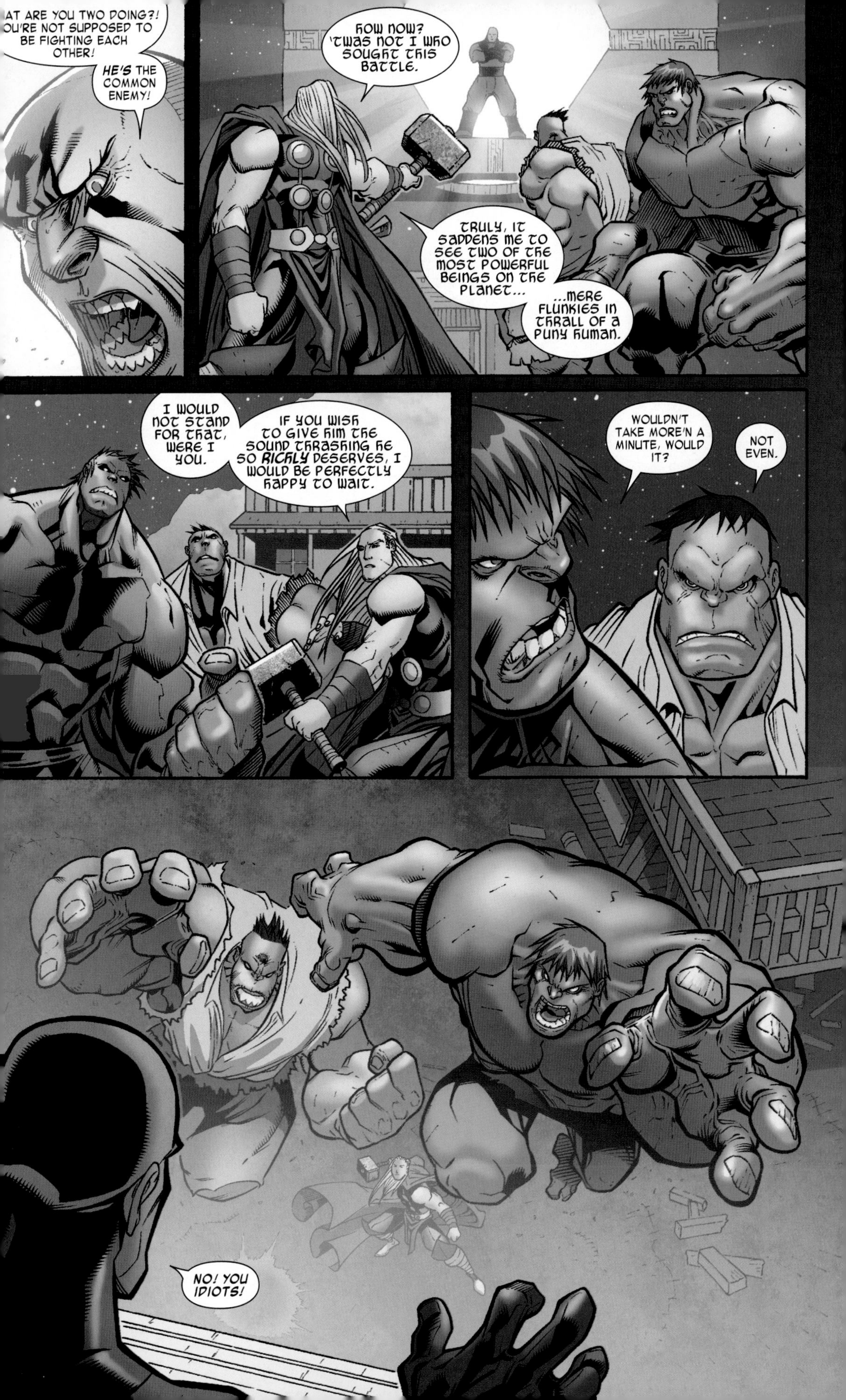
AT ARE YOU TWO DOING?! OU'RE NOT SUPPOSED TO BE FIGHTING EACH OTHER!
HE'S THE COMMON ENEMY!
HOW NOW? 'TWAS NOT I WHO SOUGHT THIS BATTLE.
TRULY, IT SADDENS ME TO SEE TWO OF THE MOST POWERFUL BEINGS ON THE PLANET...
...MERE FLUNKIES IN THRALL OF A PUNY HUMAN.
I WOULD NOT STAND FOR THAT, WERE I YOU.
IF YOU WISH TO GIVE HIM THE SOUND THRASHING HE SO RICHLY DESERVES, I WOULD BE PERFECTLY HAPPY TO WAIT.
WOULDN'T TAKE MORE'N A MINUTE, WOULD IT?
NOT EVEN.
NO! YOU IDIOTS!

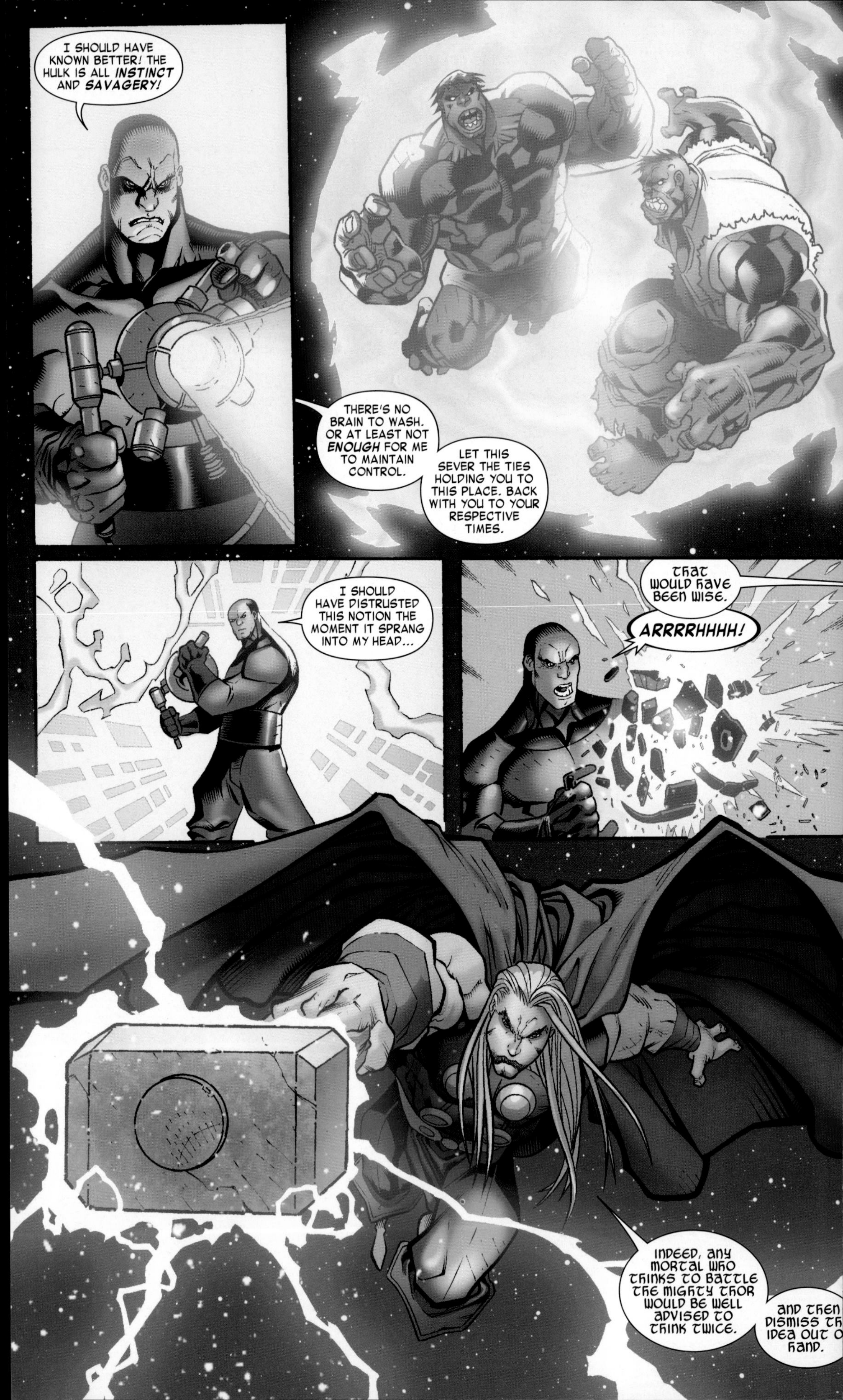
I SHOULD HAVE KNOWN BETTER! THE HULK IS ALL INSTINCT AND SAVAGERY!
THERE'S NO BRAIN TO WASH. OR AT LEAST NOT ENOUGH FOR ME TO MAINTAIN CONTROL.
LET THIS SEVER THE TIES HOLDING YOU TO THIS PLACE. BACK WITH YOU TO YOUR RESPECTIVE TIMES.
I SHOULD HAVE DISTRUSTED THIS NOTION THE MOMENT IT SPRANG INTO MY HEAD...
THAT WOULD HAVE BEEN WISE.
ARRRRHHHH!
INDEED, ANY MORTAL WHO THINKS TO BATTLE THE MIGHTY THOR WOULD BE WELL ADVISED TO THINK TWICE.

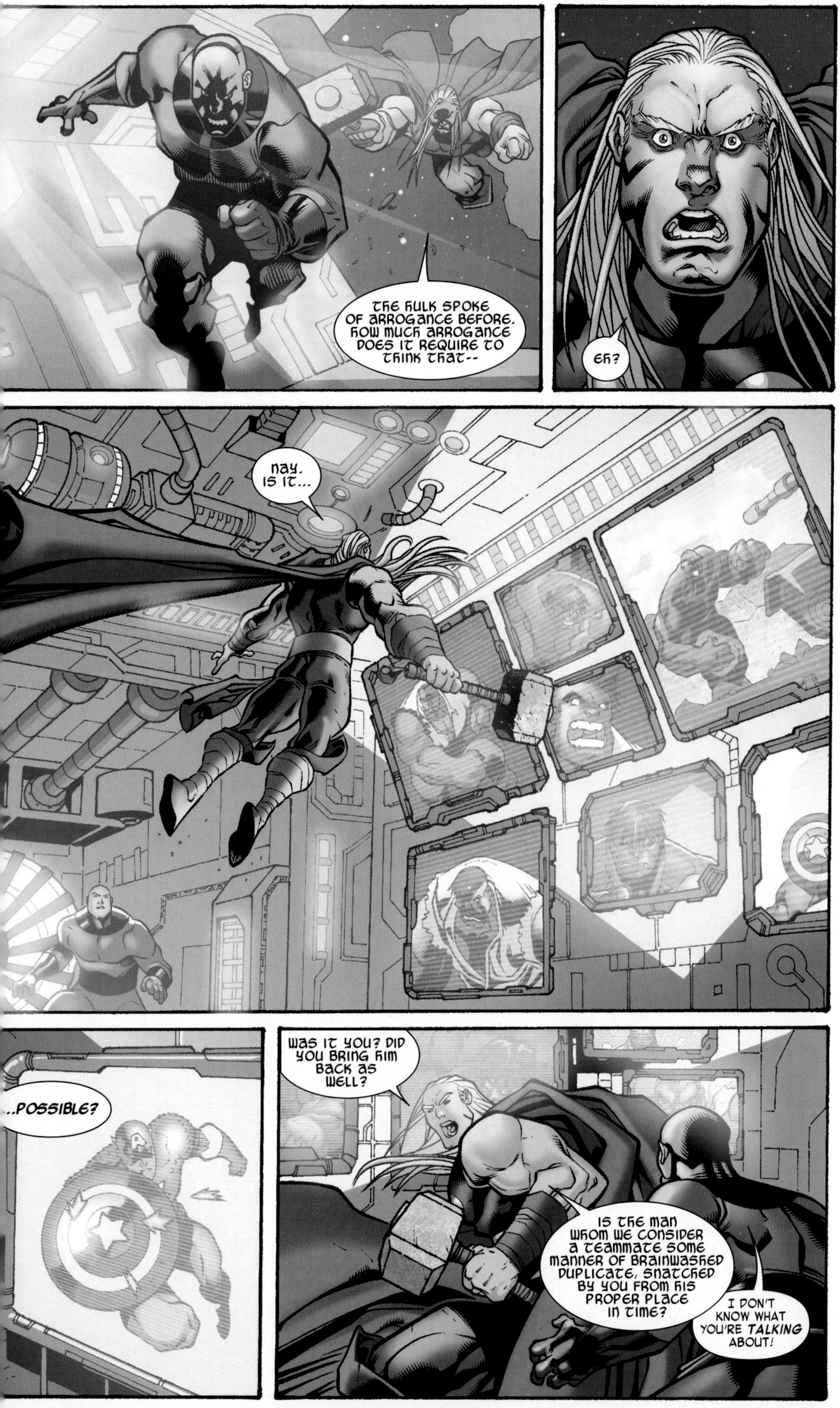
THE HULK SPOKE OF ARROGANCE BEFORE. HOW MUCH ARROGANCE DOES IT REQUIRE TO THINK THAT--
EH?
NAY. IS IT...
...POSSIBLE?
WAS IT YOU? DID YOU BRING HIM BACK AS WELL?
IS THE MAN WHOM WE CONSIDER A TEAMMATE SOME MANNER OF BRAINWASHED DUPLICATE, SNATCHED BY YOU FROM HIS PROPER PLACE IN TIME?
I DON'T KNOW WHAT YOU'RE *TALKING* ABOUT!

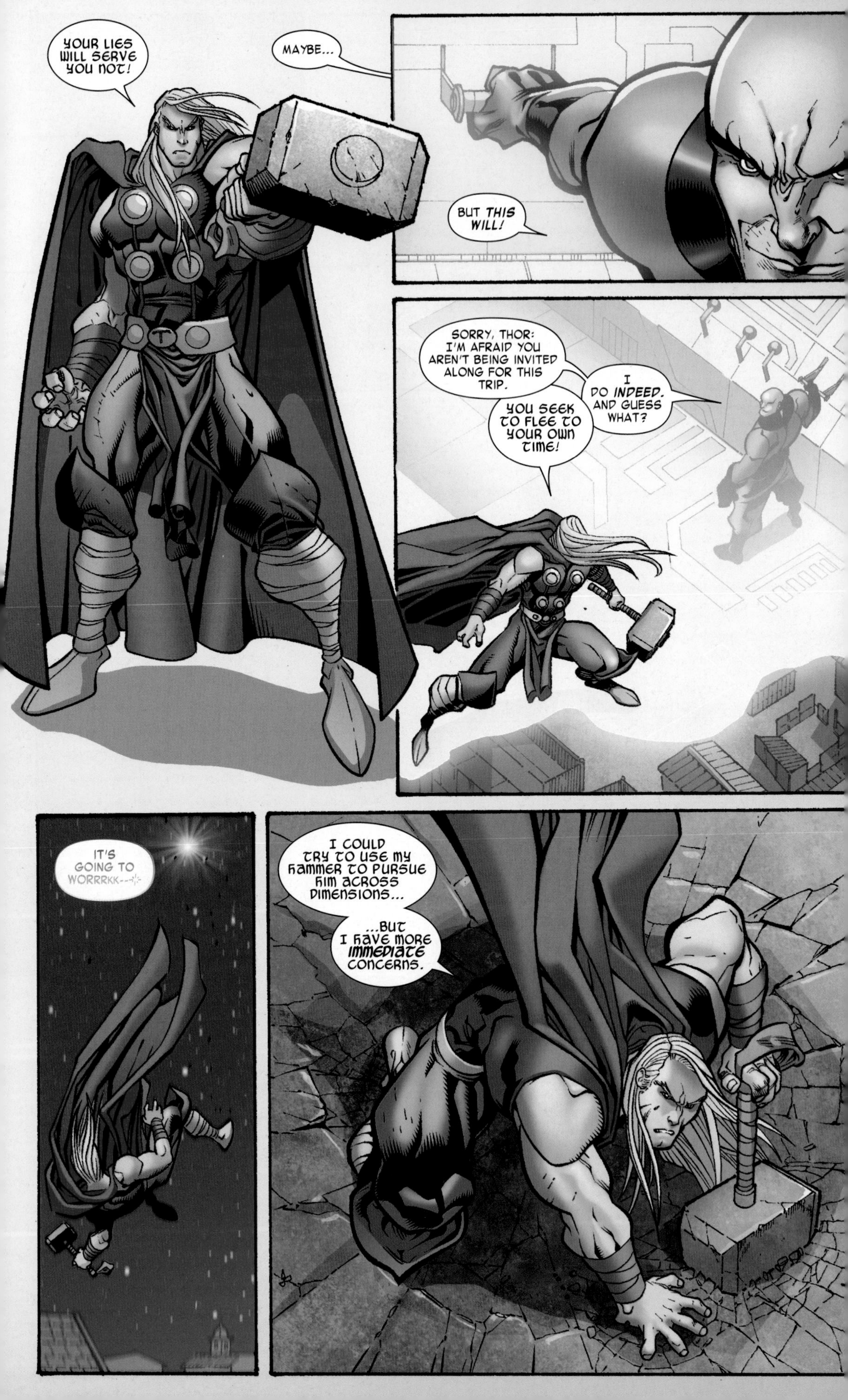

YOUR LIES WILL SERVE YOU NOT!
MAYBE...
BUT THIS WILL!
SORRY, THOR: I'M AFRAID YOU AREN'T BEING INVITED ALONG FOR THIS TRIP.
YOU SEEK TO FLEE TO YOUR OWN TIME!
I DO INDEED. AND GUESS WHAT?
IT'S GOING TO WORRRKK--
I COULD TRY TO USE MY HAMMER TO PURSUE HIM ACROSS DIMENSIONS...
...BUT I HAVE MORE IMMEDIATE CONCERNS.

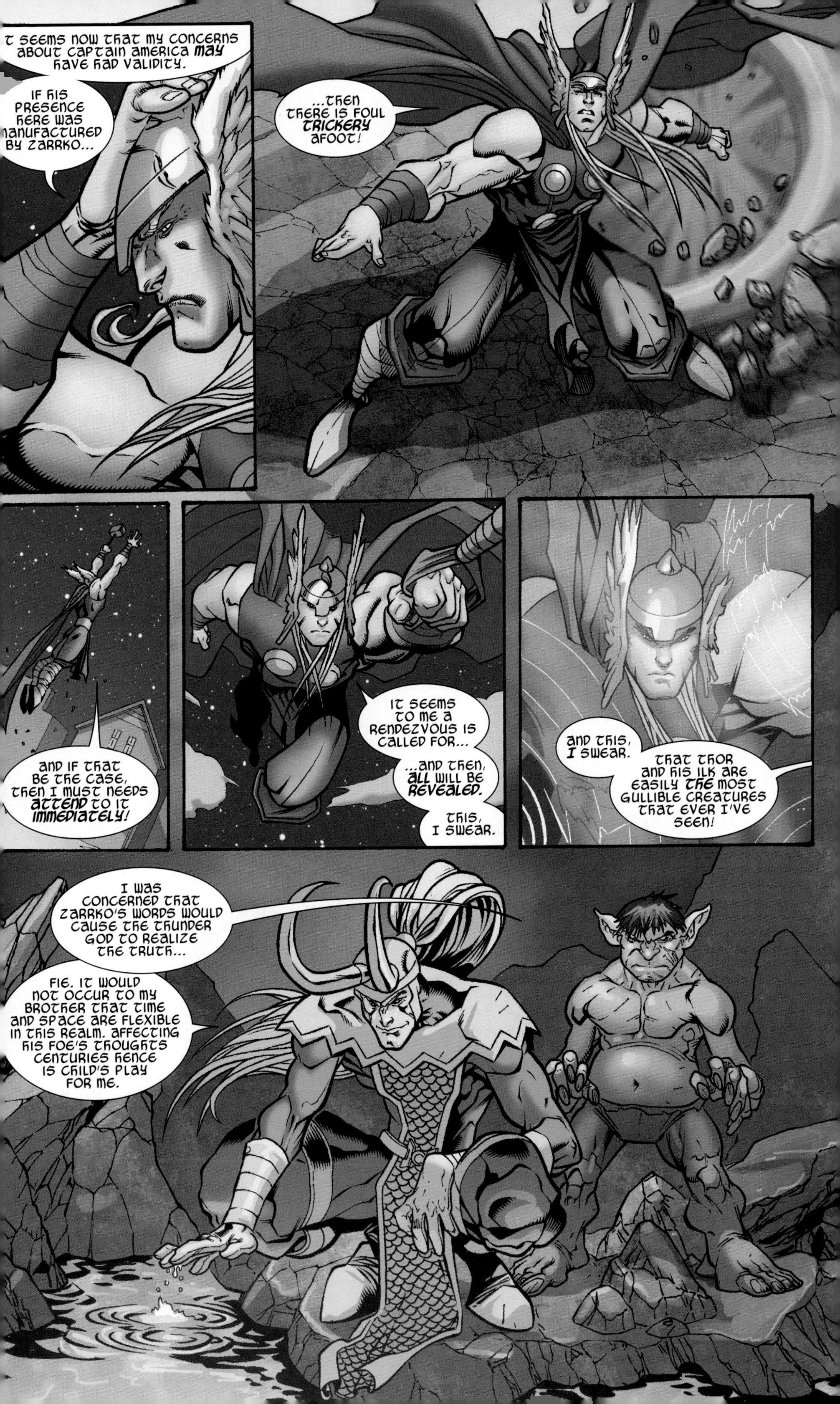

IT SEEMS NOW THAT MY CONCERNS ABOUT CAPTAIN AMERICA MAY HAVE HAD VALIDITY.
IF HIS PRESENCE HERE WAS MANUFACTURED BY ZARRKO...
...THEN THERE IS FOUL TRICKERY AFOOT!
AND IF THAT BE THE CASE, THEN I MUST NEEDS ATTEND TO IT IMMEDIATELY!
IT SEEMS TO ME A RENDEZVOUS IS CALLED FOR...
...AND THEN, ALL WILL BE REVEALED.
THIS, I SWEAR.
AND THIS, I SWEAR.
THAT THOR AND HIS ILK ARE EASILY THE MOST GULLIBLE CREATURES THAT EVER I'VE SEEN!
I WAS CONCERNED THAT ZARRKO'S WORDS WOULD CAUSE THE THUNDER GOD TO REALIZE THE TRUTH...
FIE. IT WOULD NOT OCCUR TO MY BROTHER THAT TIME AND SPACE ARE FLEXIBLE IN THIS REALM. AFFECTING HIS FOE'S THOUGHTS CENTURIES HENCE IS CHILD'S PLAY FOR ME.

I WAS CONCERNED THAT IF I EMPLOYED MAGICKS WITH THOR TO THE DEGREE I DID WITH HIS ALLIES, HE WOULD PERCEIVE MY HAND.

SO ZARRKO AND HIS MACHINATIONS WITH THE HULKS WERE GENUINE ENOUGH...

...WHILE A SIMPLE ILLUSION PROVIDED THOR HIS GLIMPSE OF CAPTAIN AMERICA ON THE SCREEN, TO ZARRKO'S GENUINE CONFUSION.

AS FOR THOR'S ASSOCIATES, ALLIES OF MINE WERE HAPPY TO DO MY BIDDING, AIDED BY SIMPLE GLAMOURS AND ILLUSIONS.

THE ENCHANTRESS ATTENDED TO CAPTAIN AMERICA, IN A WORLD THAT AT NO TIME WAS EVER WHAT HE PERCEIVED IT TO BE...

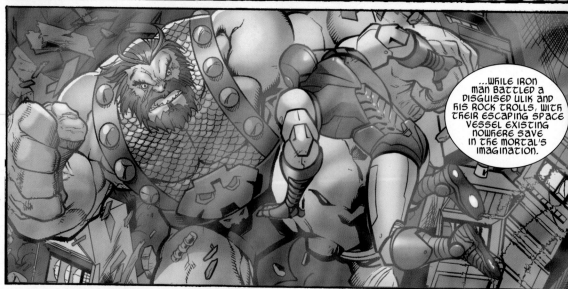

...WHILE IRON MAN BATTLED A DISGUISED ULIK AND HIS ROCK TROLLS, WITH THEIR ESCAPING SPACE VESSEL EXISTING NOWHERE SAVE IN THE MORTAL'S IMAGINATION.

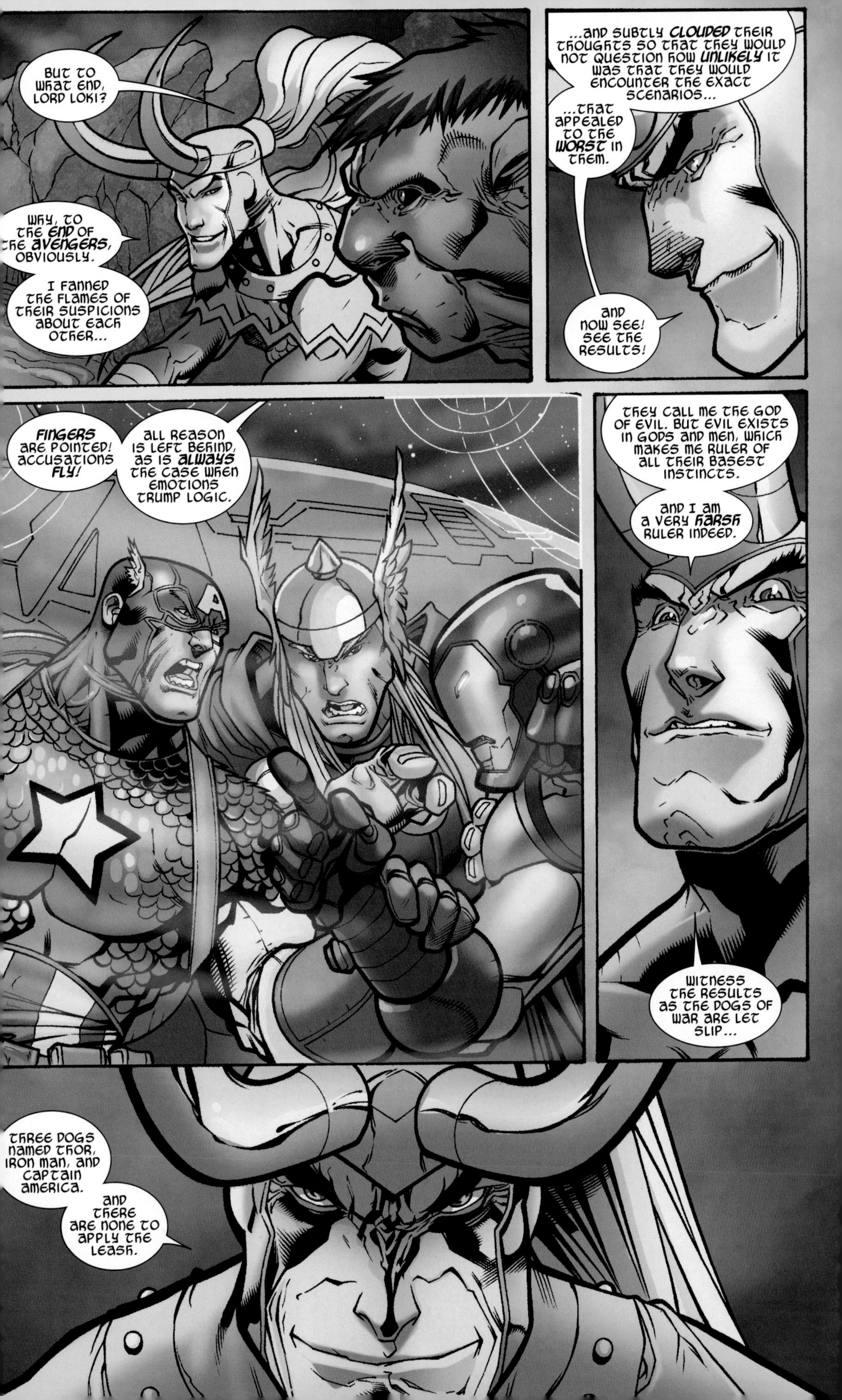

BUT TO WHAT END, LORD LOKI?
WHY, TO THE END OF THE AVENGERS, OBVIOUSLY.
I FANNED THE FLAMES OF THEIR SUSPICIONS ABOUT EACH OTHER...
...AND SUBTLY CLOUDED THEIR THOUGHTS SO THAT THEY WOULD NOT QUESTION HOW UNLIKELY IT WAS THAT THEY WOULD ENCOUNTER THE EXACT SCENARIOS...
...THAT APPEALED TO THE WORST IN THEM.
AND NOW SEE! SEE THE RESULTS!
FINGERS ARE POINTED! ACCUSATIONS FLY!
ALL REASON IS LEFT BEHIND, AS IS ALWAYS THE CASE WHEN EMOTIONS TRUMP LOGIC.
THEY CALL ME THE GOD OF EVIL. BUT EVIL EXISTS IN GODS AND MEN, WHICH MAKES ME RULER OF ALL THEIR BASEST INSTINCTS.
AND I AM A VERY HARSH RULER INDEED.
WITNESS THE RESULTS AS THE DOGS OF WAR ARE LET SLIP...
THREE DOGS NAMED THOR, IRON MAN, AND CAPTAIN AMERICA.
AND THERE ARE NONE TO APPLY THE LEASH.

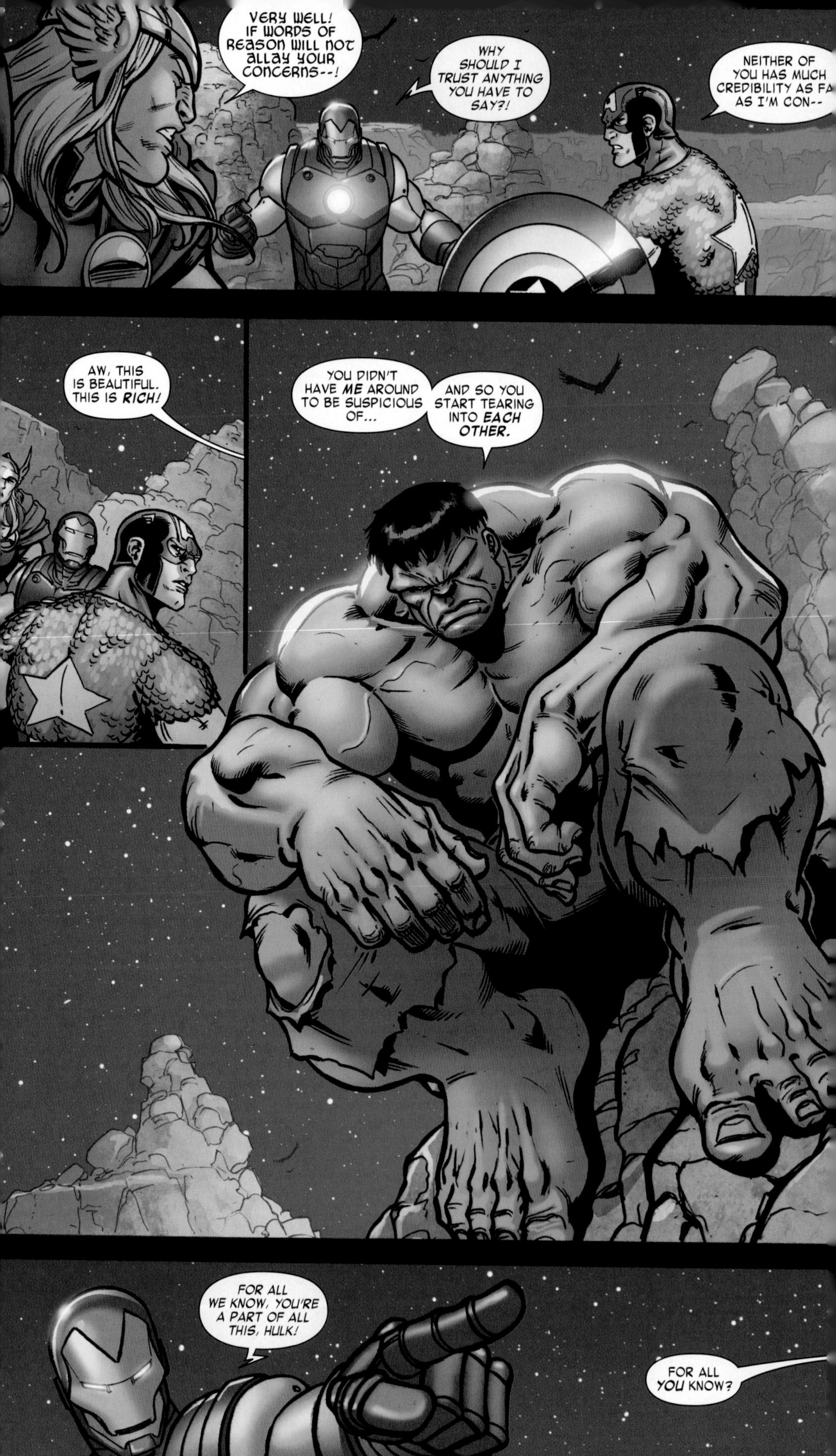

VERY WELL! IF WORDS OF REASON WILL NOT ALLAY YOUR CONCERNS--!
WHY SHOULD I TRUST ANYTHING YOU HAVE TO SAY?!
NEITHER OF YOU HAS MUCH CREDIBILITY AS FA AS I'M CON--
AW, THIS IS BEAUTIFUL. THIS IS RICH!
YOU DIDN'T HAVE ME AROUND TO BE SUSPICIOUS OF...
AND SO YOU START TEARING INTO EACH OTHER.
FOR ALL WE KNOW, YOU'RE A PART OF ALL THIS, HULK!
FOR ALL YOU KNOW?

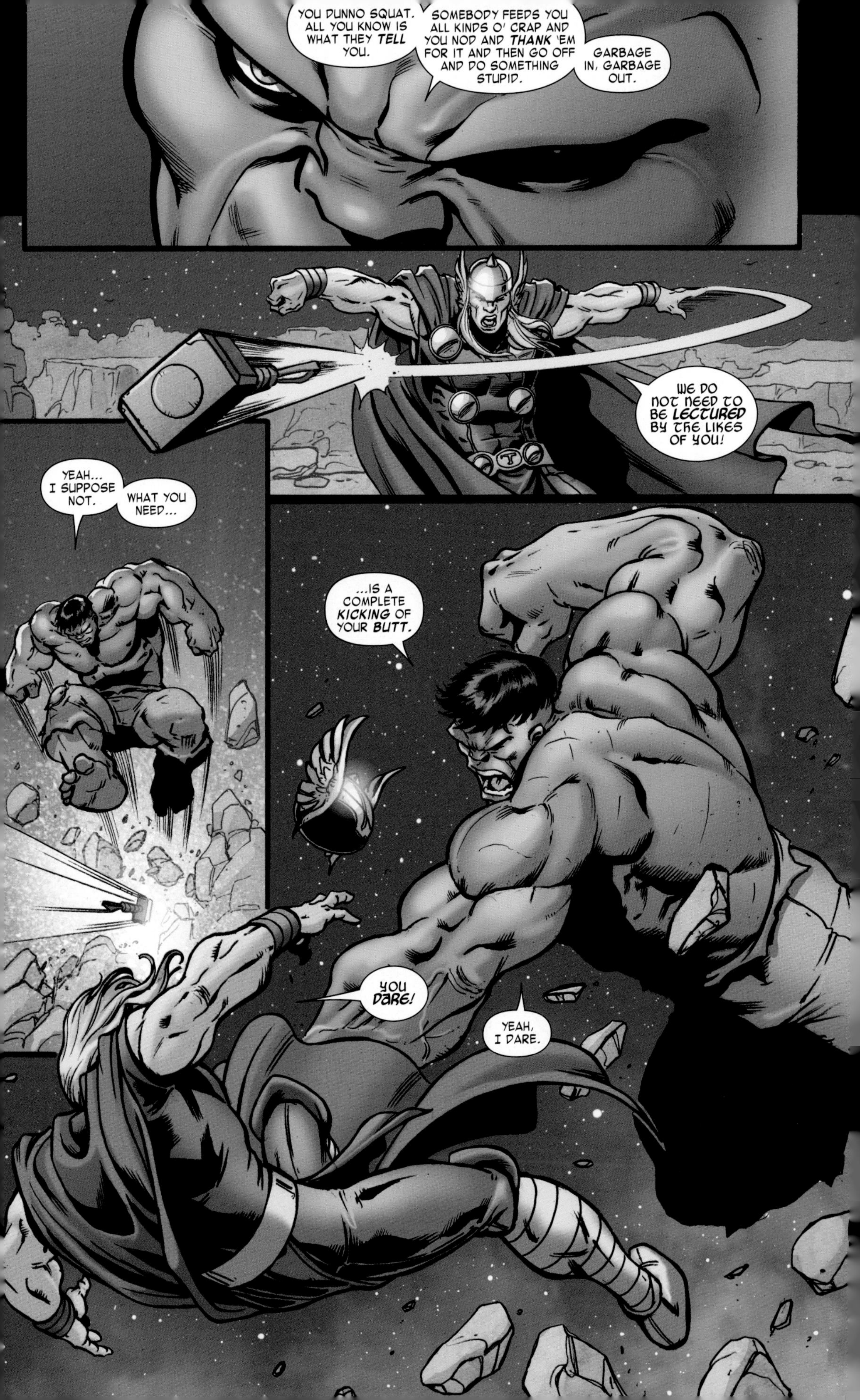
YOU DUNNO SQUAT. ALL YOU KNOW IS WHAT THEY TELL YOU.
SOMEBODY FEEDS YOU ALL KINDS O' CRAP AND YOU NOD AND THANK 'EM FOR IT AND THEN GO OFF AND DO SOMETHING STUPID.
GARBAGE IN, GARBAGE OUT.
WE DO NOT NEED TO BE LECTURED BY THE LIKES OF YOU!
YEAH... I SUPPOSE NOT.
WHAT YOU NEED...
...IS A COMPLETE KICKING OF YOUR BUTT.
YOU DARE!
YEAH, I DARE.

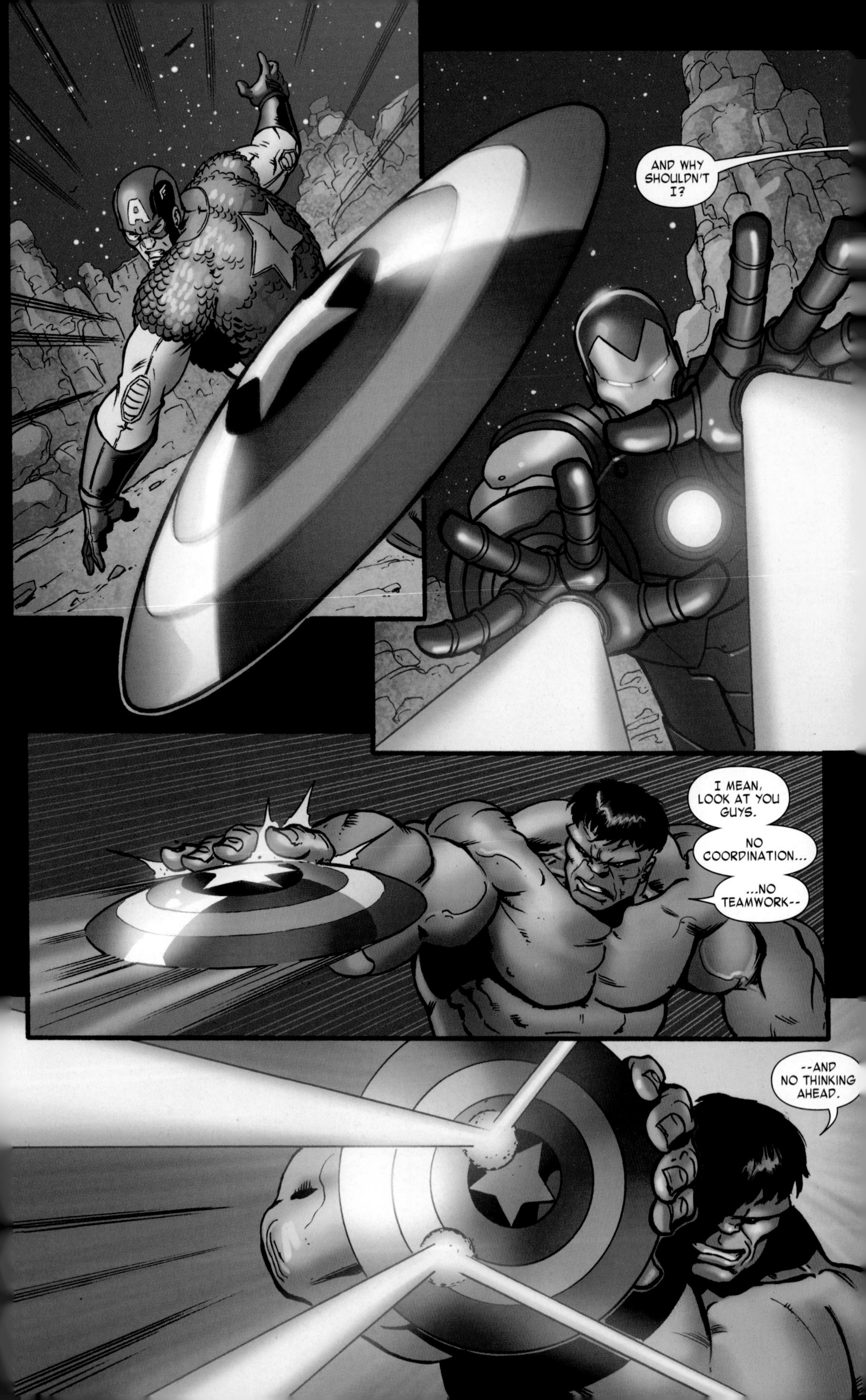
AND WHY SHOULDN'T I?
I MEAN, LOOK AT YOU GUYS.
NO COORDINATION...
...NO TEAMWORK--
--AND NO THINKING AHEAD.

HERE, CAPPY. YOU NEED THIS MORE'N I DO.

I DON'T HAVE TO HIDE BEHIND SHIELDS...

OR SUITS OF ARMOR...

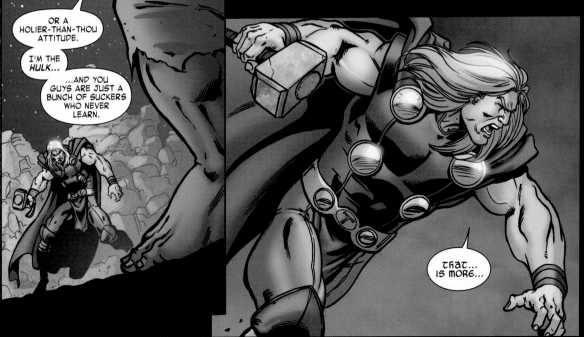

OR A HOLIER-THAN-THOU ATTITUDE.

I'M THE HULK...

...AND YOU GUYS ARE JUST A BUNCH OF SUCKERS WHO NEVER LEARN.

THAT... IS MORE...

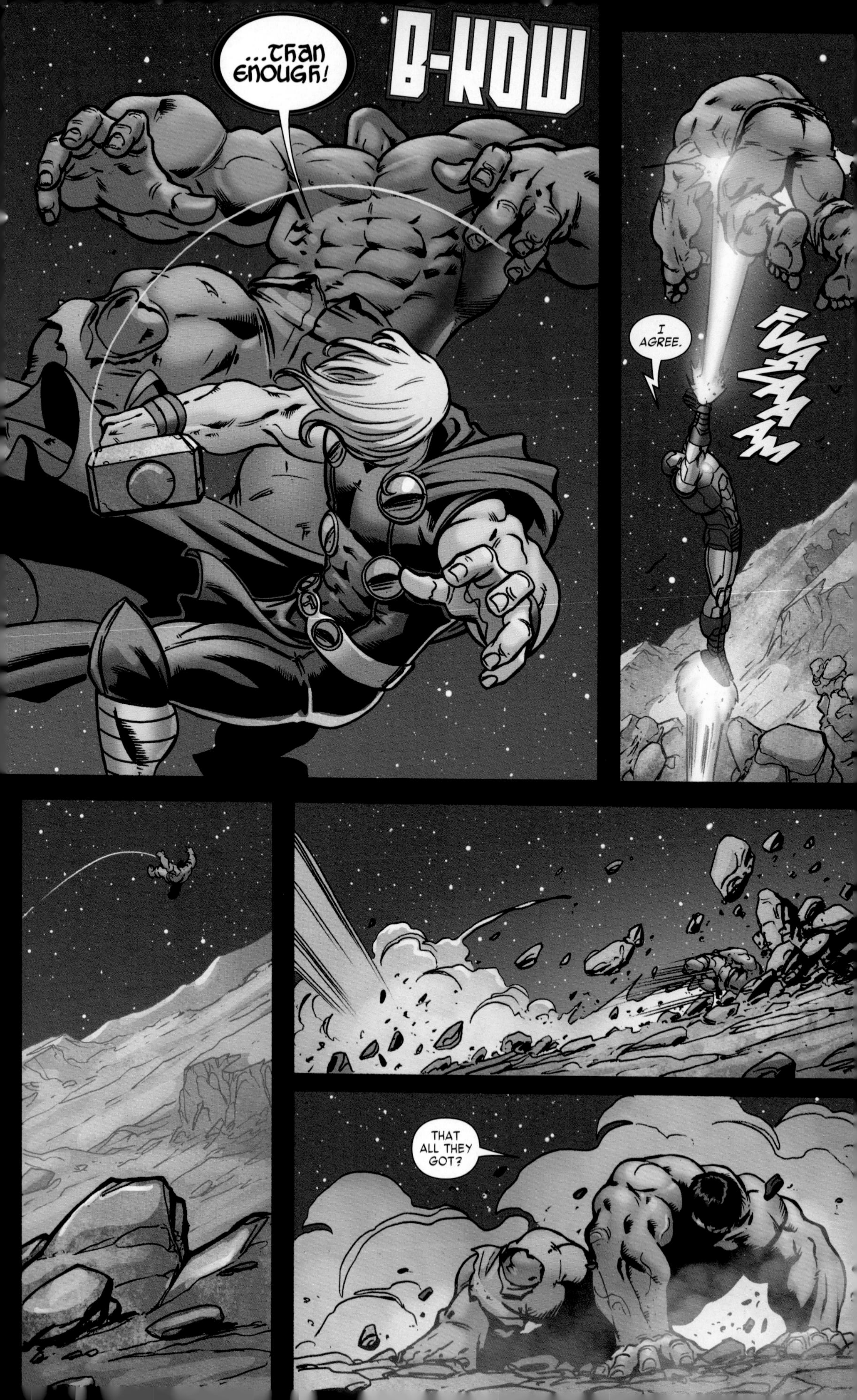

...THAN ENOUGH!
B-KOW
I AGREE.
FWAAAAM
THAT ALL THEY GOT?

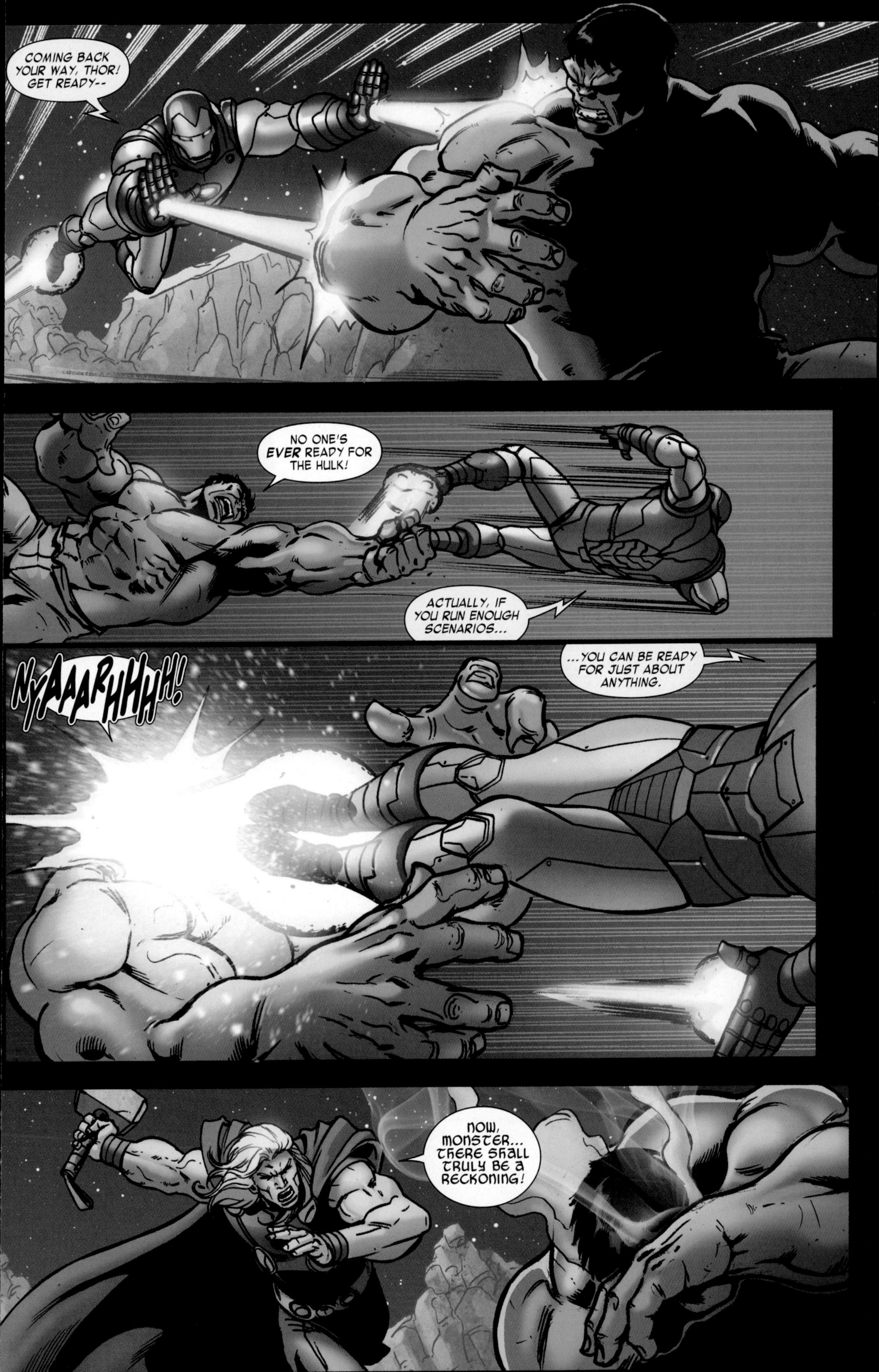
COMING BACK YOUR WAY, THOR! GET READY--
NO ONE'S EVER READY FOR THE HULK!
ACTUALLY, IF YOU RUN ENOUGH SCENARIOS...
NYAAARHHHH!
...YOU CAN BE READY FOR JUST ABOUT ANYTHING.
NOW, MONSTER... THERE SHALL TRULY BE A RECKONING!

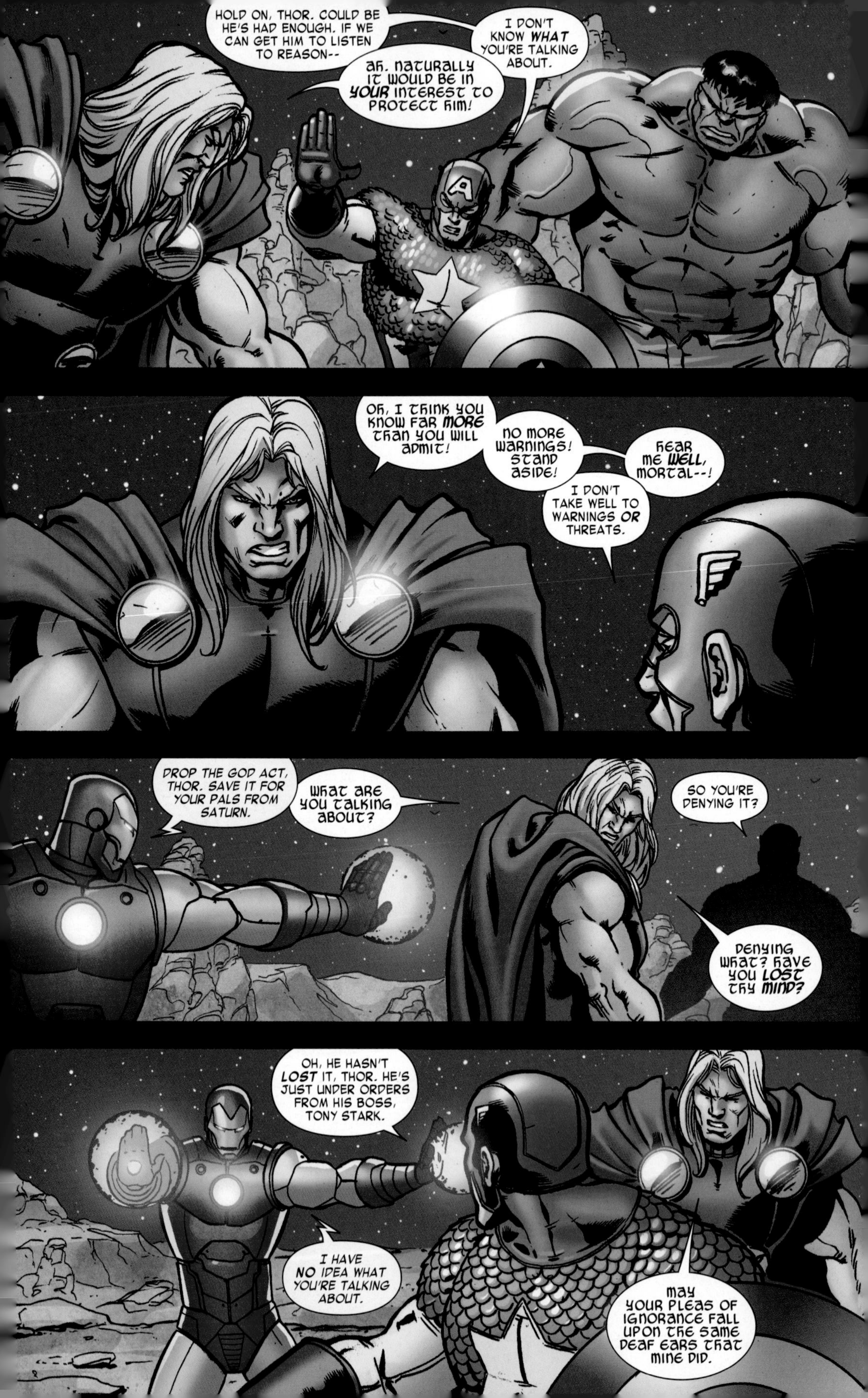
HOLD ON, THOR. COULD BE HE'S HAD ENOUGH. IF WE CAN GET HIM TO LISTEN TO REASON--
I DON'T KNOW WHAT YOU'RE TALKING ABOUT.
AH. NATURALLY IT WOULD BE IN YOUR INTEREST TO PROTECT HIM!
OH, I THINK YOU KNOW FAR MORE THAN YOU WILL ADMIT!
NO MORE WARNINGS! STAND ASIDE!
HEAR ME WELL, MORTAL--!
I DON'T TAKE WELL TO WARNINGS OR THREATS.
DROP THE GOD ACT, THOR. SAVE IT FOR YOUR PALS FROM SATURN.
WHAT ARE YOU TALKING ABOUT?
SO YOU'RE DENYING IT?
DENYING WHAT? HAVE YOU LOST THY MIND?
OH, HE HASN'T LOST IT, THOR. HE'S JUST UNDER ORDERS FROM HIS BOSS, TONY STARK.
I HAVE NO IDEA WHAT YOU'RE TALKING ABOUT.
MAY YOUR PLEAS OF IGNORANCE FALL UPON THE SAME DEAF EARS THAT MINE DID.

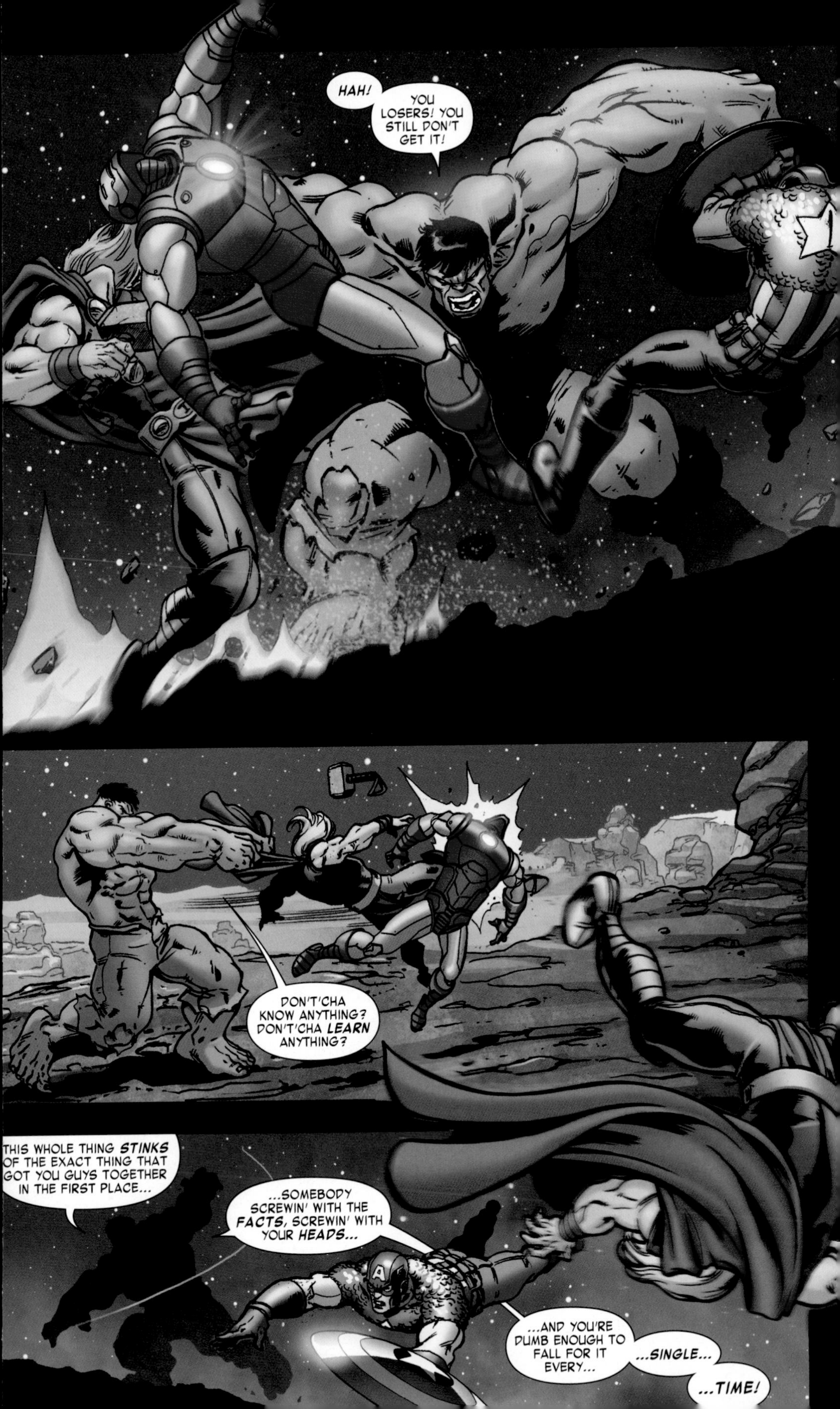
HAH!
YOU LOSERS! YOU STILL DON'T GET IT!
DON'T'CHA KNOW ANYTHING? DON'T'CHA LEARN ANYTHING?
THIS WHOLE THING STINKS OF THE EXACT THING THAT GOT YOU GUYS TOGETHER IN THE FIRST PLACE...
...SOMEBODY SCREWIN' WITH THE FACTS, SCREWIN' WITH YOUR HEADS...
...AND YOU'RE DUMB ENOUGH TO FALL FOR IT EVERY...
...SINGLE...
...TIME!

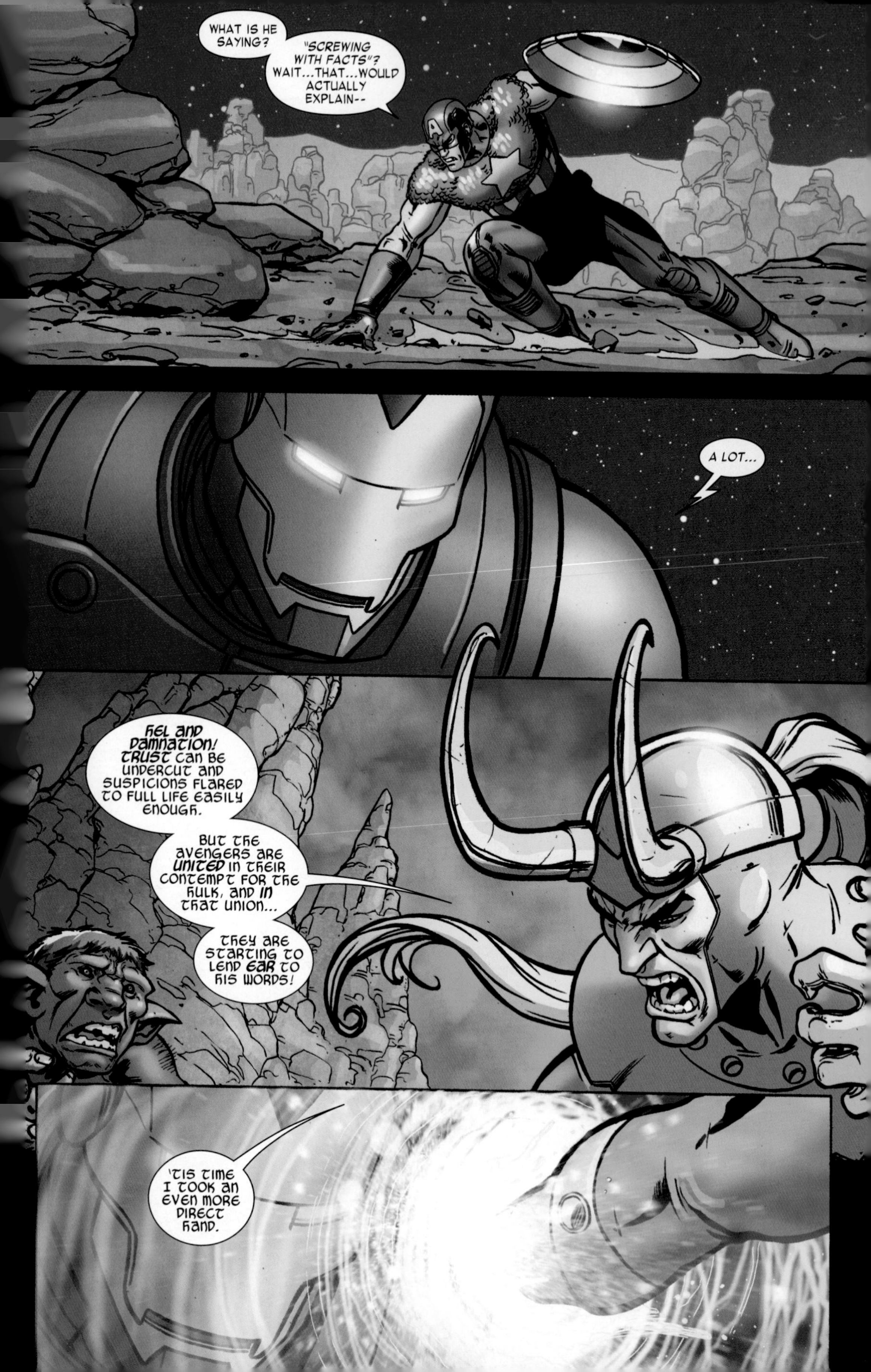
WHAT IS HE SAYING?
"SCREWING WITH FACTS"? WAIT...THAT...WOULD ACTUALLY EXPLAIN--
A LOT...
HEL AND DAMNATION! TRUST CAN BE UNDERCUT AND SUSPICIONS FLARED TO FULL LIFE EASILY ENOUGH.
BUT THE AVENGERS ARE UNITED IN THEIR CONTEMPT FOR THE HULK, AND IN THAT UNION...
THEY ARE STARTING TO LEND EAR TO HIS WORDS!
'TIS TIME I TOOK AN EVEN MORE DIRECT HAND.

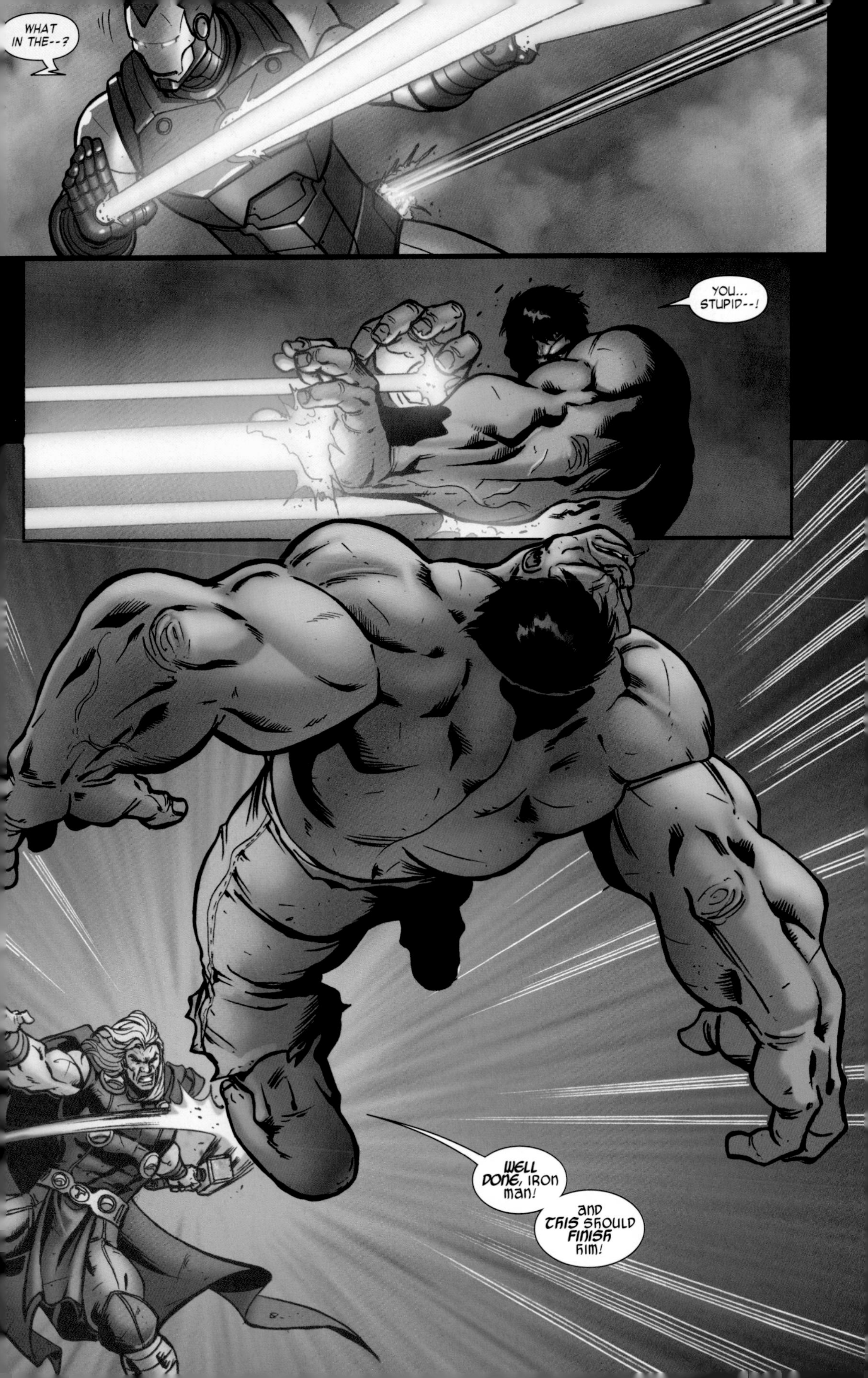
WHAT IN THE--?
YOU... STUPID--!
WELL DONE, IRON MAN!
AND THIS SHOULD FINISH HIM!

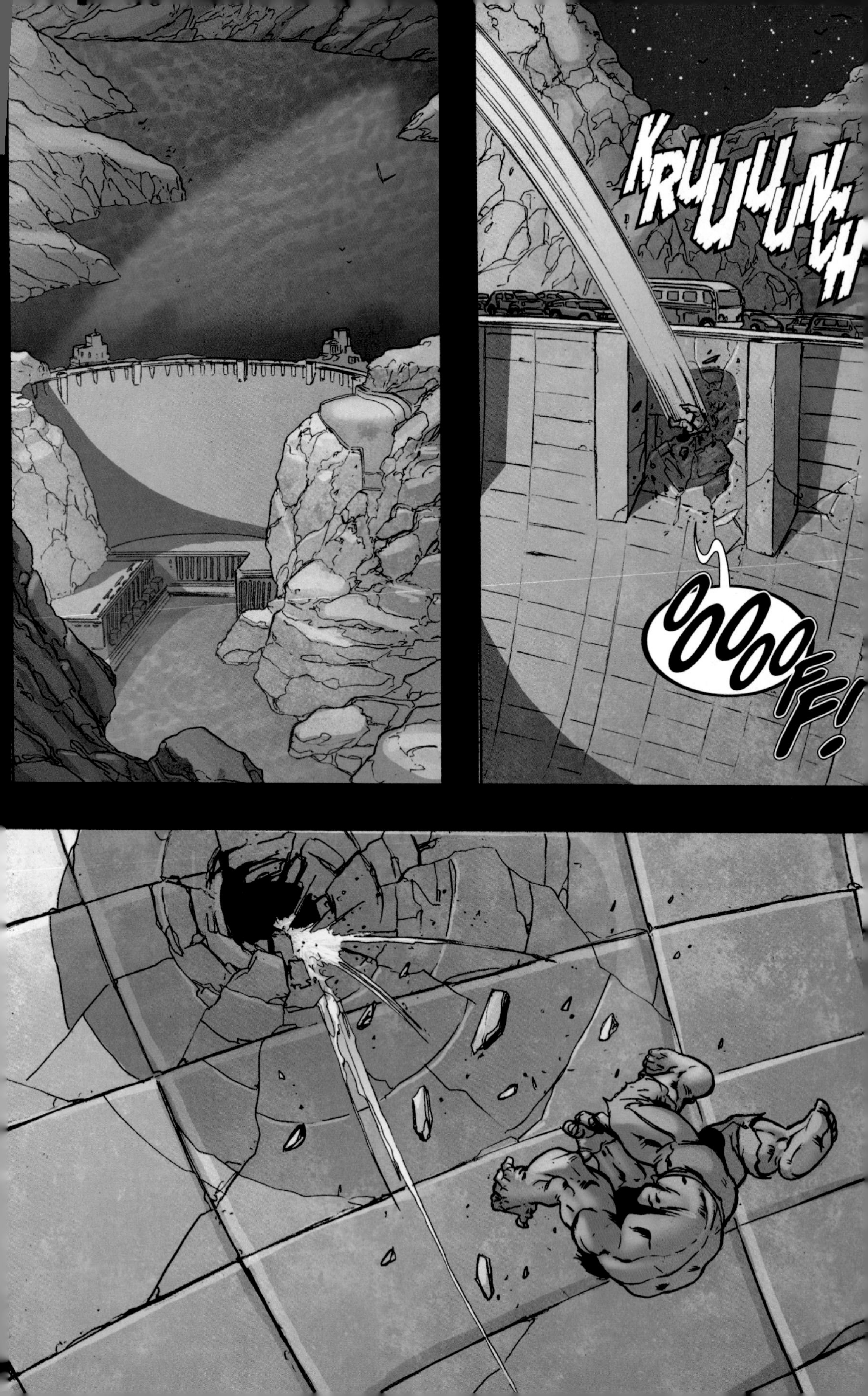
KRUUUUNCH
OOOOOFF!

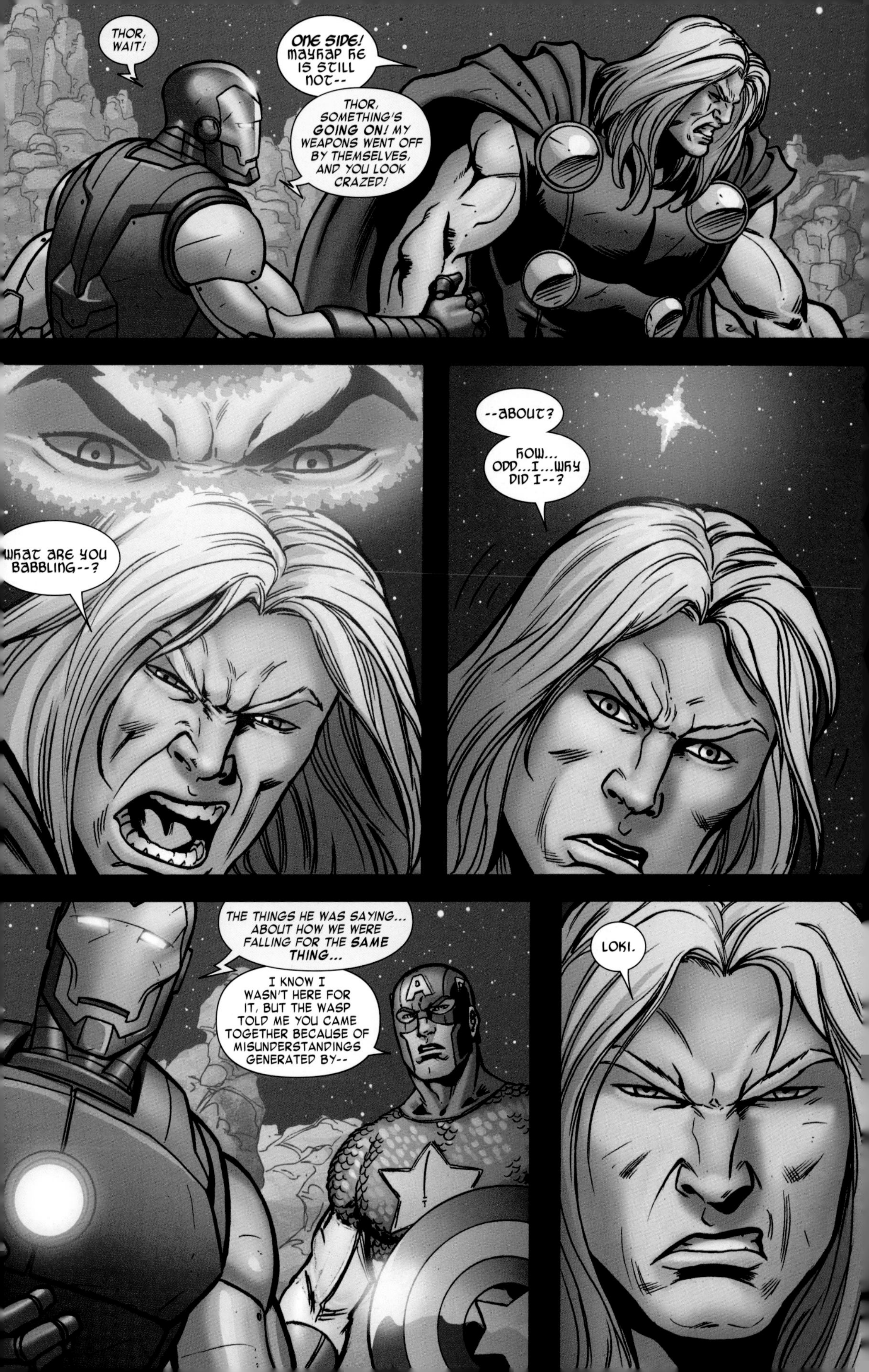
THOR, WAIT!
ONE SIDE! MAYHAP HE IS STILL NOT--
THOR, SOMETHING'S GOING ON! MY WEAPONS WENT OFF BY THEMSELVES, AND YOU LOOK CRAZED!
WHAT ARE YOU BABBLING--?
--ABOUT?
HOW... ODD...I...WHY DID I--?
THE THINGS HE WAS SAYING... ABOUT HOW WE WERE FALLING FOR THE SAME THING...
I KNOW I WASN'T HERE FOR IT, BUT THE WASP TOLD ME YOU CAME TOGETHER BECAUSE OF MISUNDERSTANDINGS GENERATED BY--
LOKI.

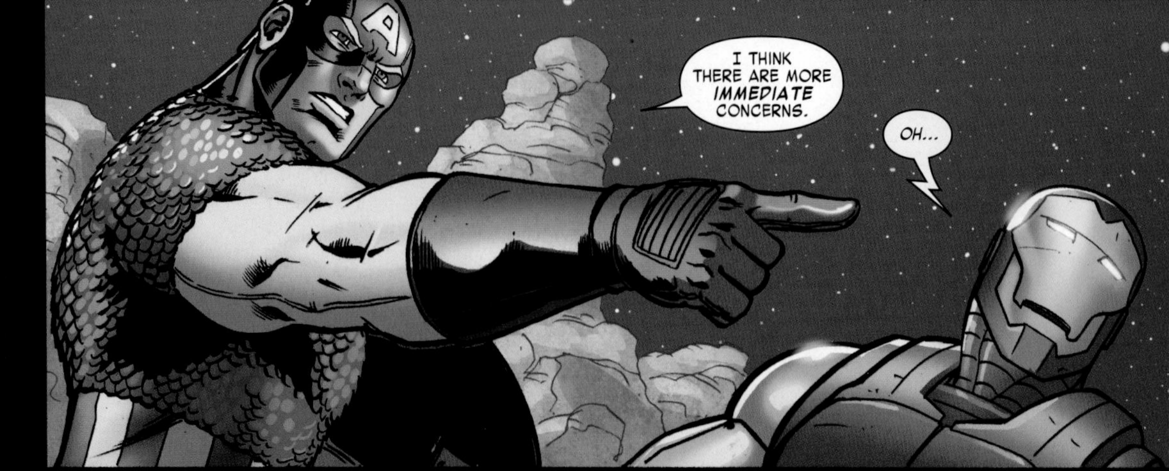
I THINK THERE ARE MORE IMMEDIATE CONCERNS.
OH...

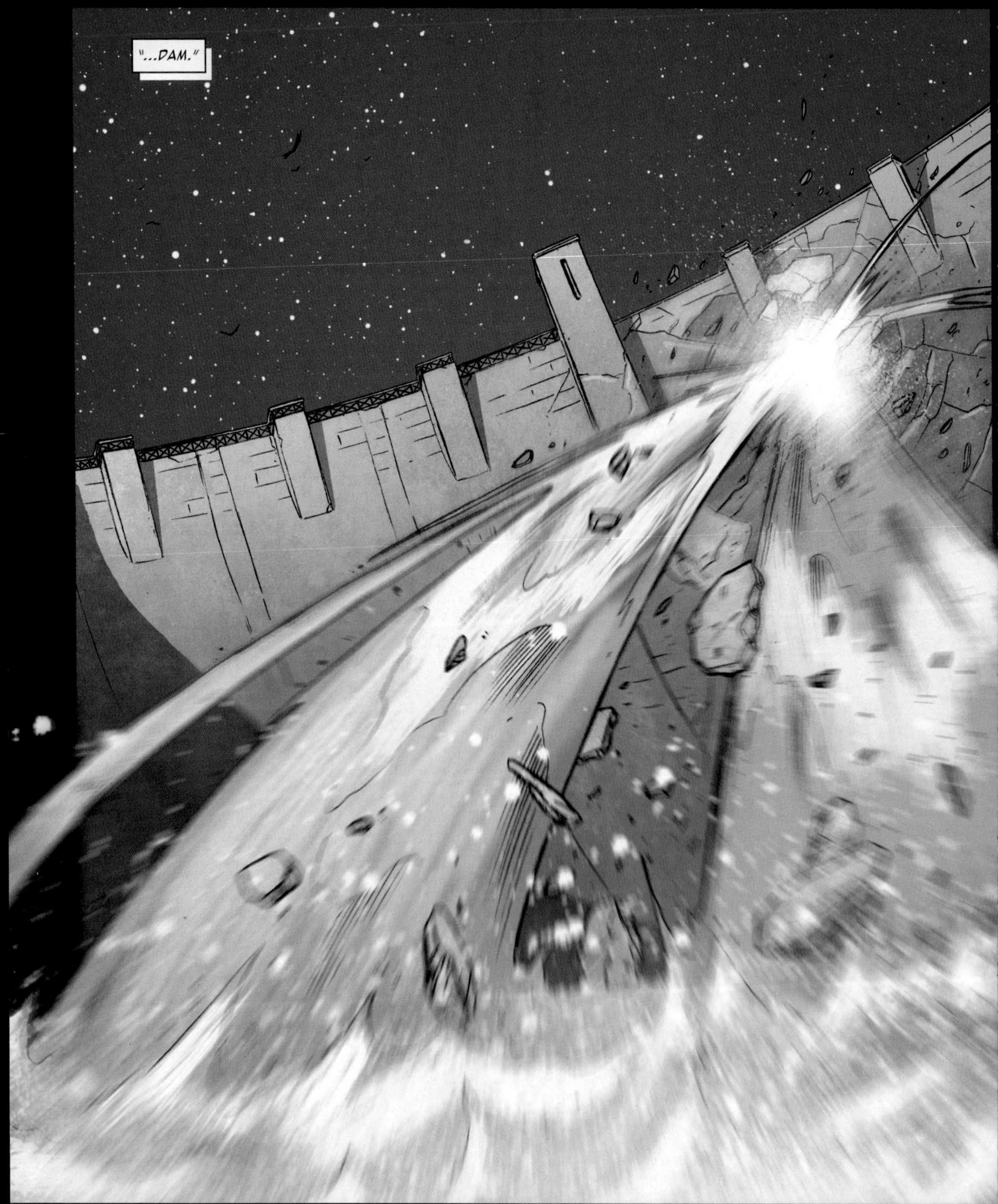
"...DAM."

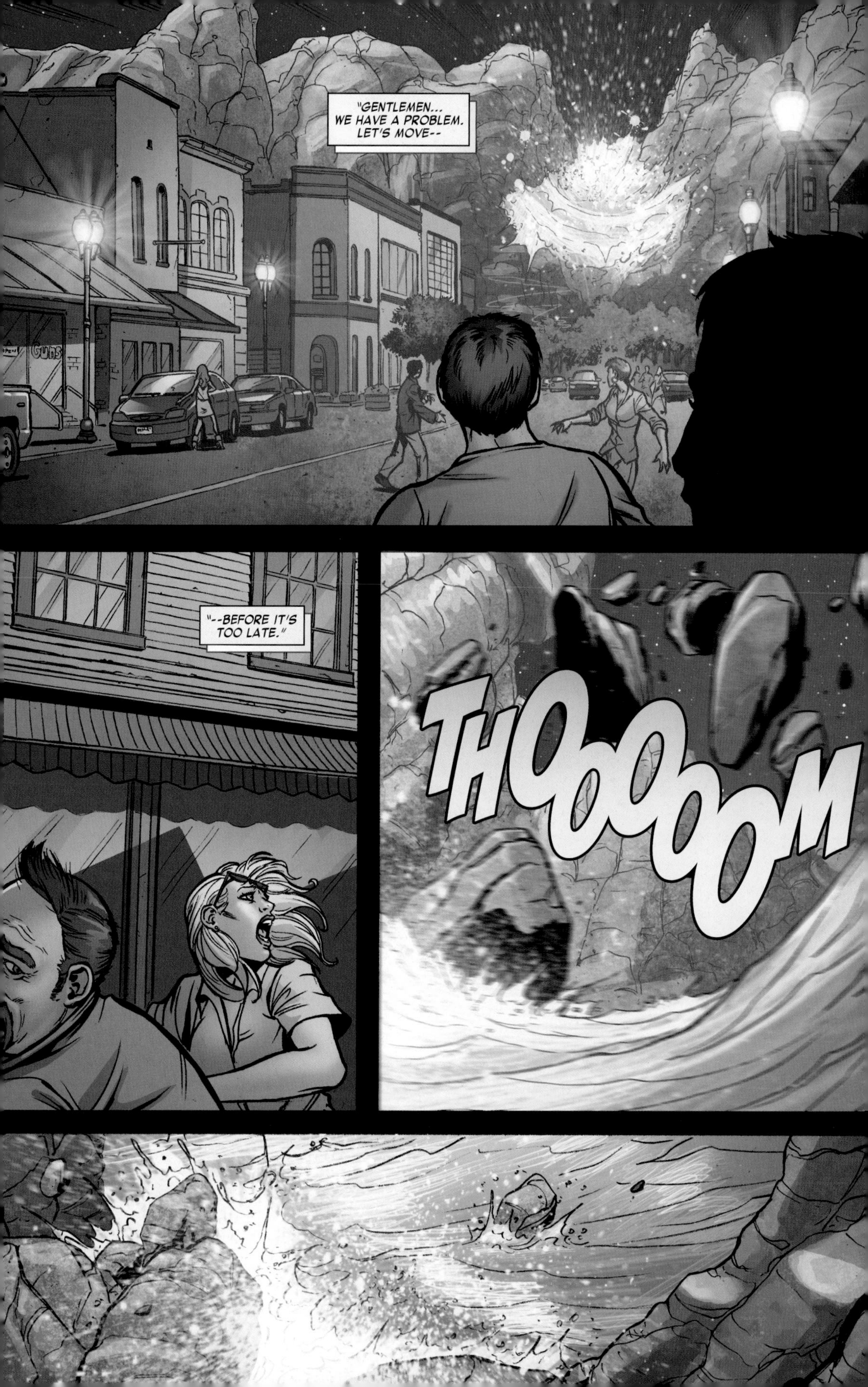
"GENTLEMEN... WE HAVE A PROBLEM. LET'S MOVE--
GUNS
"--BEFORE IT'S TOO LATE."
THOOOOOM

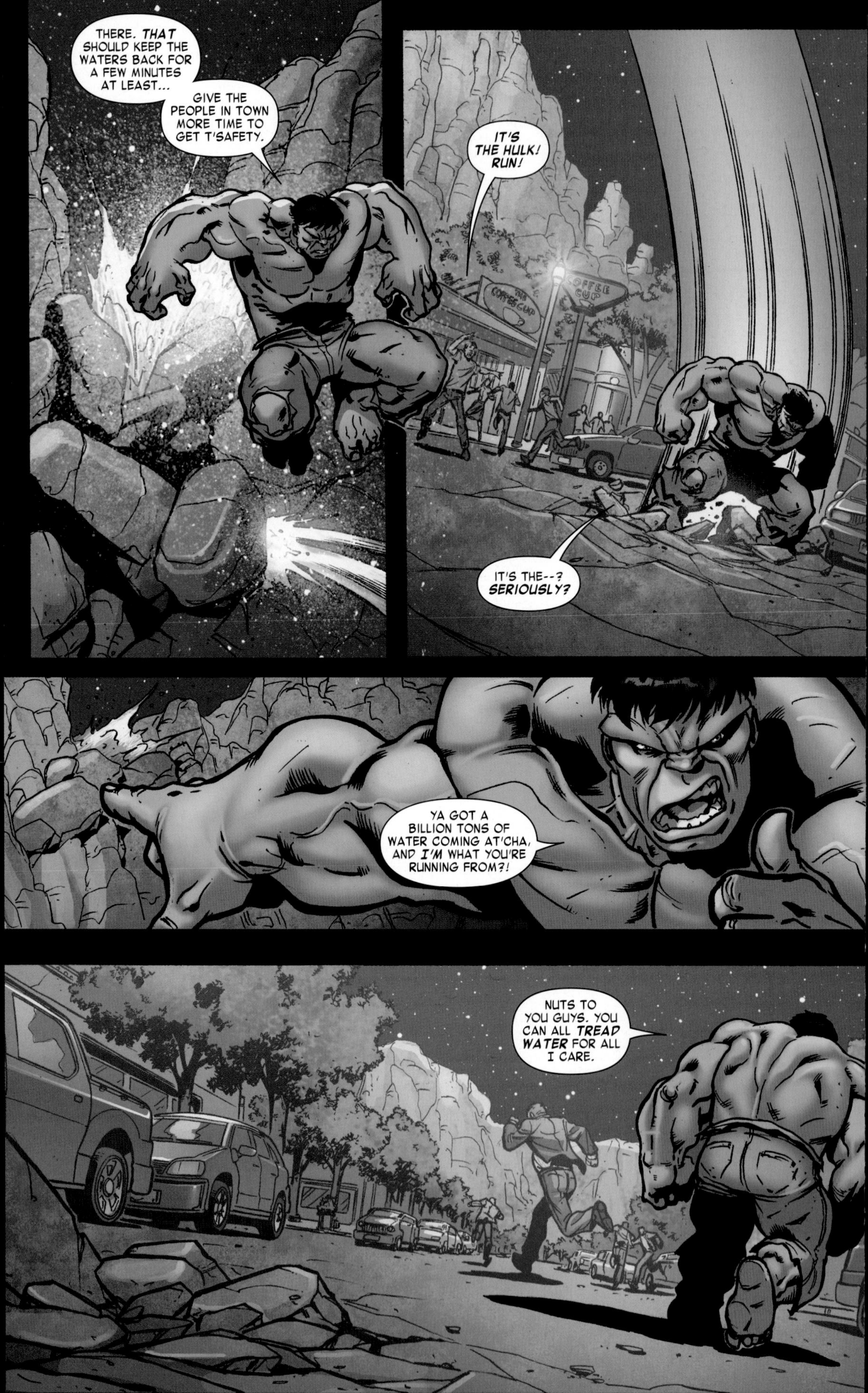
THERE. *THAT* SHOULD KEEP THE WATERS BACK FOR A FEW MINUTES AT LEAST...
GIVE THE PEOPLE IN TOWN MORE TIME TO GET T'SAFETY.
IT'S THE HULK! RUN!
THE COFFEE CUP
COFFEE CUP
IT'S THE--? *SERIOUSLY?*
YA GOT A BILLION TONS OF WATER COMING AT'CHA, AND *I'M* WHAT YOU'RE RUNNING FROM?!
NUTS TO YOU GUYS. YOU CAN ALL *TREAD WATER* FOR ALL I CARE.

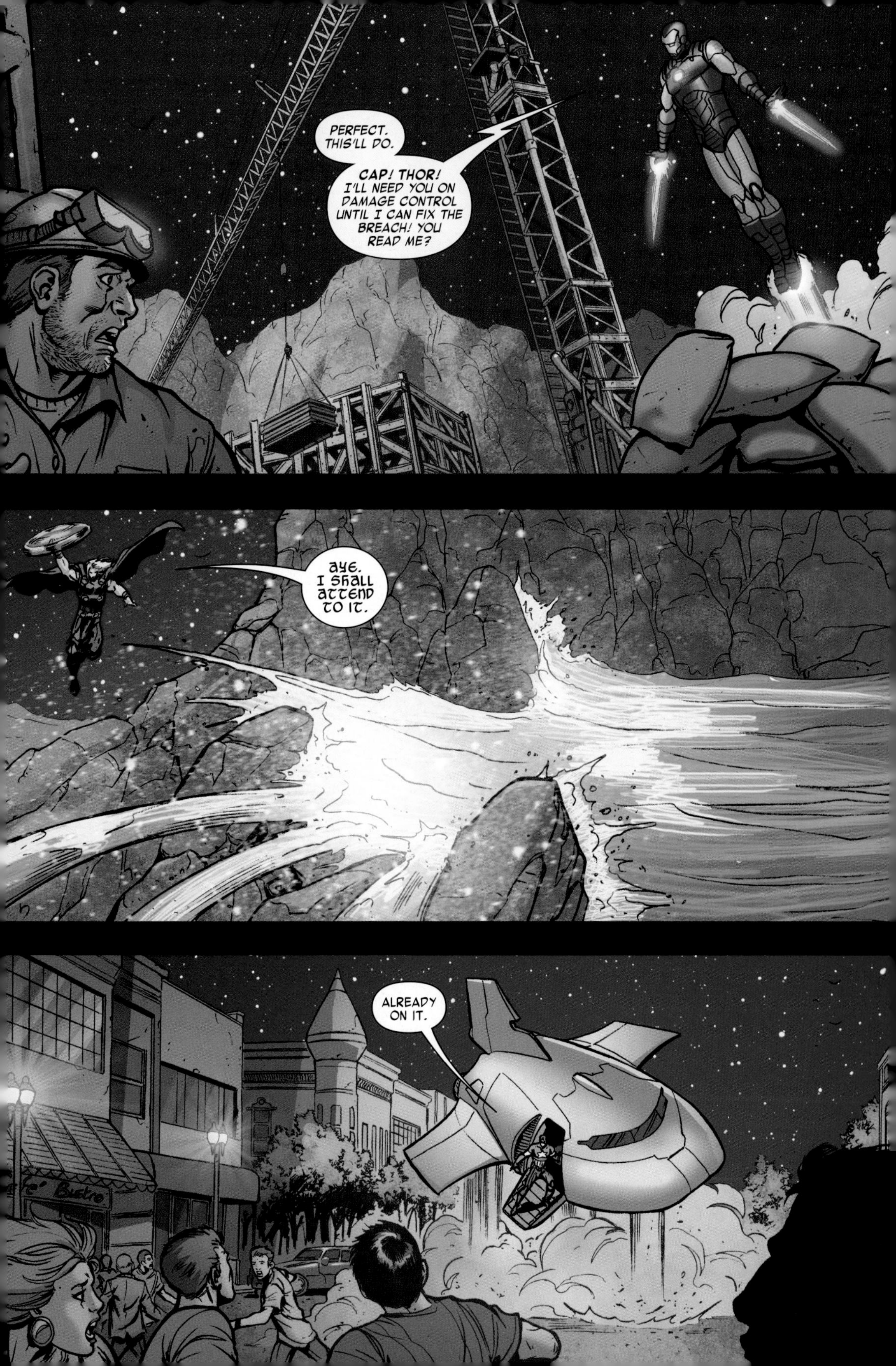
PERFECT. THIS'LL DO.
CAP! THOR! I'LL NEED YOU ON DAMAGE CONTROL UNTIL I CAN FIX THE BREACH! YOU READ ME?
AYE. I SHALL ATTEND TO IT.
ALREADY ON IT.

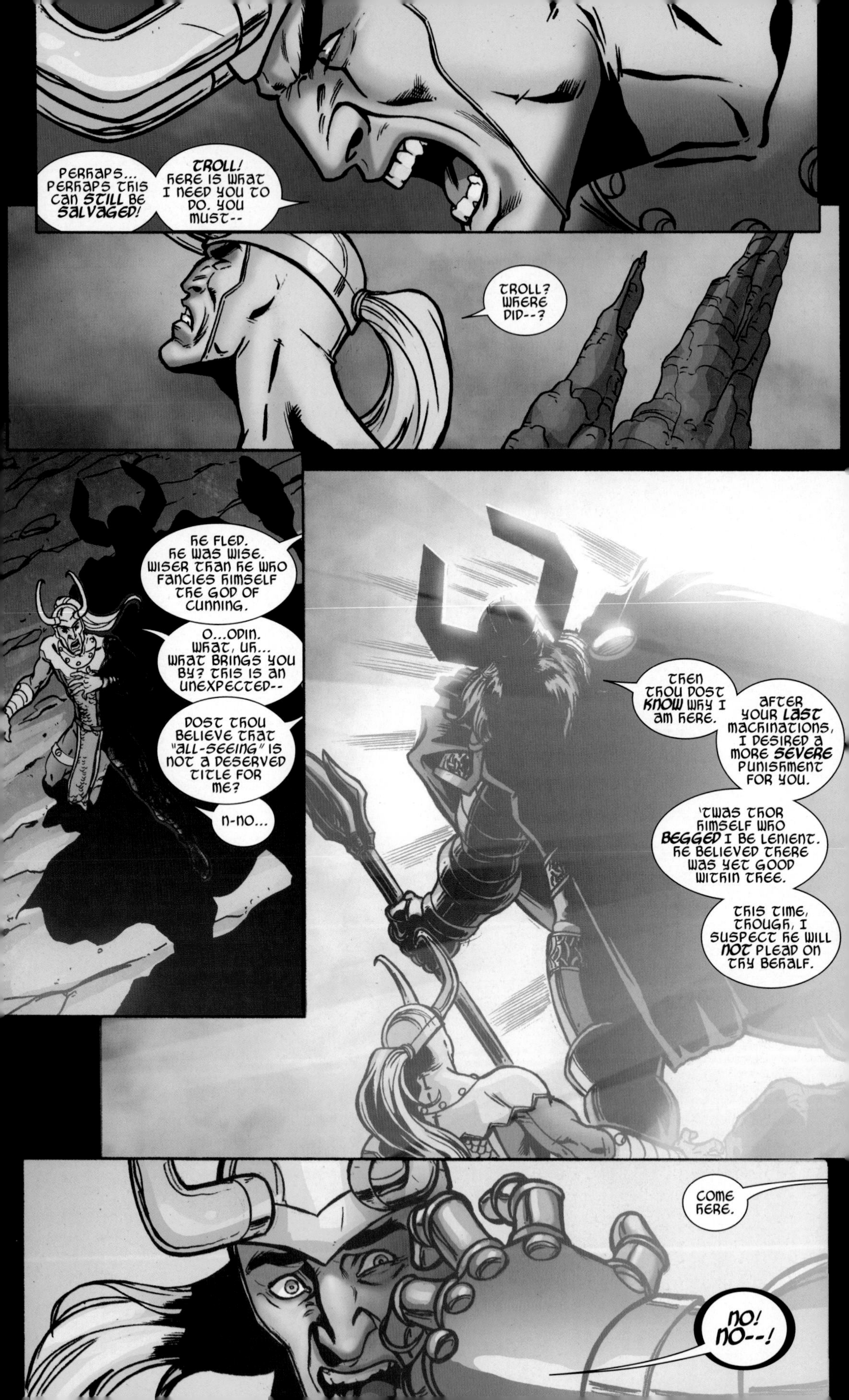
PERHAPS... PERHAPS THIS CAN STILL BE SALVAGED!
TROLL! HERE IS WHAT I NEED YOU TO DO. YOU MUST--
TROLL? WHERE DID--?
HE FLED. HE WAS WISE. WISER THAN HE WHO FANCIES HIMSELF THE GOD OF CUNNING.
O...ODIN. WHAT, UH... WHAT BRINGS YOU BY? THIS IS AN UNEXPECTED--
DOST THOU BELIEVE THAT "ALL-SEEING" IS NOT A DESERVED TITLE FOR ME?
N-NO...
THEN THOU DOST KNOW WHY I AM HERE.
AFTER YOUR LAST MACHINATIONS, I DESIRED A MORE SEVERE PUNISHMENT FOR YOU.
'TWAS THOR HIMSELF WHO BEGGED I BE LENIENT. HE BELIEVED THERE WAS YET GOOD WITHIN THEE.
THIS TIME, THOUGH, I SUSPECT HE WILL NOT PLEAD ON THY BEHALF.
COME HERE.
NO! NO--!

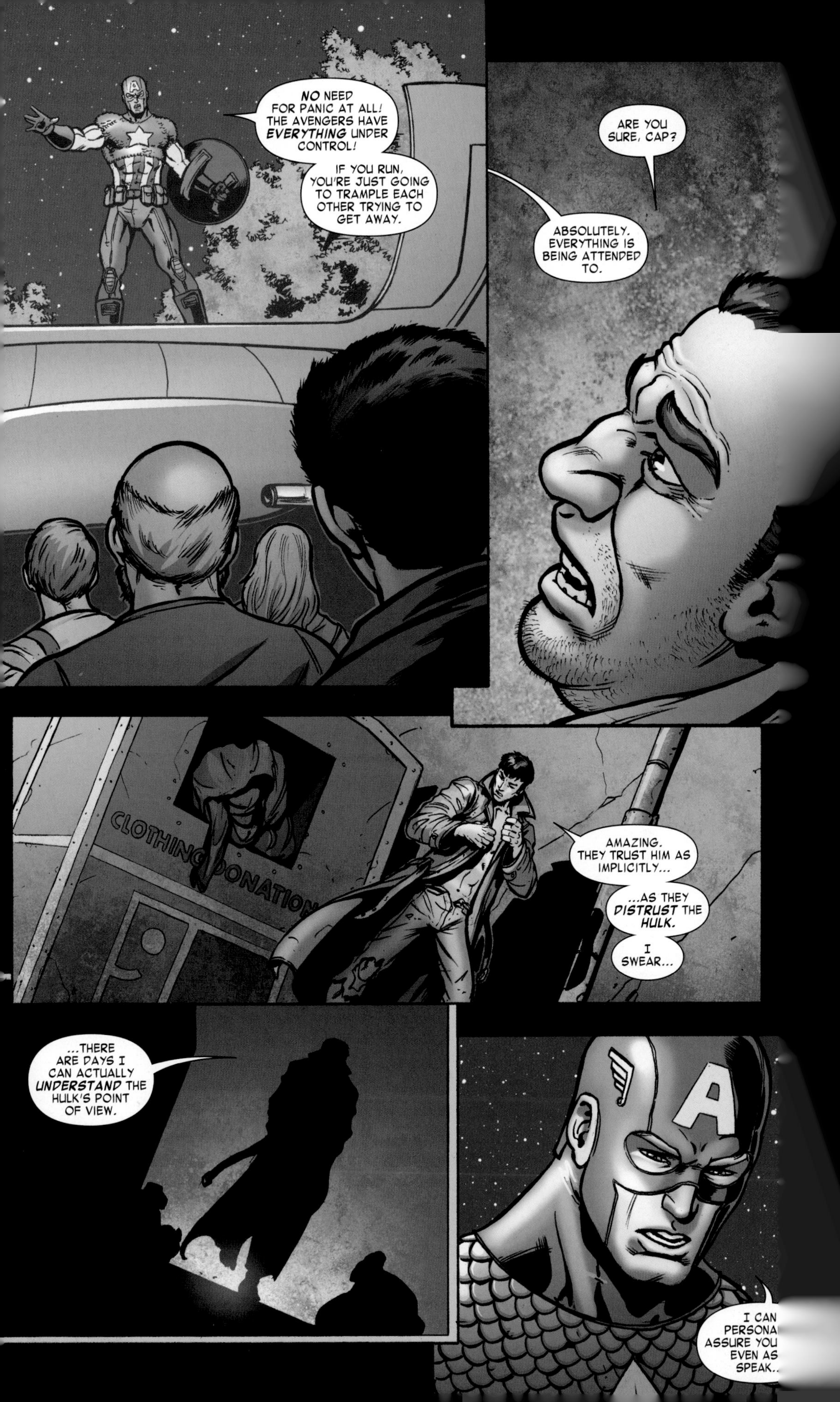
NO NEED FOR PANIC AT ALL! THE AVENGERS HAVE EVERYTHING UNDER CONTROL!
IF YOU RUN, YOU'RE JUST GOING TO TRAMPLE EACH OTHER TRYING TO GET AWAY.
ARE YOU SURE, CAP?
ABSOLUTELY. EVERYTHING IS BEING ATTENDED TO.
CLOTHING DONATION
AMAZING. THEY TRUST HIM AS IMPLICITLY...
...AS THEY DISTRUST THE HULK.
I SWEAR...
...THERE ARE DAYS I CAN ACTUALLY UNDERSTAND THE HULK'S POINT OF VIEW.
I CAN PERSONA ASSURE YOU EVEN AS SPEAK..

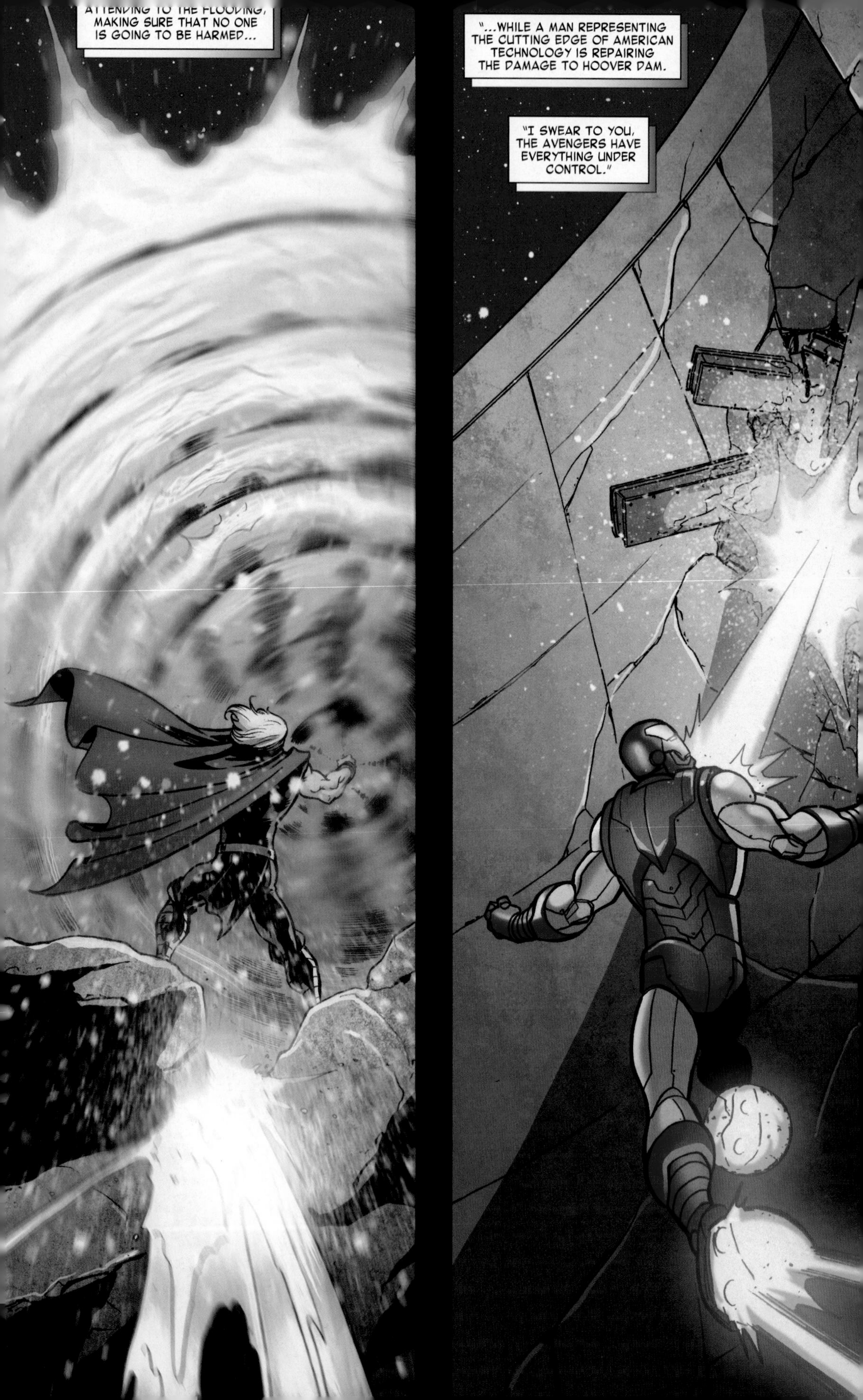
ATTENDING TO THE FLOODING, MAKING SURE THAT NO ONE IS GOING TO BE HARMED...
"...WHILE A MAN REPRESENTING THE CUTTING EDGE OF AMERICAN TECHNOLOGY IS REPAIRING THE DAMAGE TO HOOVER DAM.
"I SWEAR TO YOU, THE AVENGERS HAVE EVERYTHING UNDER CONTROL."

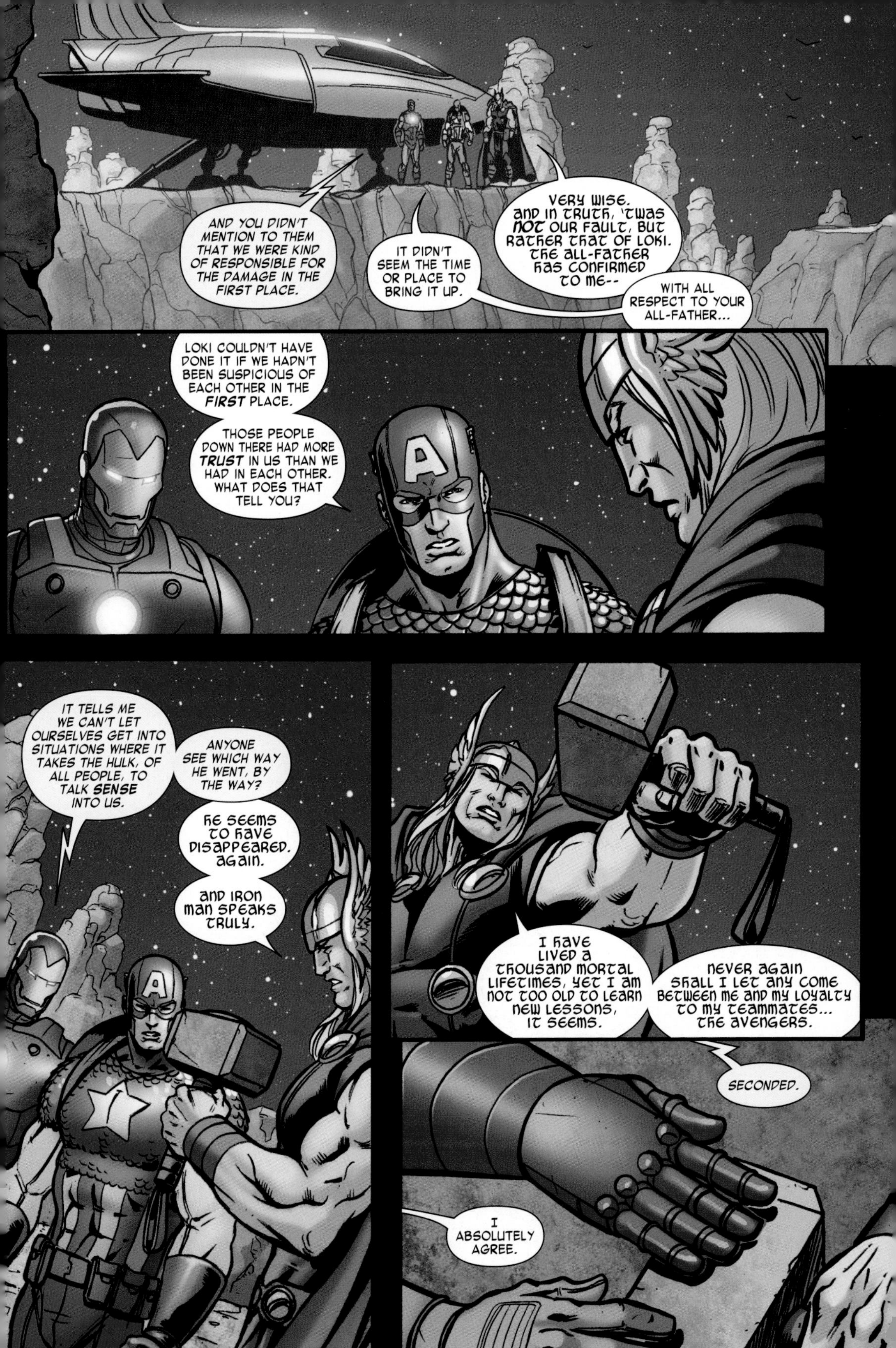
AND YOU DIDN'T MENTION TO THEM THAT WE WERE KIND OF RESPONSIBLE FOR THE DAMAGE IN THE FIRST PLACE.
IT DIDN'T SEEM THE TIME OR PLACE TO BRING IT UP.
VERY WISE. AND IN TRUTH, 'TWAS NOT OUR FAULT, BUT RATHER THAT OF LOKI. THE ALL-FATHER HAS CONFIRMED TO ME--
WITH ALL RESPECT TO YOUR ALL-FATHER...
LOKI COULDN'T HAVE DONE IT IF WE HADN'T BEEN SUSPICIOUS OF EACH OTHER IN THE FIRST PLACE.
THOSE PEOPLE DOWN THERE HAD MORE TRUST IN US THAN WE HAD IN EACH OTHER. WHAT DOES THAT TELL YOU?
IT TELLS ME WE CAN'T LET OURSELVES GET INTO SITUATIONS WHERE IT TAKES THE HULK, OF ALL PEOPLE, TO TALK SENSE INTO US.
ANYONE SEE WHICH WAY HE WENT, BY THE WAY?
HE SEEMS TO HAVE DISAPPEARED. AGAIN.
AND IRON MAN SPEAKS TRULY.
I HAVE LIVED A THOUSAND MORTAL LIFETIMES, YET I AM NOT TOO OLD TO LEARN NEW LESSONS, IT SEEMS.
NEVER AGAIN SHALL I LET ANY COME BETWEEN ME AND MY LOYALTY TO MY TEAMMATES... THE AVENGERS.
SECONDED.
I ABSOLUTELY AGREE.

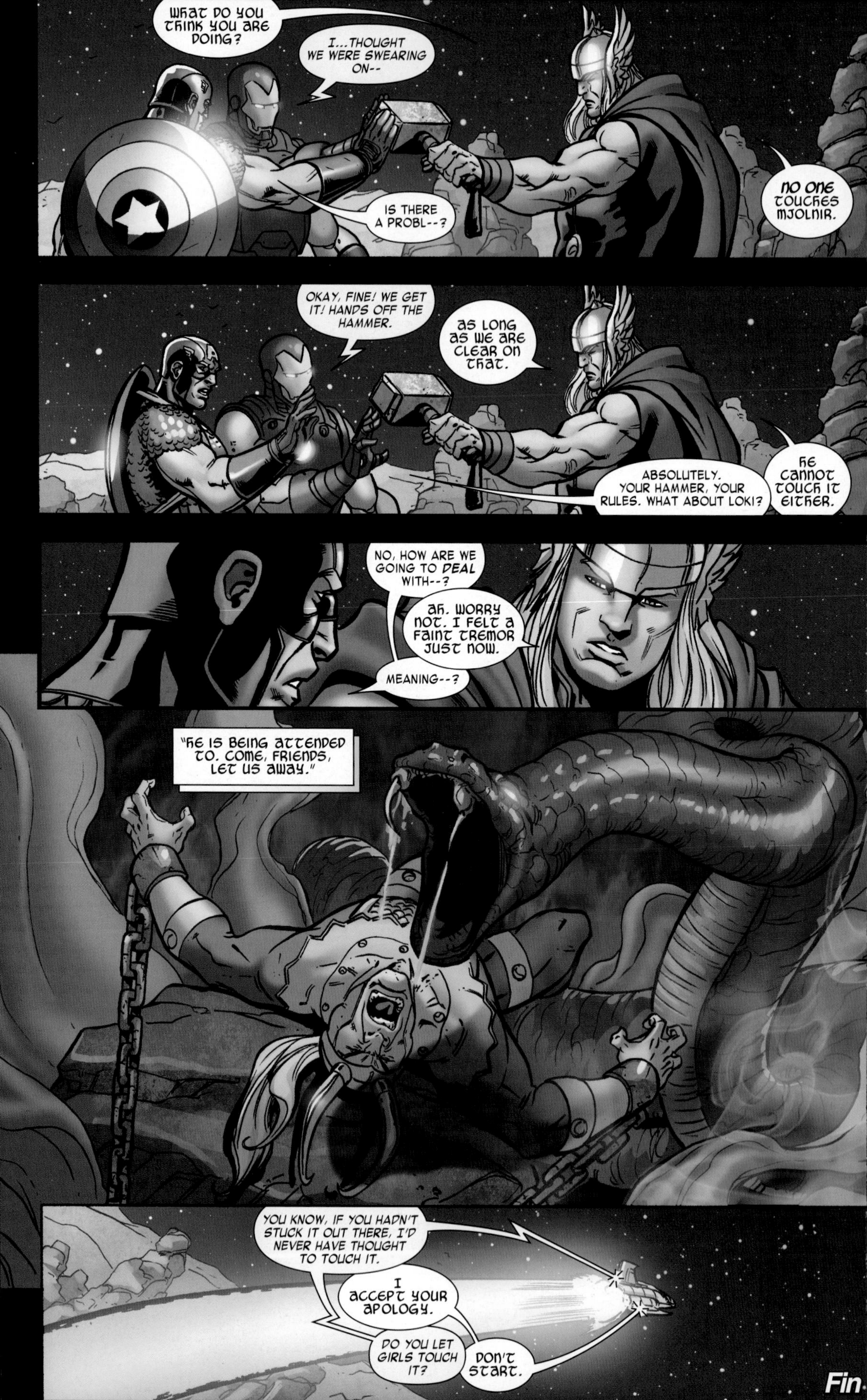
WHAT DO YOU THINK YOU ARE DOING?
I...THOUGHT WE WERE SWEARING ON--
IS THERE A PROBL--?
NO ONE TOUCHES MJOLNIR.
OKAY, FINE! WE GET IT! HANDS OFF THE HAMMER.
AS LONG AS WE ARE CLEAR ON THAT.
ABSOLUTELY. YOUR HAMMER, YOUR RULES. WHAT ABOUT LOKI?
HE CANNOT TOUCH IT EITHER.
NO, HOW ARE WE GOING TO DEAL WITH--?
AH. WORRY NOT. I FELT A FAINT TREMOR JUST NOW.
MEANING--?
"HE IS BEING ATTENDED TO. COME, FRIENDS, LET US AWAY."
YOU KNOW, IF YOU HADN'T STUCK IT OUT THERE, I'D NEVER HAVE THOUGHT TO TOUCH IT.
I ACCEPT YOUR APOLOGY.
DO YOU LET GIRLS TOUCH IT?
DON'T START.
Fin

WHERE ARE THEY NOW? *AVENGERS ASSEMBLE #1* ONE OF THE GREATEST AVENGERS VILLAINS OF ALL TIME GETS REINVENTED FOR THE MODERN AGE IN THIS PERFECT JUMPING-ON POINT FEATURING THE CAST OF THE BLOCKBUSTER MOVIE BUT IN MARVEL UNIVERSE CONTINUITY!

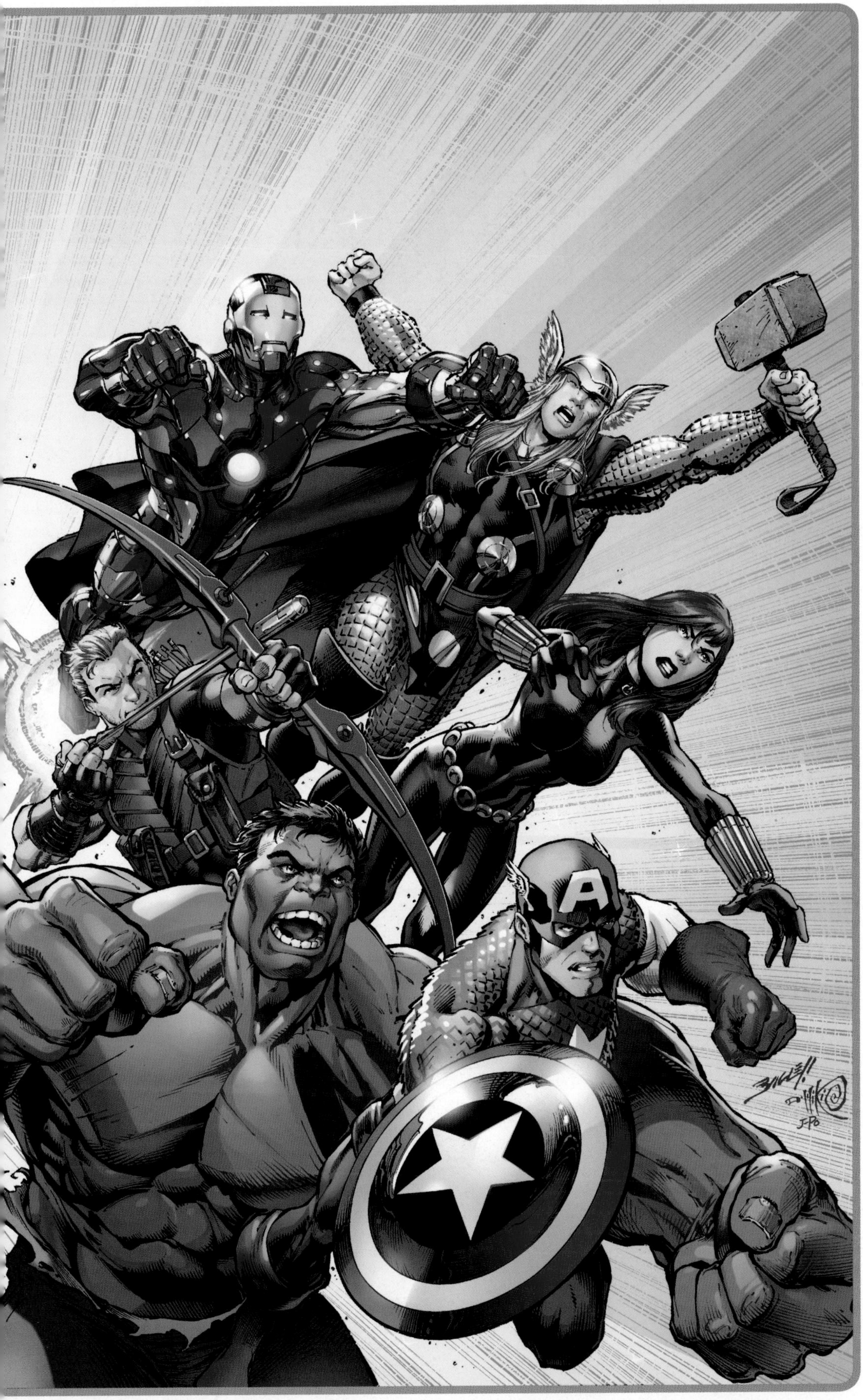

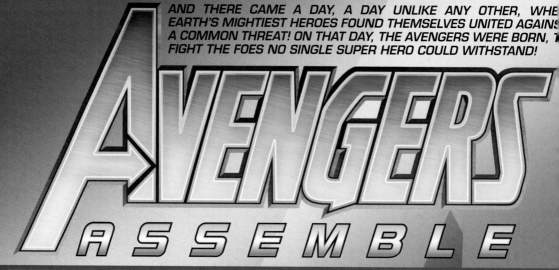

AND THERE CAME A DAY, A DAY UNLIKE ANY OTHER, WHE
EARTH'S MIGHTIEST HEROES FOUND THEMSELVES UNITED AGAINS
A COMMON THREAT! ON THAT DAY, THE AVENGERS WERE BORN, T
FIGHT THE FOES NO SINGLE SUPER HERO COULD WITHSTAND!

AVENGERS
ASSEMBLE

CAPTAIN AMERICA
STEVE ROGERS
SUPER-SOLDIER

THOR
GOD OF THUNDER

IRON MAN
TONY STARK
BILLIONAIRE TECHNOLOGIST,
HIGH-TECH ARMOR

BLACK WIDOW
NATASHA ROMANOFF
EX-KGB SPY,
COVERT SPECIALIST

HULK
BRUCE BANNER
BRILLIANT MAN,
GAMMA-CHARGED MONSTER

HAWKEYE
CLINT BARTO
EXPERT MARKS

BRIAN MICHAEL
BENDIS
WRITER

MARK
BAGLEY
PENCILER

DANNY
MIKI
INKER

PAUL
MOUNTS
COLORS

VC'S CLAYTON
COWLES
LETTERER

JOHN
DENNING
ASST. EDITOR

LAUREN
SANKOVITCH
ASSOC. EDITOR

TOM
BREVOORT
EXEC. EDITOR

AXEL
ALONSO
EDITOR IN CHIEF

JOE
QUESADA
CHIEF CREATIVE OFFICER

DAN
BUCKLEY
PUBLISHER

ALAN
FINE
EXECUTIVE PRODUCER

HAWKEYE'S COSTUME DESIGNED BY **BRYAN HITC**

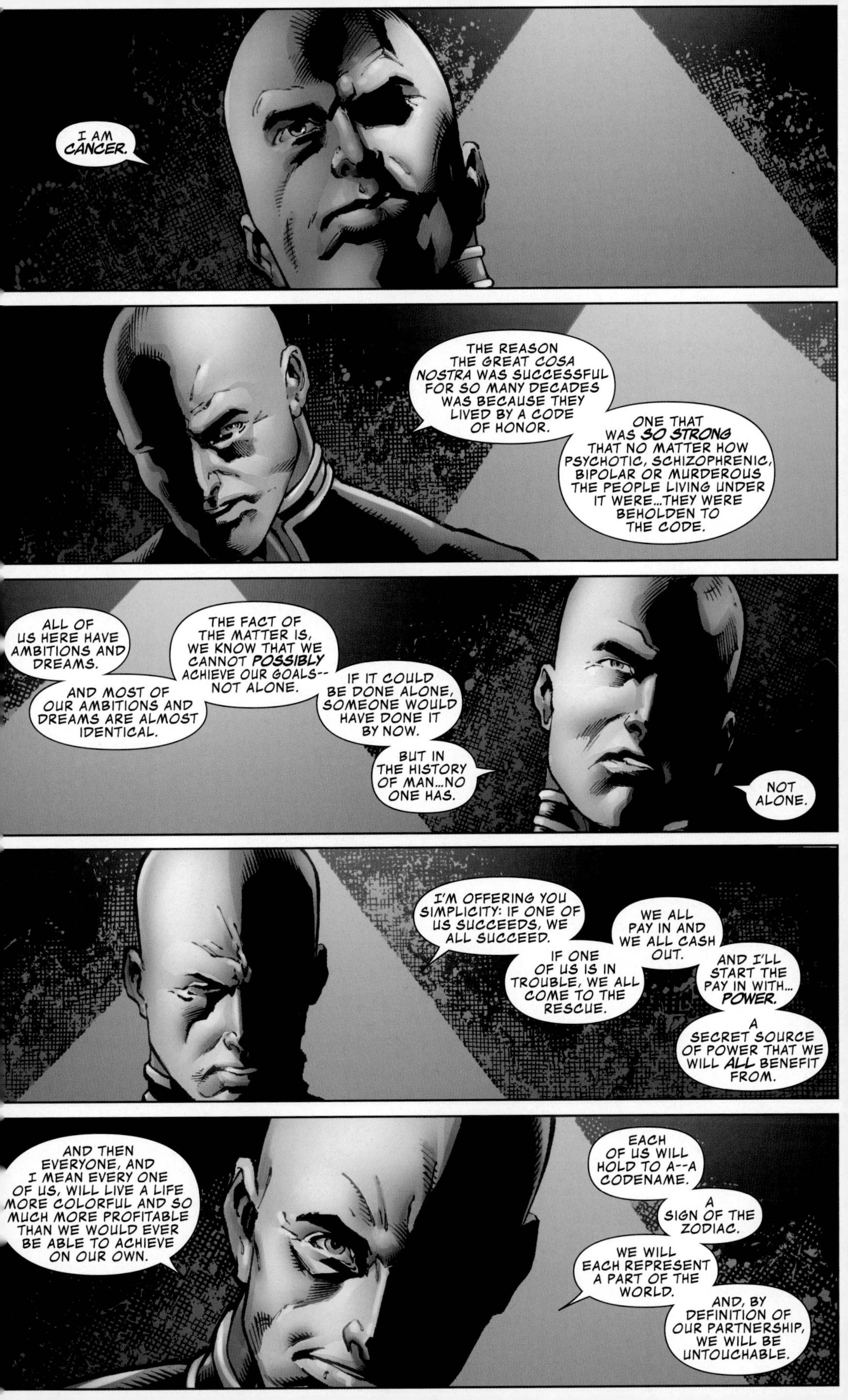
I AM CANCER.
THE REASON THE GREAT COSA NOSTRA WAS SUCCESSFUL FOR SO MANY DECADES WAS BECAUSE THEY LIVED BY A CODE OF HONOR.
ONE THAT WAS SO STRONG THAT NO MATTER HOW PSYCHOTIC, SCHIZOPHRENIC, BIPOLAR OR MURDEROUS THE PEOPLE LIVING UNDER IT WERE...THEY WERE BEHOLDEN TO THE CODE.
ALL OF US HERE HAVE AMBITIONS AND DREAMS.
AND MOST OF OUR AMBITIONS AND DREAMS ARE ALMOST IDENTICAL.
THE FACT OF THE MATTER IS, WE KNOW THAT WE CANNOT POSSIBLY ACHIEVE OUR GOALS--NOT ALONE.
IF IT COULD BE DONE ALONE, SOMEONE WOULD HAVE DONE IT BY NOW.
BUT IN THE HISTORY OF MAN...NO ONE HAS.
NOT ALONE.
I'M OFFERING YOU SIMPLICITY: IF ONE OF US SUCCEEDS, WE ALL SUCCEED.
IF ONE OF US IS IN TROUBLE, WE ALL COME TO THE RESCUE.
WE ALL PAY IN AND WE ALL CASH OUT.
AND I'LL START THE PAY IN WITH... POWER.
A SECRET SOURCE OF POWER THAT WE WILL ALL BENEFIT FROM.
AND THEN EVERYONE, AND I MEAN EVERY ONE OF US, WILL LIVE A LIFE MORE COLORFUL AND SO MUCH MORE PROFITABLE THAN WE WOULD EVER BE ABLE TO ACHIEVE ON OUR OWN.
EACH OF US WILL HOLD TO A--A CODENAME.
A SIGN OF THE ZODIAC.
WE WILL EACH REPRESENT A PART OF THE WORLD.
AND, BY DEFINITION OF OUR PARTNERSHIP, WE WILL BE UNTOUCHABLE.

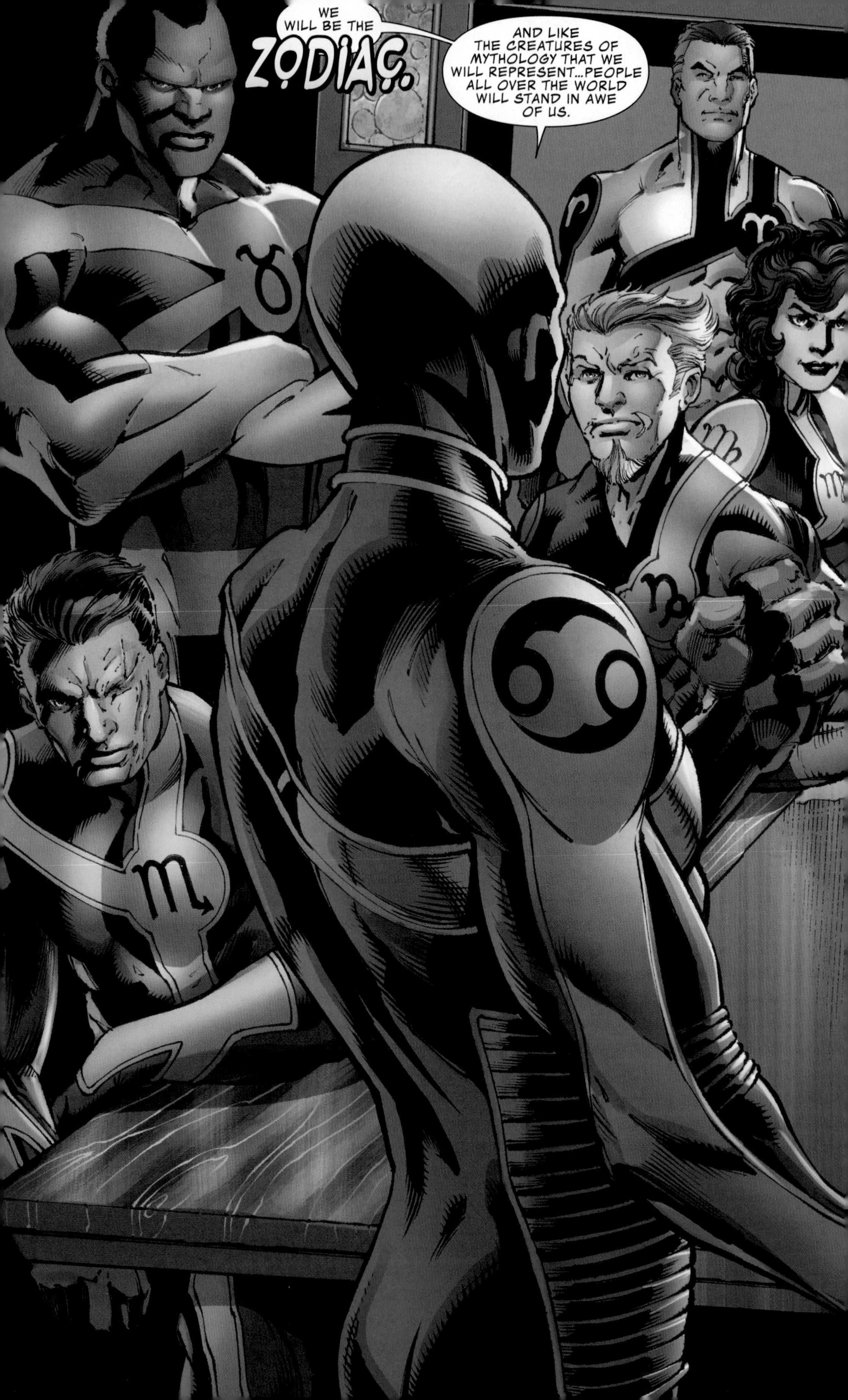
WE WILL BE THE
ZODIAC.
AND LIKE THE CREATURES OF MYTHOLOGY THAT WE WILL REPRESENT...PEOPLE ALL OVER THE WORLD WILL STAND IN AWE OF US.

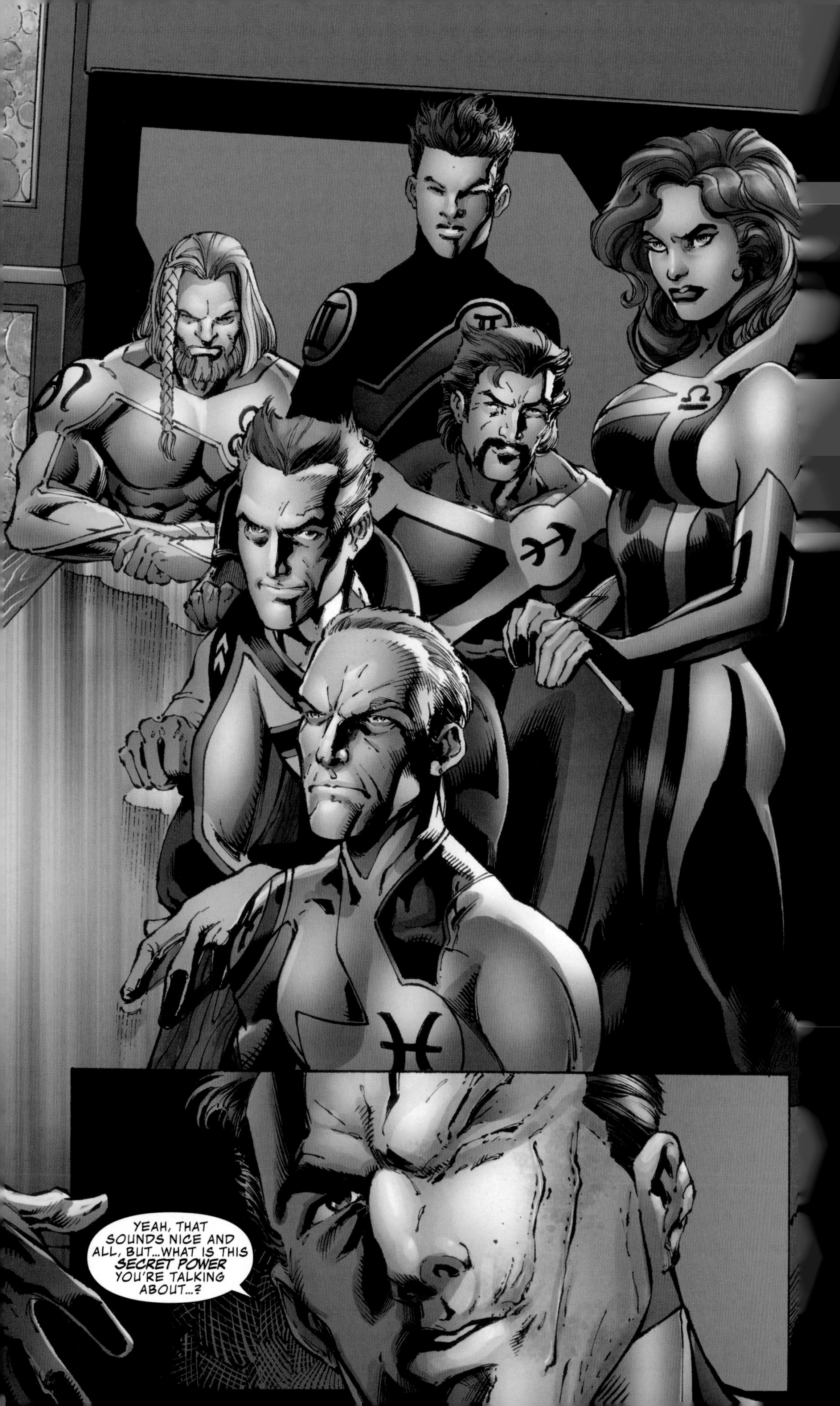
YEAH, THAT SOUNDS NICE AND ALL, BUT...WHAT IS THIS SECRET POWER YOU'RE TALKING ABOUT...?

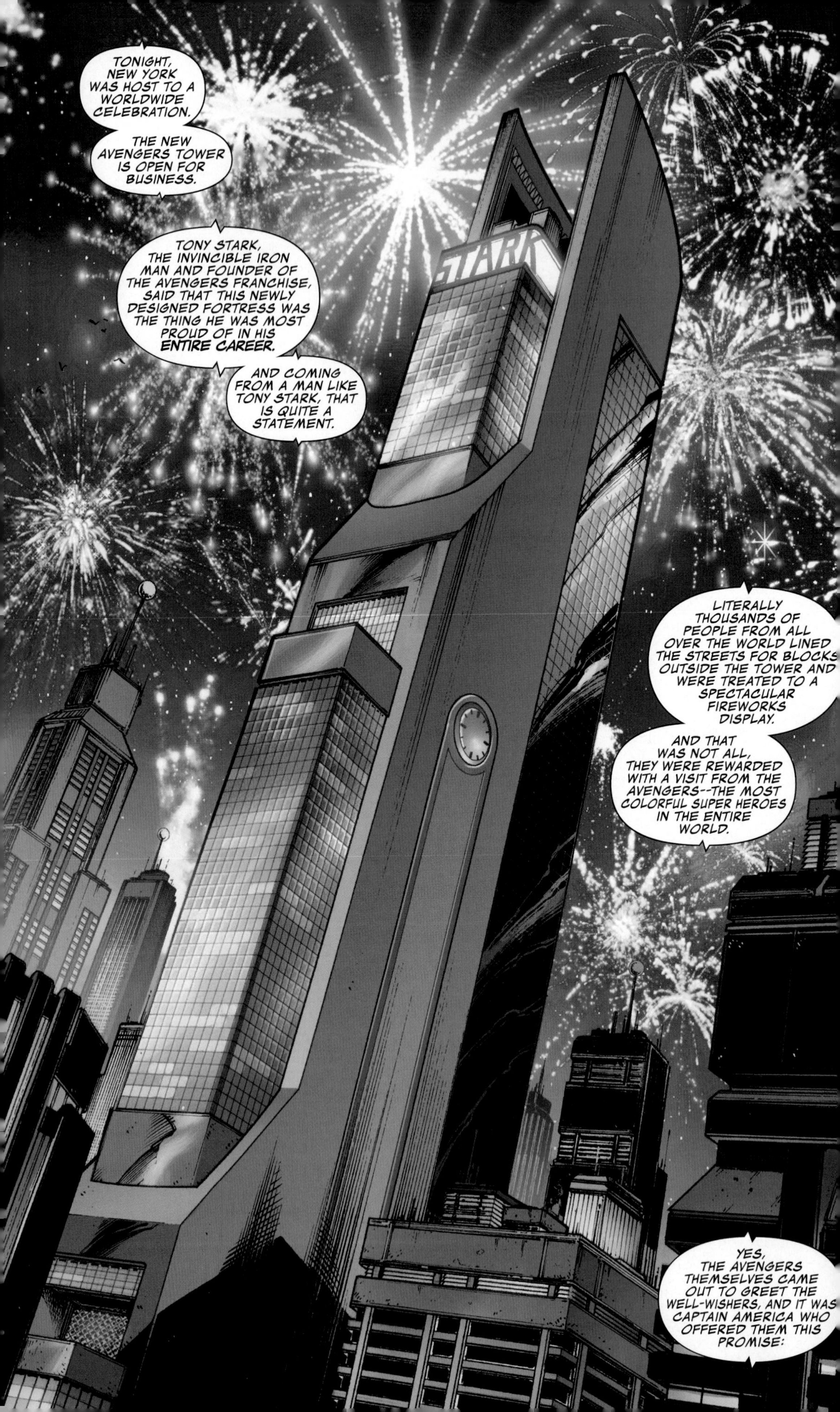
TONIGHT, NEW YORK WAS HOST TO A WORLDWIDE CELEBRATION.
THE NEW AVENGERS TOWER IS OPEN FOR BUSINESS.
TONY STARK, THE INVINCIBLE IRON MAN AND FOUNDER OF THE AVENGERS FRANCHISE, SAID THAT THIS NEWLY DESIGNED FORTRESS WAS THE THING HE WAS MOST PROUD OF IN HIS **ENTIRE CAREER.**
AND COMING FROM A MAN LIKE TONY STARK, THAT IS QUITE A STATEMENT.
STARK
LITERALLY THOUSANDS OF PEOPLE FROM ALL OVER THE WORLD LINED THE STREETS FOR BLOCKS OUTSIDE THE TOWER AND WERE TREATED TO A SPECTACULAR FIREWORKS DISPLAY.
AND THAT WAS NOT ALL, THEY WERE REWARDED WITH A VISIT FROM THE AVENGERS--THE MOST COLORFUL SUPER HEROES IN THE ENTIRE WORLD.
YES, THE AVENGERS THEMSELVES CAME OUT TO GREET THE WELL-WISHERS, AND IT WAS CAPTAIN AMERICA WHO OFFERED THEM THIS PROMISE:

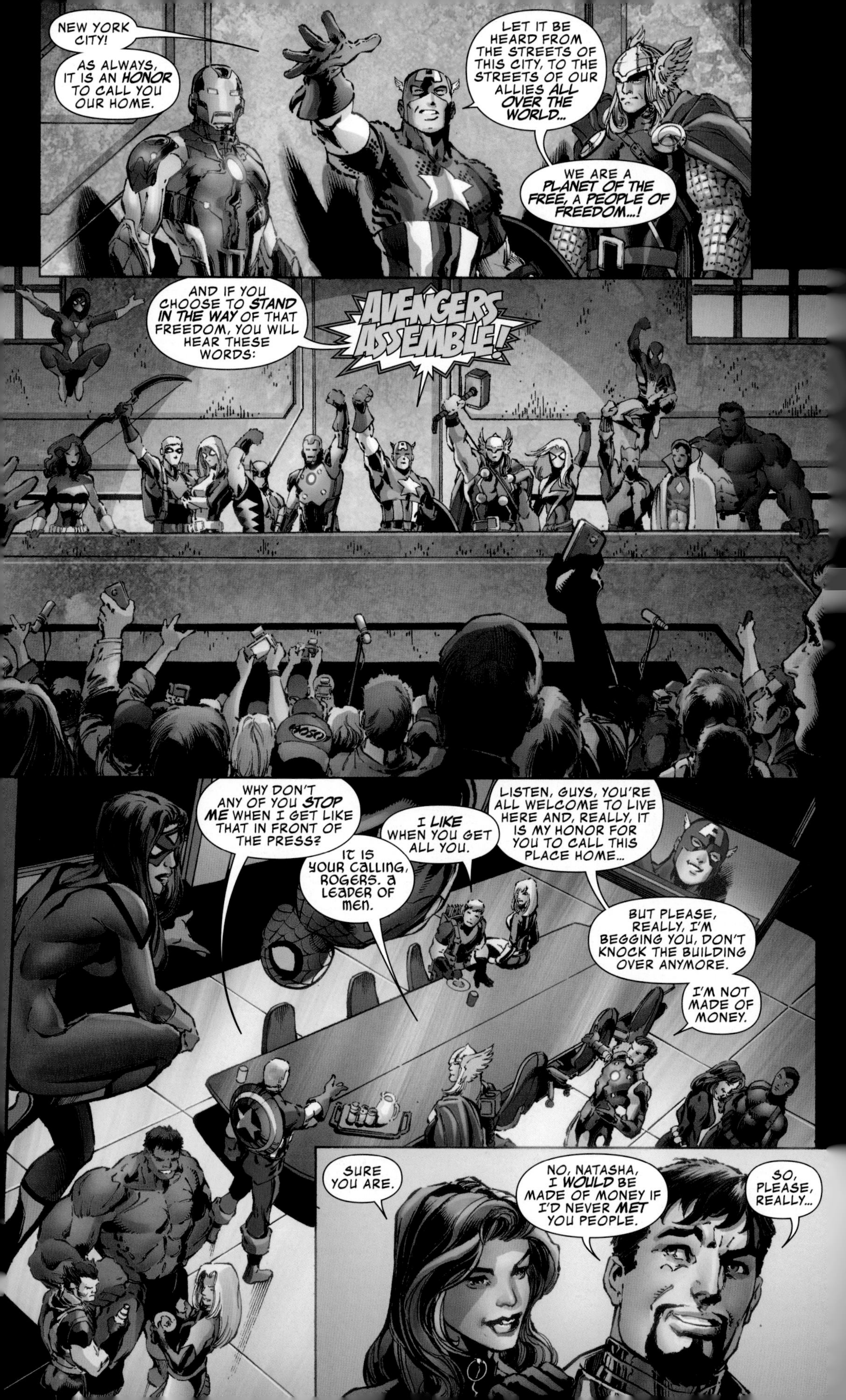
NEW YORK CITY!
AS ALWAYS, IT IS AN HONOR TO CALL YOU OUR HOME.
LET IT BE HEARD FROM THE STREETS OF THIS CITY, TO THE STREETS OF OUR ALLIES ALL OVER THE WORLD...
WE ARE A PLANET OF THE FREE, A PEOPLE OF FREEDOM...!
AND IF YOU CHOOSE TO STAND IN THE WAY OF THAT FREEDOM, YOU WILL HEAR THESE WORDS:
AVENGERS ASSEMBLE!
WHY DON'T ANY OF YOU STOP ME WHEN I GET LIKE THAT IN FRONT OF THE PRESS?
IT IS YOUR CALLING, ROGERS. A LEADER OF MEN.
I LIKE WHEN YOU GET ALL YOU.
LISTEN, GUYS, YOU'RE ALL WELCOME TO LIVE HERE AND, REALLY, IT IS MY HONOR FOR YOU TO CALL THIS PLACE HOME...
BUT PLEASE, REALLY, I'M BEGGING YOU, DON'T KNOCK THE BUILDING OVER ANYMORE.
I'M NOT MADE OF MONEY.
SURE YOU ARE.
NO, NATASHA, I WOULD BE MADE OF MONEY IF I'D NEVER MET YOU PEOPLE.
SO, PLEASE, REALLY...

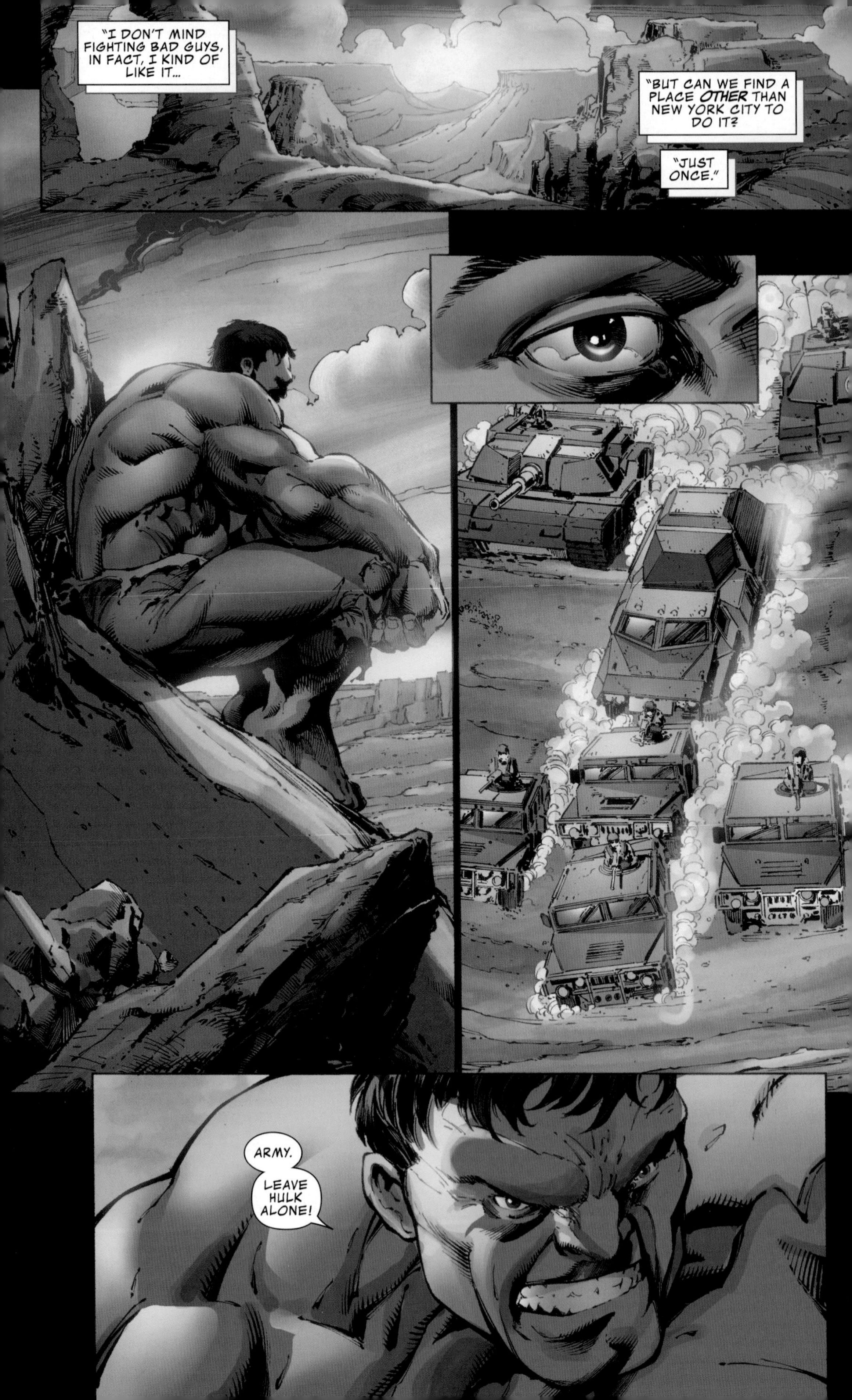
"I DON'T MIND FIGHTING BAD GUYS, IN FACT, I KIND OF LIKE IT...
"BUT CAN WE FIND A PLACE OTHER THAN NEW YORK CITY TO DO IT?
"JUST ONCE."
ARMY.
LEAVE HULK ALONE!

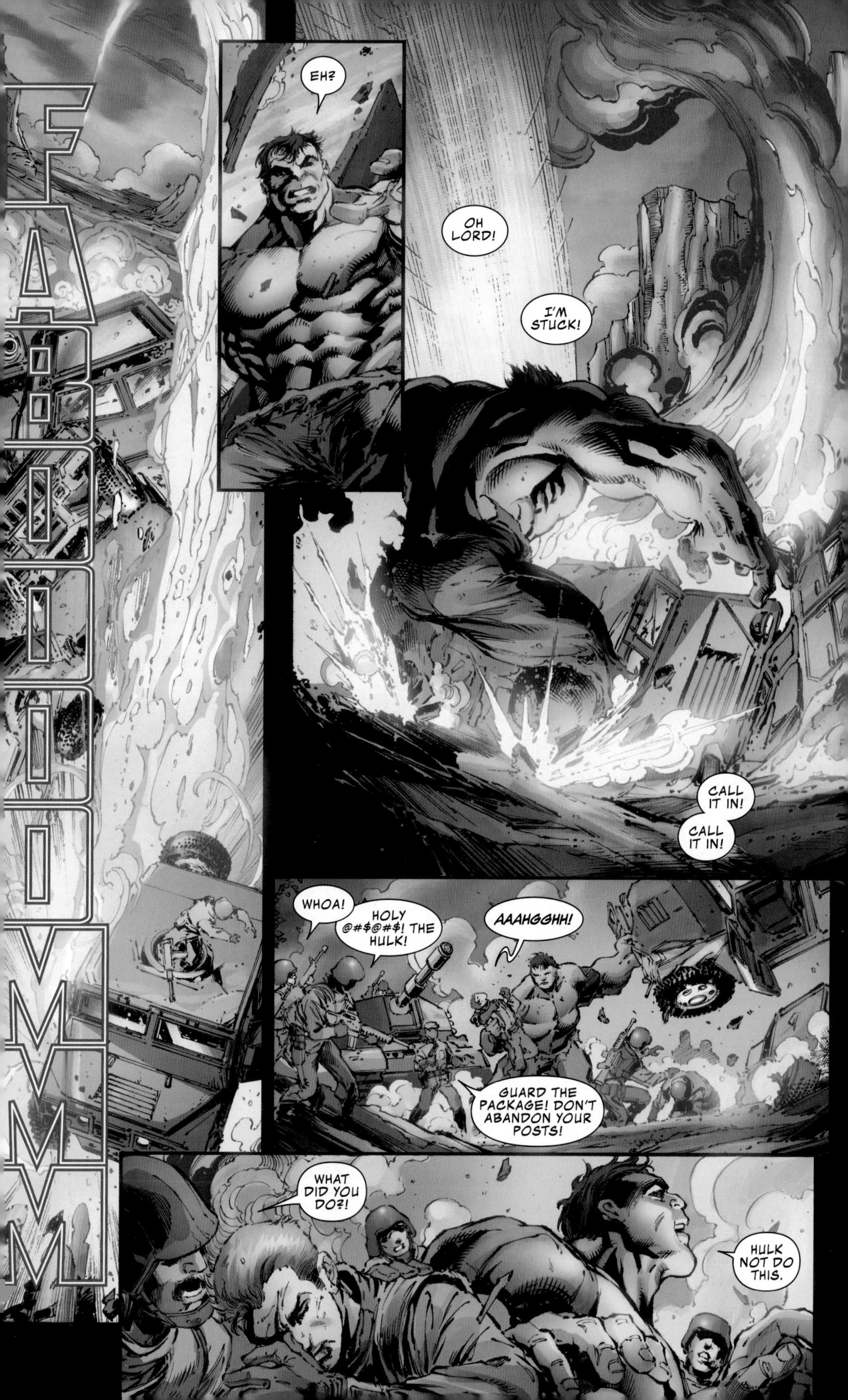

EH?
OH LORD!
I'M STUCK!
CALL IT IN!
CALL IT IN!
WHOA!
HOLY @#$@#$! THE HULK!
AAAHGGHH!
GUARD THE PACKAGE! DON'T ABANDON YOUR POSTS!
WHAT DID YOU DO?!
HULK NOT DO THIS.

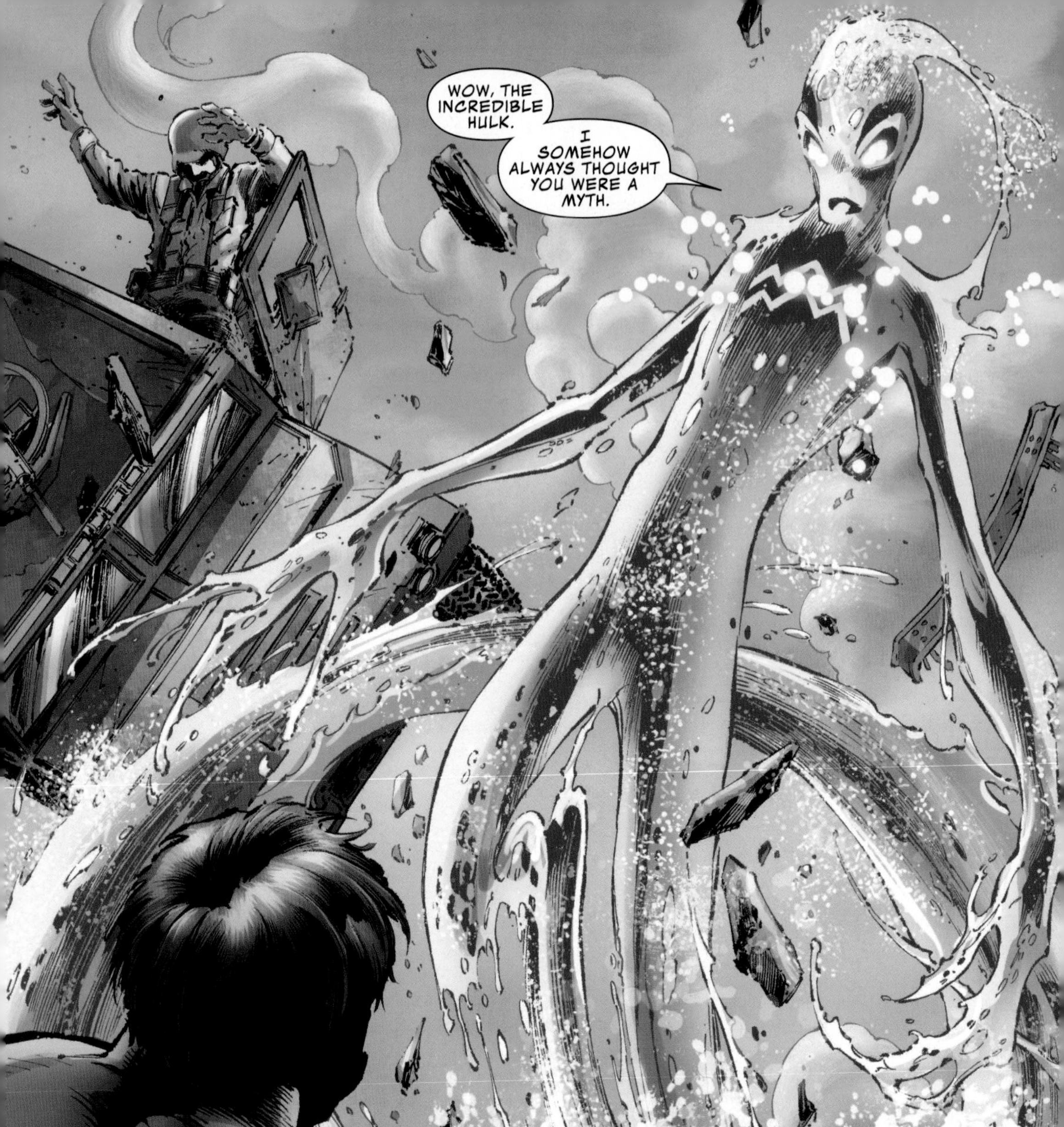
WOW, THE INCREDIBLE HULK.
I SOMEHOW ALWAYS THOUGHT YOU WERE A MYTH.

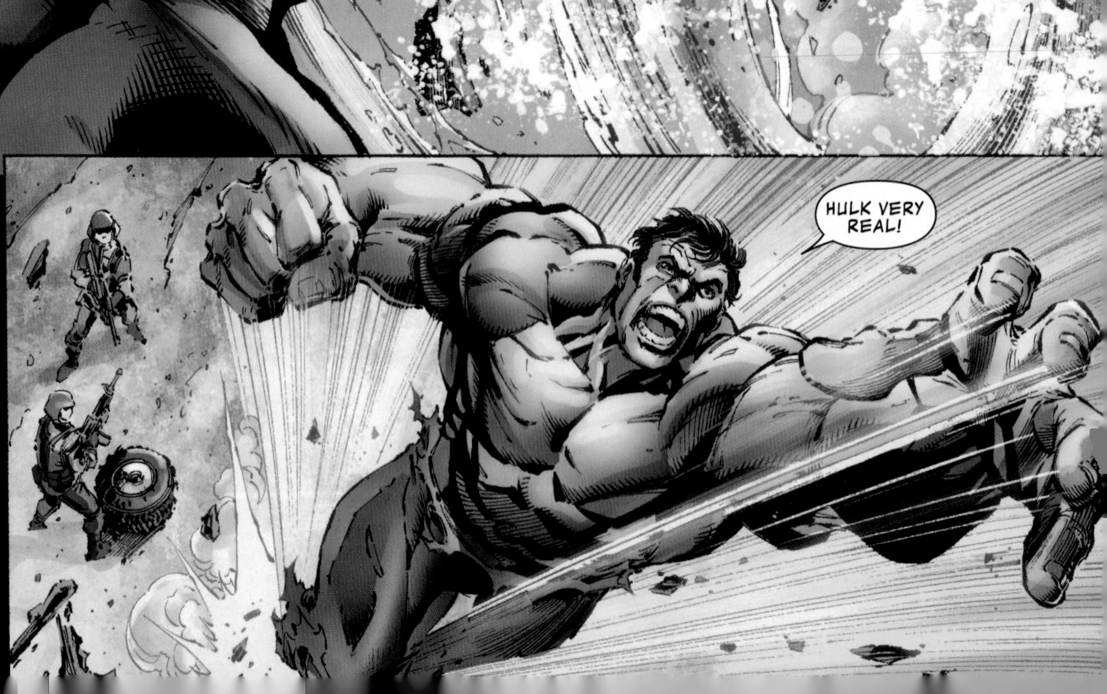
HULK VERY REAL!

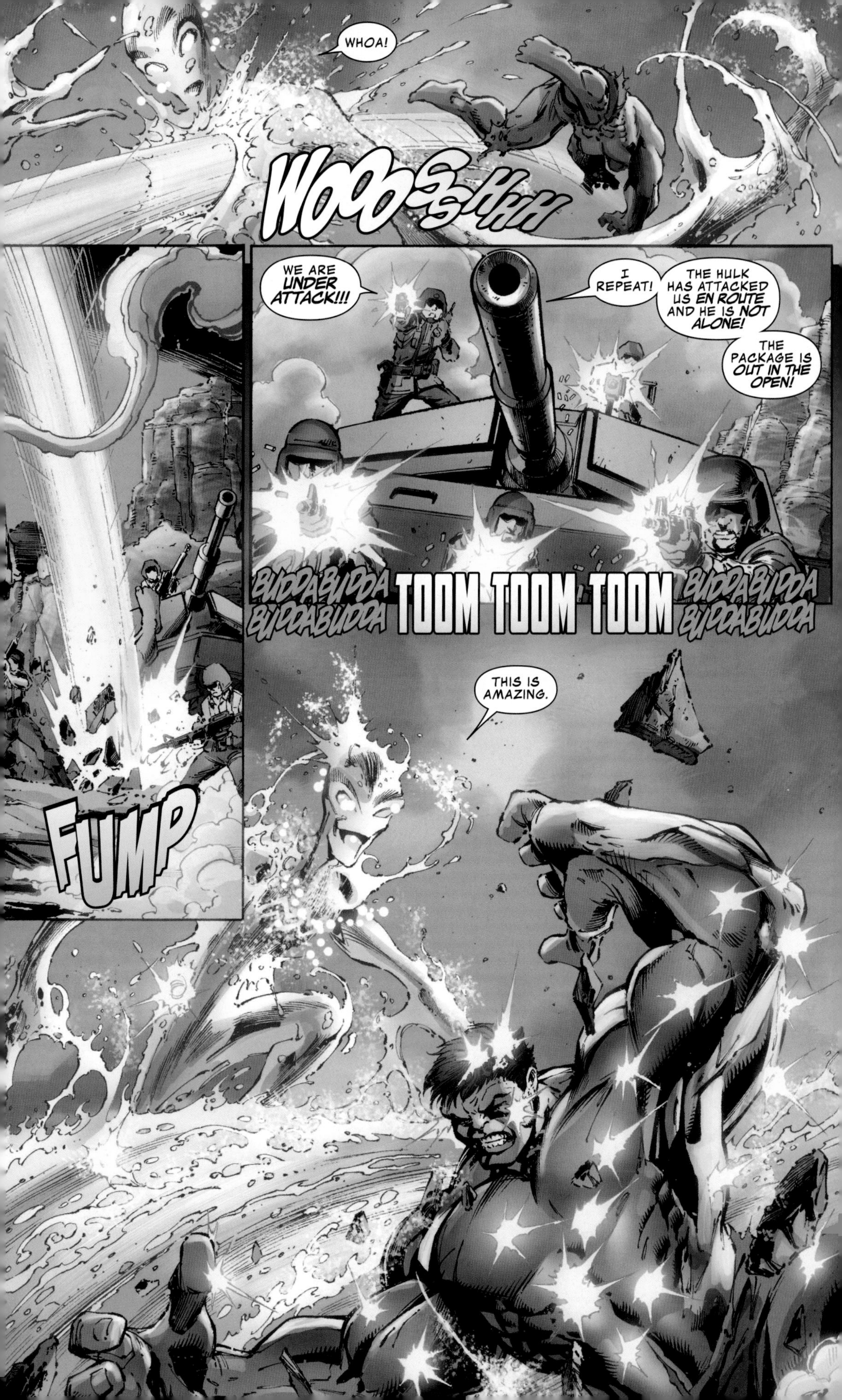
WHOA!
WOOOSSHHH
WE ARE UNDER ATTACK!!!
I REPEAT!
THE HULK HAS ATTACKED US EN ROUTE AND HE IS NOT ALONE!
THE PACKAGE IS OUT IN THE OPEN!
BUDDABUDDA BUDDABUDDA
TOOM TOOM TOOM
BUDDABUDDA BUDDABUDDA
FUMP
THIS IS AMAZING.

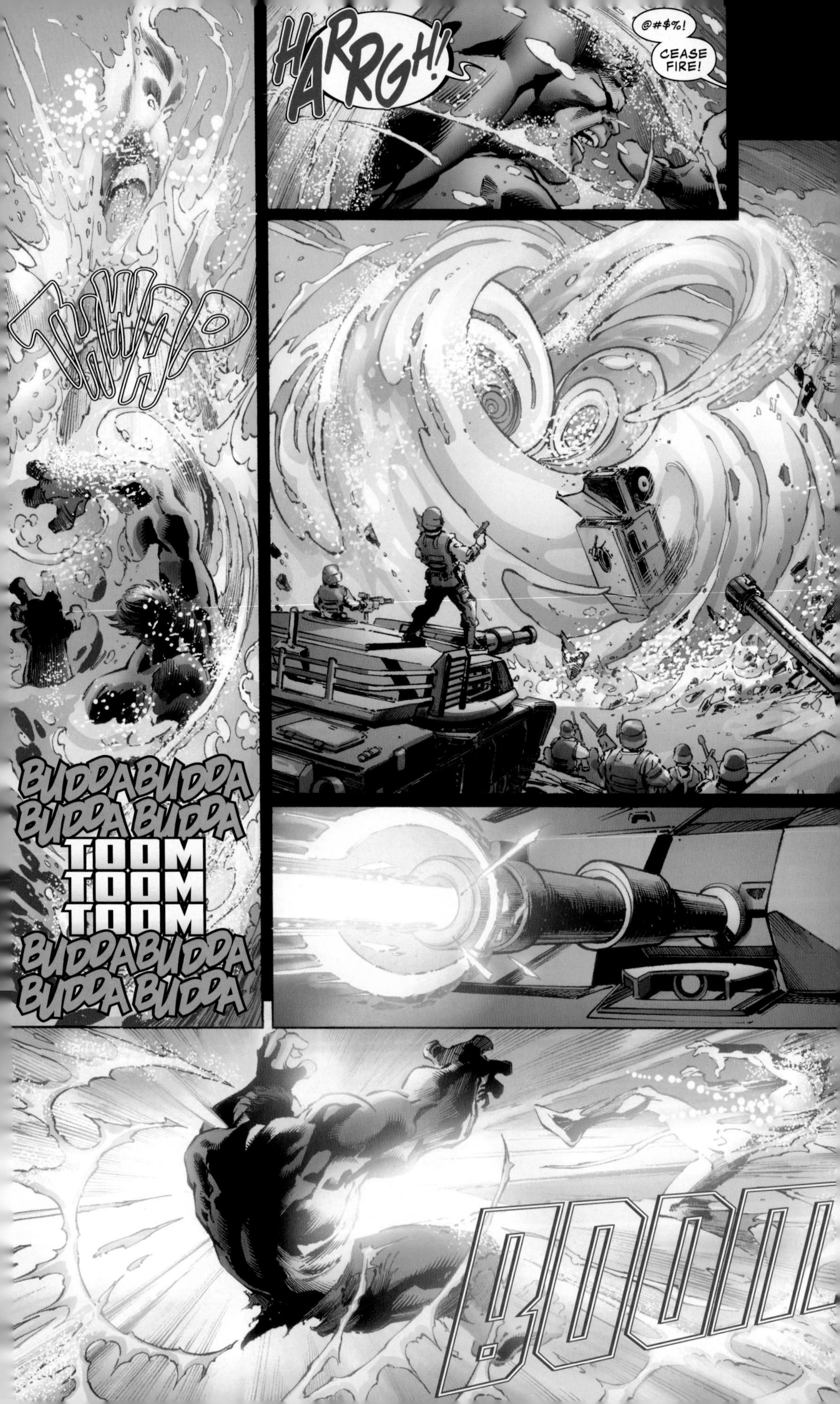
HARRGH!
@#$%! CEASE FIRE!
THWAP
BUDDABUDDA BUDDA BUDDA
TOOM TOOM TOOM
BUDDABUDDA BUDDA BUDDA

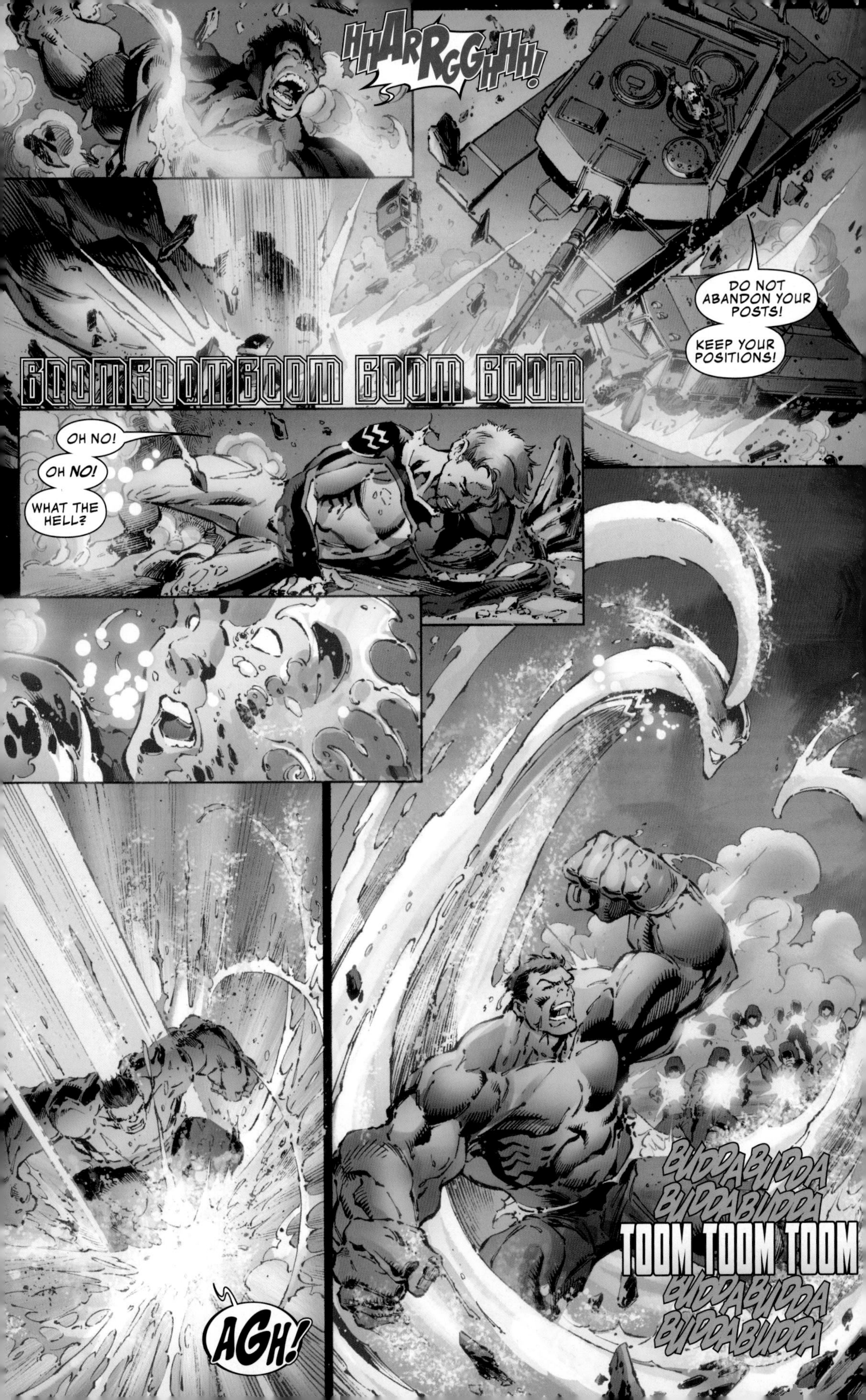
HHARRGGHHH!
DO NOT ABANDON YOUR POSTS!
KEEP YOUR POSITIONS!
BOOMBOOMBOOM BOOM BOOM
OH NO!
OH NO!
WHAT THE HELL?
BUDDABUDDA
BUDDABUDDA
TOOM TOOM TOOM
BUDDABUDDA
BUDDABUDDA
AGH!

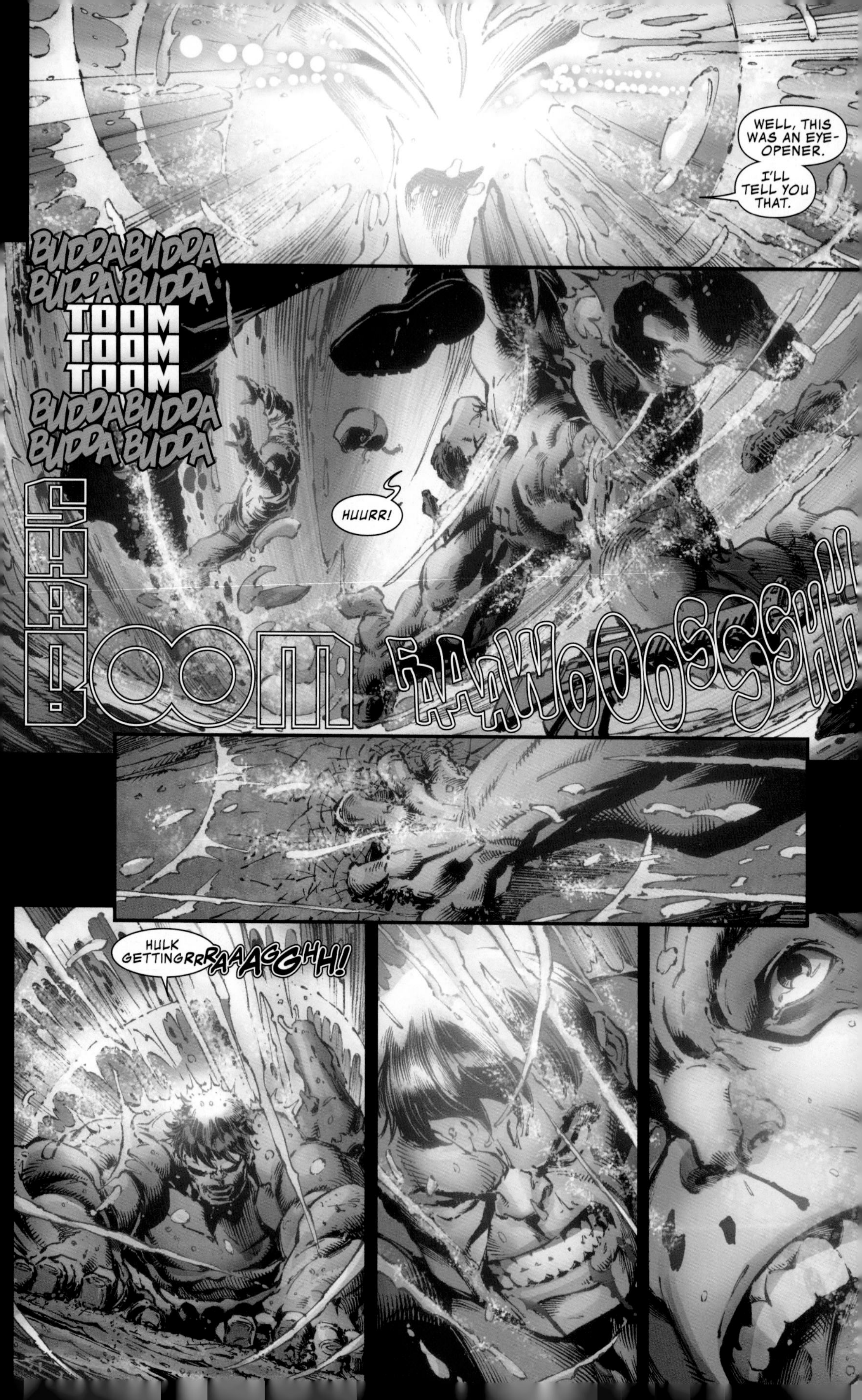
WELL, THIS WAS AN EYE-OPENER.
I'LL TELL YOU THAT.
BUDDABUDDA BUDDA BUDDA
TOOM TOOM TOOM
BUDDABUDDA BUDDA BUDDA
HUURR!
SHRA-BOOM
FRAAWOOOSSSH
HULK GETTINGRRRAAAGGHH!

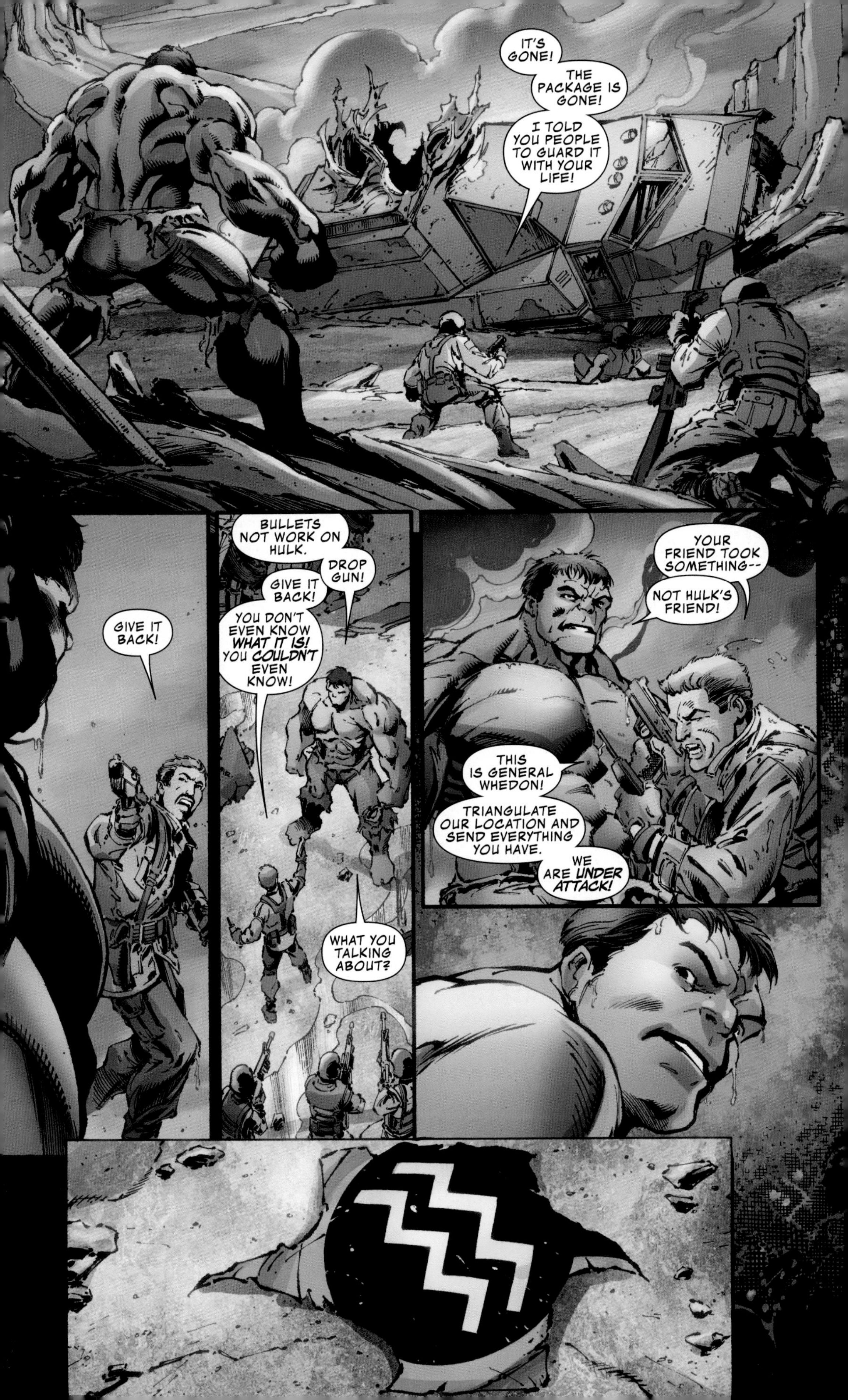
IT'S GONE!
THE PACKAGE IS GONE!
I TOLD YOU PEOPLE TO GUARD IT WITH YOUR LIFE!
GIVE IT BACK!
BULLETS NOT WORK ON HULK.
DROP GUN!
GIVE IT BACK!
YOU DON'T EVEN KNOW WHAT IT IS! YOU COULDN'T EVEN KNOW!
WHAT YOU TALKING ABOUT?
YOUR FRIEND TOOK SOMETHING--
NOT HULK'S FRIEND!
THIS IS GENERAL WHEDON!
TRIANGULATE OUR LOCATION AND SEND EVERYTHING YOU HAVE.
WE ARE UNDER ATTACK!

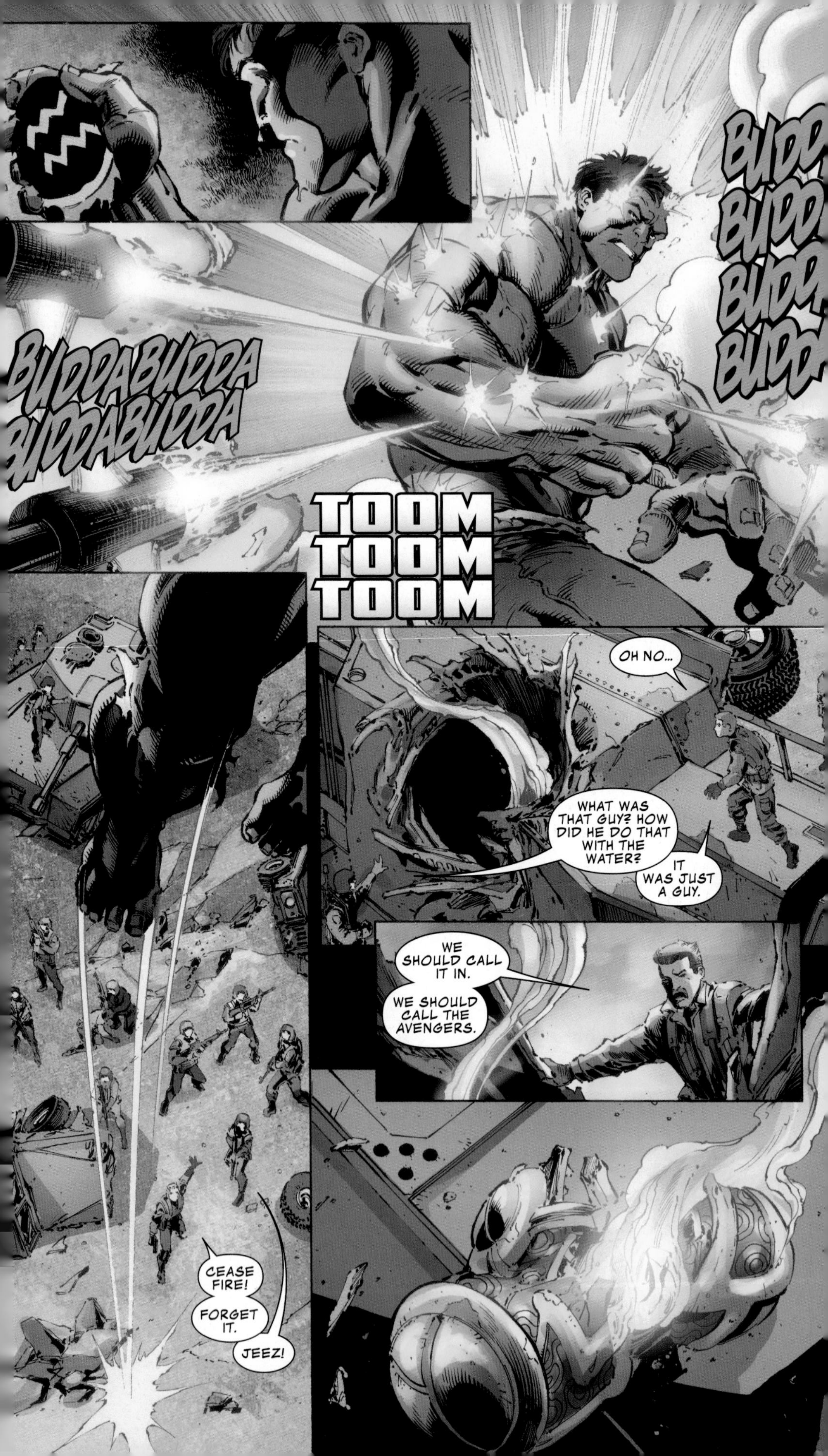

BUDDABUDDA BUDDABUDDA
TOOM TOOM TOOM
OH NO...
WHAT WAS THAT GUY? HOW DID HE DO THAT WITH THE WATER?
IT WAS JUST A GUY.
WE SHOULD CALL IT IN.
WE SHOULD CALL THE AVENGERS.
CEASE FIRE!
FORGET IT.
JEEZ!

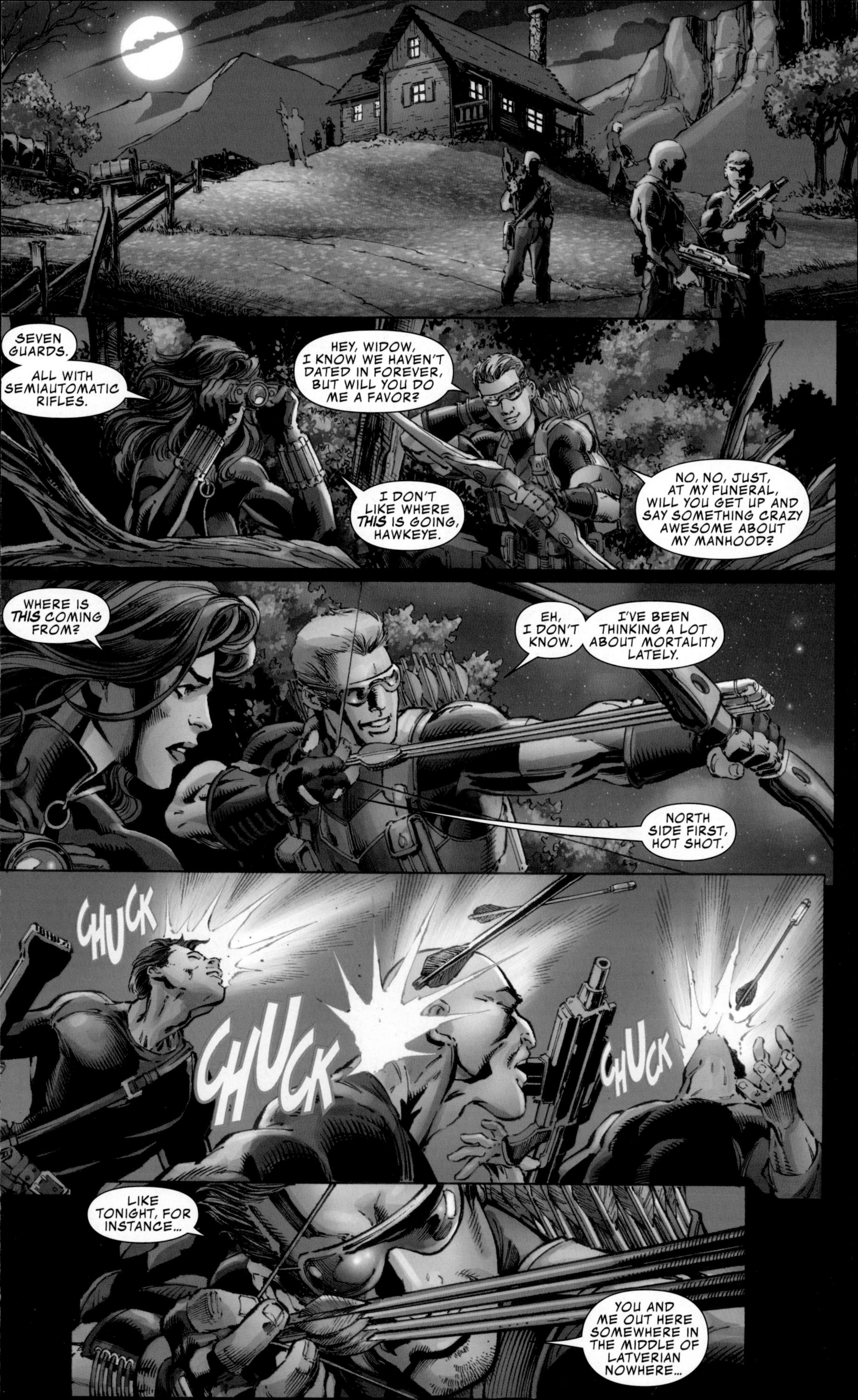
SEVEN GUARDS.
ALL WITH SEMIAUTOMATIC RIFLES.
HEY, WIDOW, I KNOW WE HAVEN'T DATED IN FOREVER, BUT WILL YOU DO ME A FAVOR?
I DON'T LIKE WHERE THIS IS GOING, HAWKEYE.
NO, NO, JUST, AT MY FUNERAL, WILL YOU GET UP AND SAY SOMETHING CRAZY AWESOME ABOUT MY MANHOOD?
WHERE IS THIS COMING FROM?
EH, I DON'T KNOW.
I'VE BEEN THINKING A LOT ABOUT MORTALITY LATELY.
NORTH SIDE FIRST, HOT SHOT.
CHUCK
CHUCK
CHUCK
LIKE TONIGHT, FOR INSTANCE...
YOU AND ME OUT HERE SOMEWHERE IN THE MIDDLE OF LATVERIAN NOWHERE...

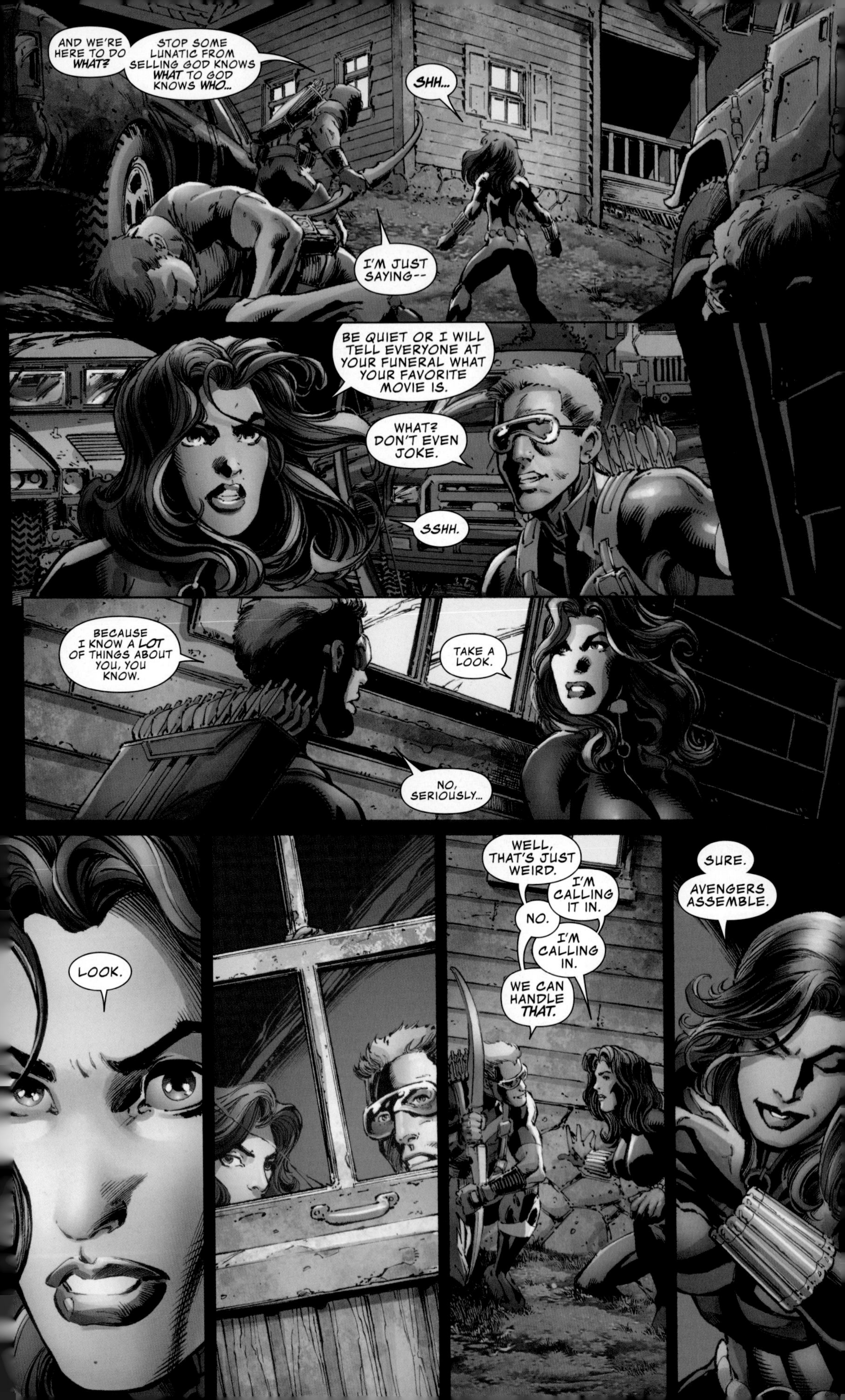
AND WE'RE HERE TO DO WHAT?
STOP SOME LUNATIC FROM SELLING GOD KNOWS WHAT TO GOD KNOWS WHO...
SHH...
I'M JUST SAYING--
BE QUIET OR I WILL TELL EVERYONE AT YOUR FUNERAL WHAT YOUR FAVORITE MOVIE IS.
WHAT? DON'T EVEN JOKE.
SSHH.
BECAUSE I KNOW A LOT OF THINGS ABOUT YOU, YOU KNOW.
TAKE A LOOK.
NO, SERIOUSLY...
LOOK.
WELL, THAT'S JUST WEIRD.
I'M CALLING IT IN.
NO.
I'M CALLING IN.
WE CAN HANDLE THAT.
SURE.
AVENGERS ASSEMBLE.

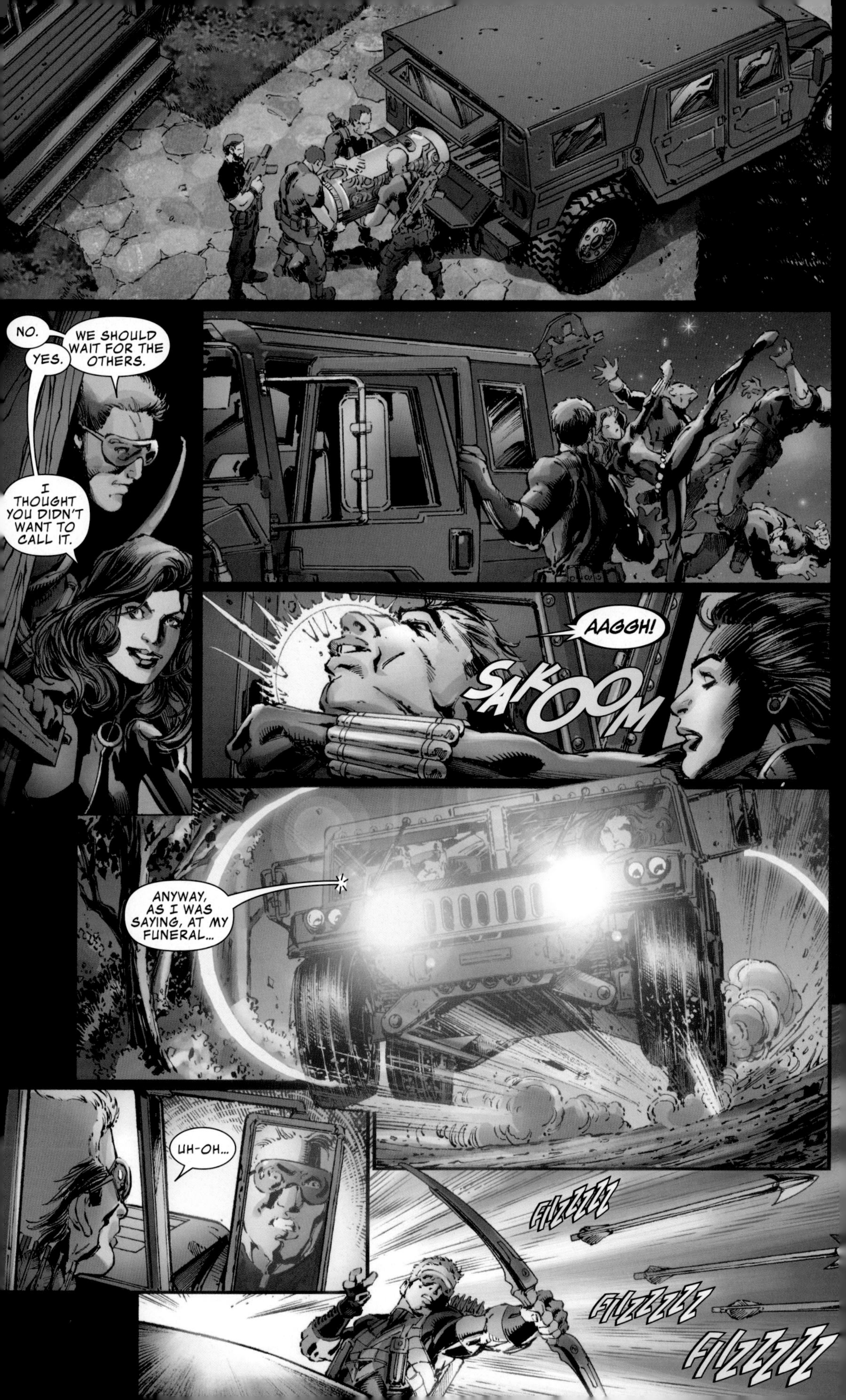
NO.
WE SHOULD WAIT FOR THE OTHERS.
YES.
I THOUGHT YOU DIDN'T WANT TO CALL IT.
AAGGH!
SAKOOM
ANYWAY, AS I WAS SAYING, AT MY FUNERAL...
UH-OH...
FIZZZZZ
FIZZZZZ
FIZZZZZ

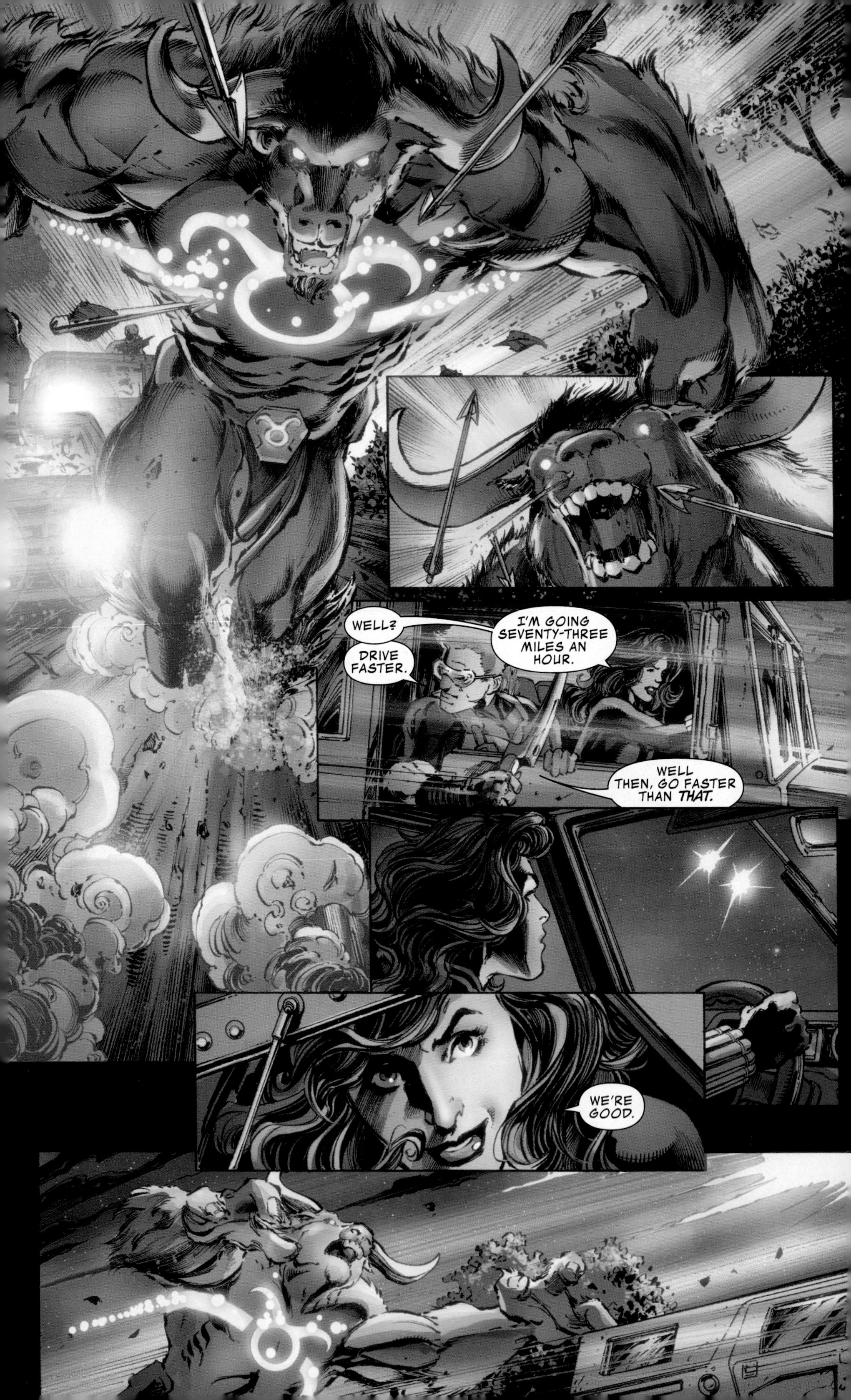
WELL?
I'M GOING SEVENTY-THREE MILES AN HOUR.
DRIVE FASTER.
WELL THEN, GO FASTER THAN *THAT.*
WE'RE GOOD.

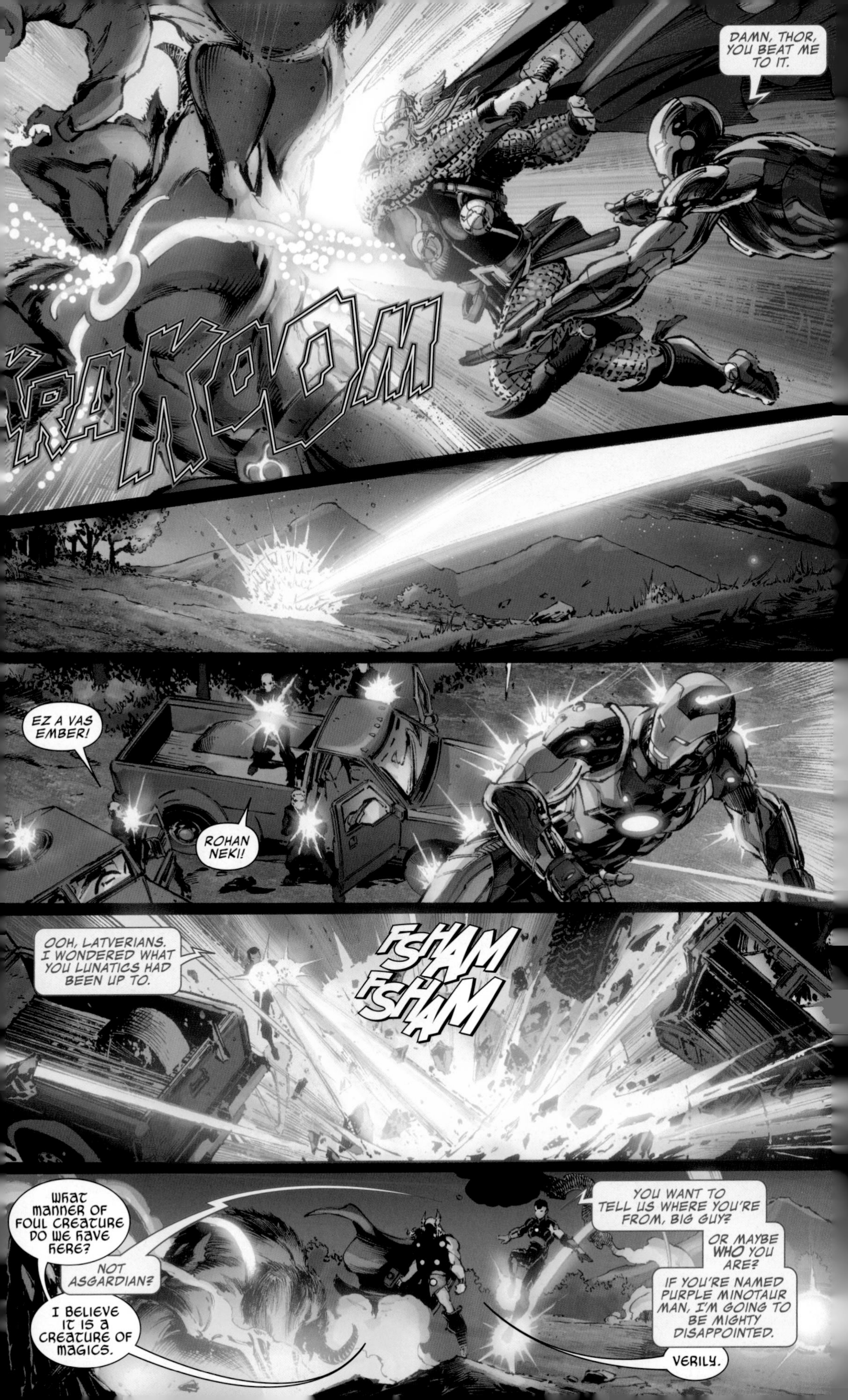
DAMN, THOR, YOU BEAT ME TO IT.
KRAKOOM
EZ A VAS EMBER!
ROHAN NEKI!
OOH, LATVERIANS. I WONDERED WHAT YOU LUNATICS HAD BEEN UP TO.
FSHAM FSHAM
WHAT MANNER OF FOUL CREATURE DO WE HAVE HERE?
NOT ASGARDIAN?
I BELIEVE IT IS A CREATURE OF MAGICS.
YOU WANT TO TELL US WHERE YOU'RE FROM, BIG GUY?
OR MAYBE WHO YOU ARE?
IF YOU'RE NAMED PURPLE MINOTAUR MAN, I'M GOING TO BE MIGHTY DISAPPOINTED.
VERILY.

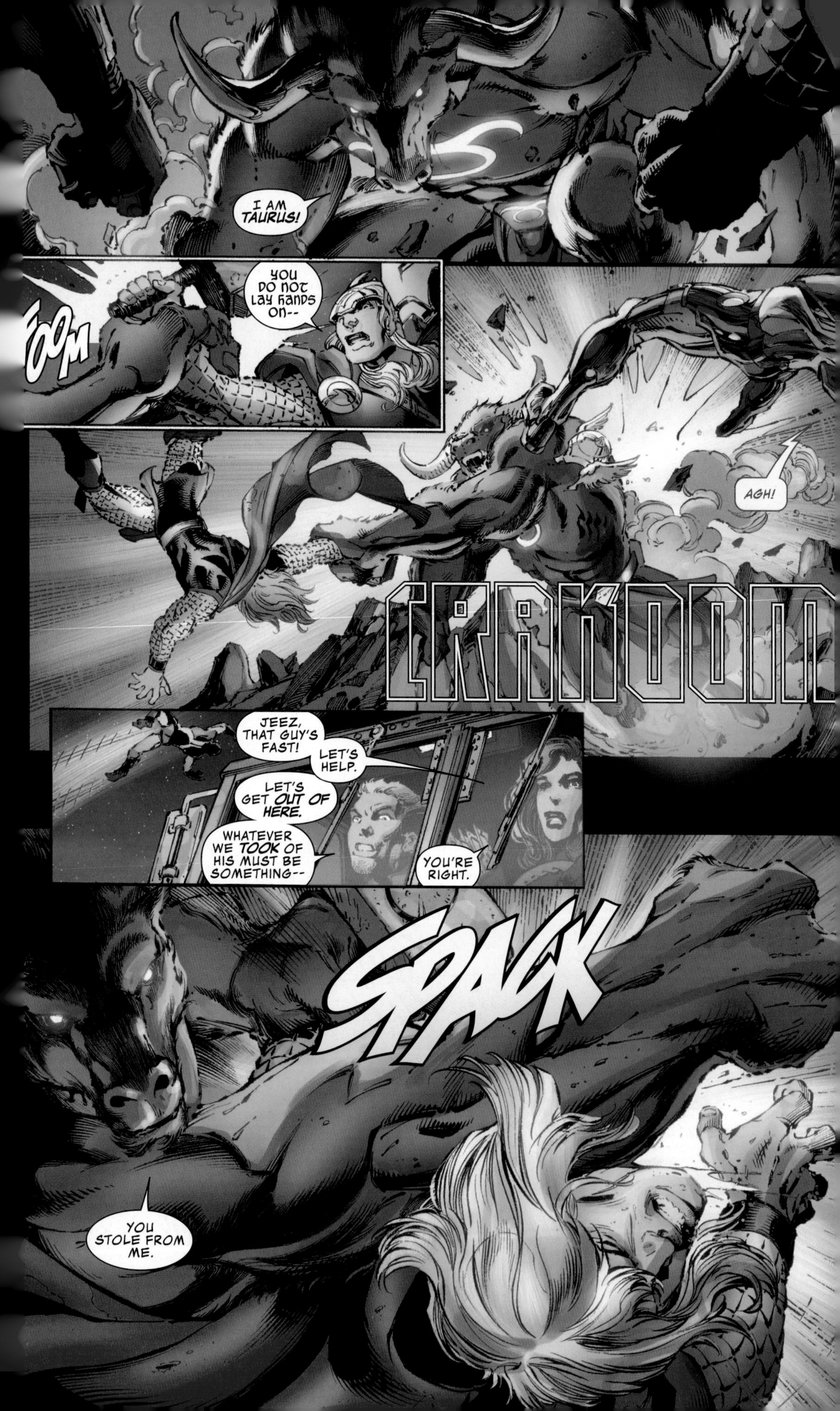
I AM TAURUS!
FOOM
YOU DO NOT LAY HANDS ON--
AGH!
CRAKOOM
JEEZ, THAT GUY'S FAST!
LET'S HELP.
LET'S GET OUT OF HERE.
WHATEVER WE TOOK OF HIS MUST BE SOMETHING--
YOU'RE RIGHT.
SPACK
YOU STOLE FROM ME.

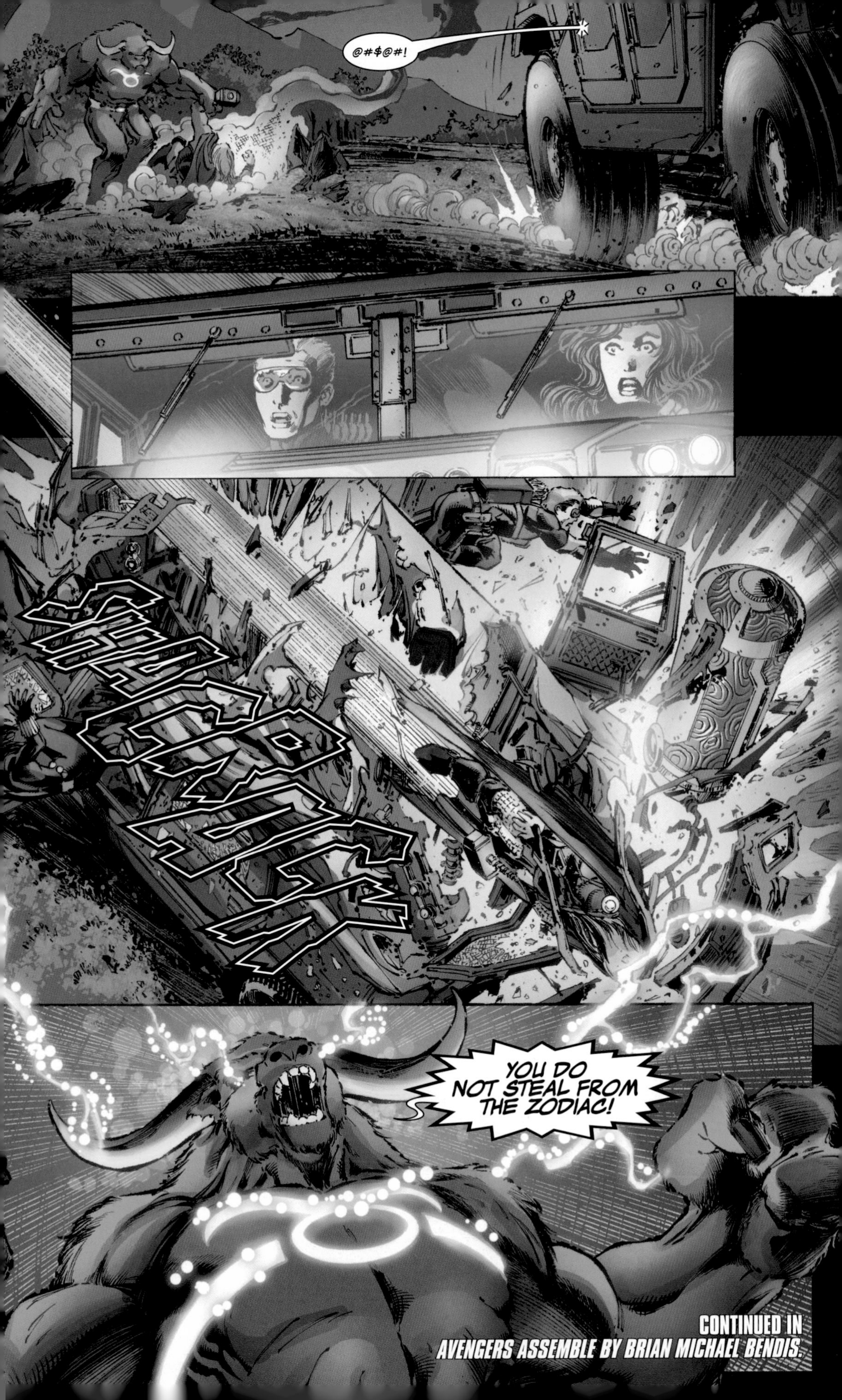
@#$@#!
YOU DO NOT STEAL FROM THE ZODIAC!
CONTINUED IN
AVENGERS ASSEMBLE BY BRIAN MICHAEL BENDIS.

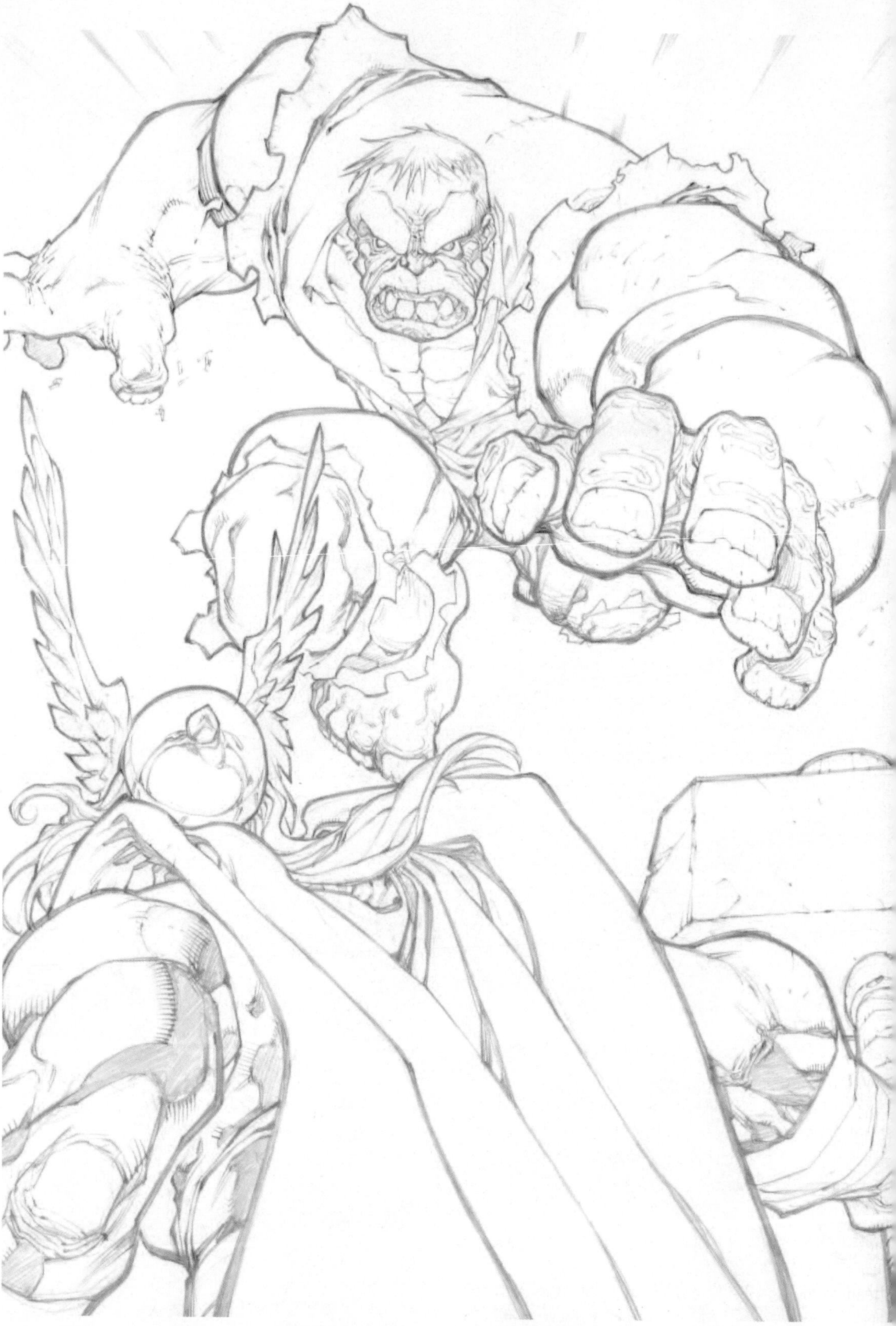

PAGE-BY-PAGE OUTLINE BY PETER DAVID

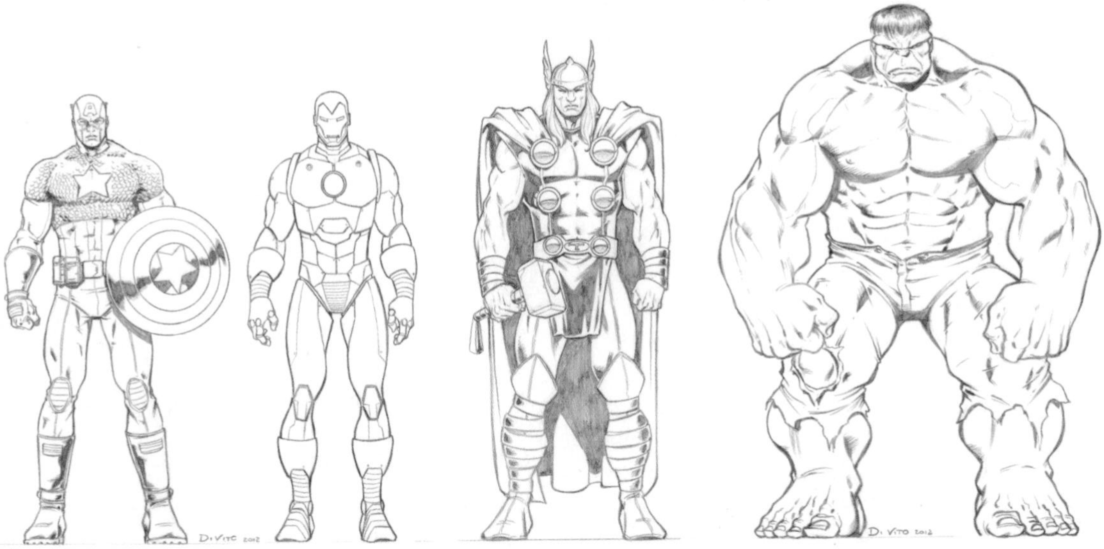

PAGES 1-19

Introduction of LOKI, pissed off while stewing in the Island of Silence. Over these pages we have a recap of the events that led to the formation of the team in the first place, and the discovery of CAPTAIN AMERICA in the ice. He considers each of the major players of the team, stewing over the situation.

CUT TO: IRON MAN is battling the HULK and winds up getting his head handed to him. We then reveal that what we've seen is Tony Stark running scenarios as to how to try and defeat him. Tony also reveals in narrative that he's suspicious of THOR, because he's learned of the existence of shape-changing aliens and is worried that Thor is actually some sort of alien with a hidden agenda, taking the form of a classic mythic hero in order to discourage suspicion. After all, the Avengers have already taken a PR hit thanks to the Hulk; the last thing they need is to be discovered to be harboring an alien spy or worse.

CUT TO: MIGHTY THOR, using his weather powers to bring water to an area that was previously suffering from a drought. A grateful elderly farmer is a WW II get, and he asks Thor if it's true that Captain America has returned. The old man figures Thor, being a god, is the one to ask about it since it can only be described as a miracle. And this alone starts Thor wondering, suspicious. After all, what a staggering coincidence it is, that enabled them to find Captain America floating along in the few hours between when the ice would have thoroughly melted in the warm Gulf Stream waters and the point where he would have drowned? Plus he hardly comes across like the determined heroic, one man army that legends spoke of. Thor doesn't see how someone who has been given a second lease on life can be moping about "poor Bucky." The teen died heroically. What more can a hero ask than that?

CUT TO: CAPTAIN AMERICA. He intervenes in a gang fight, and lectures them on the futility of fighting each other when all Americans should be united. This doesn't prompt the reaction he'd anticipated as the gang members burst into laughter at how old and out of touch this guy is. They disperse, many of them saying, "Who the hell is Captain America?" They've never heard of him. (If we can have a whole generation that doesn't know who Paul McCartney is, I figure anything's possible.) It leaves Cap wondering

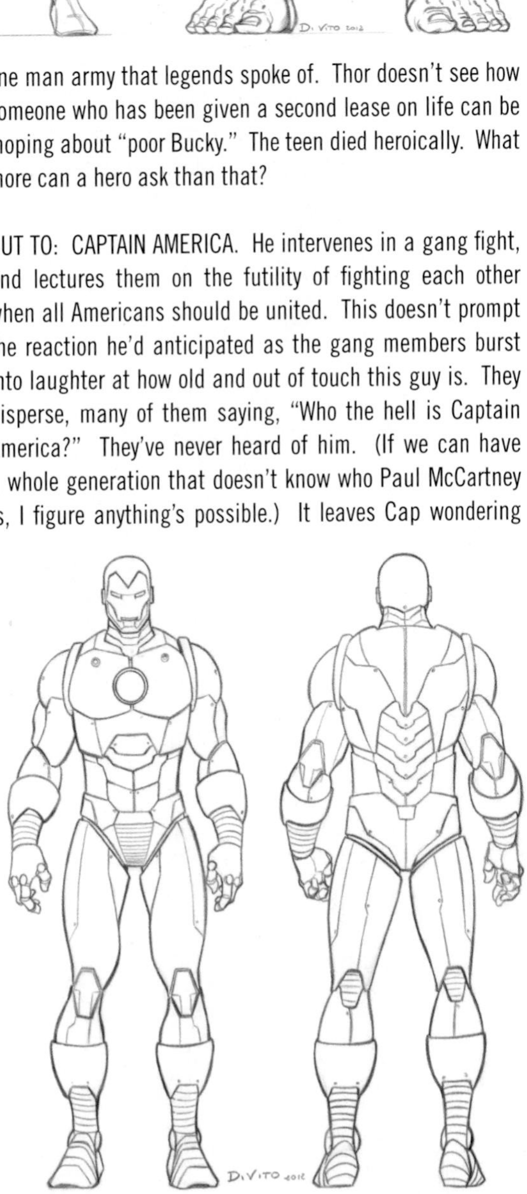

who, indeed, Captain America is. Captain America is still grief stricken over the loss of Bucky, feeling displaced and dealing with survivor's guilt.

The Avengers then receive a communication from NICK FURY (either on panel or not, depending if we want to go with Classic Fury, Movie Fury, or just leave it ambiguous). He informs them that they have reports of the Hulk stampeding around in Nevada and can localize his whereabouts for them. "You're the guys who paraded him around as being rehabbed, only to wind up looking like idiots. I figure you'd want first crack at him."

Jumping in the Avengers quinjet, the trio heads out (Giant Man and the Wasp not along for the ride since they have tickets for a cruise and thus are unavailable.) The trio is uncharacteristically quiet.

Upon arriving at the Hulk's last known location, the group spreads out so they can cover as much area as possible (Cap on a motorcycle that they brought with them in their plane.)

PAGES 20 TO 39

DiVito

As Cap approaches a small town, he suddenly feels a pinching on the back of his neck, like a mosquito bit him. He loses his balance on his motorcycle and it skids out but being Cap, he lands on his feet. The townsfolk approach him in awe, thrilled to see the living legend in their midst. This town is like Main Street in Disneyland. They can't get enough of feting Captain America. There's a parade for him down the Main Street. Also there's a lovely young girl who is the spitting image of his lost Peggy Carter. He goes on an old-fashioned date with her, everything is wonderful, they're making out...and suddenly he remembers he's supposed to be tracking the Hulk. He has a mission. He'd never turn his back on a mission. That's not who he is; that's not who Captain America is. He fights his way back to awareness and comes to, discovering he's strapped to a table, being experimented on by the Red Skull and his shock troops. The "mosquito" was a knockout dart and the Skull is working on brainwashing Cap in order to make him more controllable, "as per the desires of our billionaire ally," the Skull says to his associates, unaware that Cap's come to. Cap breaks free, battles the Skull and his forces, takes a pounding, but ultimately triumphs. The Skull and his forces escape, and Cap discovers—to his horror—that the equipment used to brainwash him was manufactured by Stark Industries. Then the bunker begins to blow up, and Cap barely escapes, but loses the proof in the process. He is, however, determined to confront Iron Man and ask him what he knows of Stark's apparent association with the Skull.

PAGES 40 TO 59

Iron Man arrives in Reno, arcing over it, and sees people running from "that horrible monster." He angles down, sees a hulking form, assumes it's the Hulk and goes after him. But no: it's MISTER HYDE. Hyde snarls, "About time," and attacks him. He's strong, but he's no match for Iron Man...but just when Iron Man figures, "That was easy," he's suddenly assaulted from all sides by alien Stone Men. These guys are unbelievably tough, and a far ranging battle annihilates an entire casino (sadly, one owned by Tony Stark.) Ultimately he manages to drive them off, but he has no idea why they were clearly gunning for him. He goes back to find the unconscious Hyde is just coming around and has morphed back into Calvin Zabo. Zabo, pleading, says he had nothing to do with it; he barely remembers any of it. "I think...they said something about Thor." "About attacking me to get to him?" "No, about...protecting him. That's all I know, I swear!" Patching into SHIELD's global monitoring computers (easy enough; they got them from Stark) he finds a photo readout that shows the Stone Men landing on Earth in Norway and then leaving just as quickly...with a satellite photo of Thor watching them go. Holy crap: Thor IS an alien. They dropped him off and somehow Thor figured out that Stark is growing suspicious of him and wanted him taken out.

PAGES 60 TO 79

Thor is cruising along when a missile comes screaming toward him. He dispatches it with his hammer and heads for the site from which they were fired, a ghost town. Waiting for him there? ZARRKO the Tomorrow Man, who fires more missiles at him that Thor is able to batter his way past. Zarrko, seeking vengeance for Thor's having defeated his plans before, airily informs Thor that this is just to warm him up and suddenly Thor is under assault by the Hulk. Except...not just one Hulk. Several Hulks, who Zarko claims have been taken by him from several different points in the Hulk's past and brainwashed to dispose of Thor once and for all. We have the gray Hulk in tattered clothing, the green Hulk in slacks, and the Green Hulk in purple trunks, all of them battling furiously. They're battering the living crap out of Thor. He manages to overcome them and Zarrko, who wasn't expecting that, tries to flee in his vessel, but Thor comes crashing into it. He closes in on Zarrko, and sees various video screens trained on Hulks from the past...and then, to his shock, he sees one trained on the 1940s, and there's Captain America. Then, before Thor can take any sort of action, the time ship literally disappears all around him, leaving him alone...and convinced that the Captain America they found, the one with only a sketchy memory of his past, is there courtesy of Zaarko, brainwashed and a danger to everyone.

PAGES 80 TO 96 OR HIGHER (but not to exceed 100)

And now we cut back to Loki, and we reveal the truth: everyone they've encountered have been foot soldiers of Loki's, their true natures disguised by glamours provided by the trickster god. (Hyde, for instance, was the Executioner; the multiple Hulks were rock trolls, etc.) Now, Loki reasons, all he has to do is sit back and let them destroy each other. Indeed the heroes now come together. Cross accusations are getting thrown around, and fundamental uncertainties

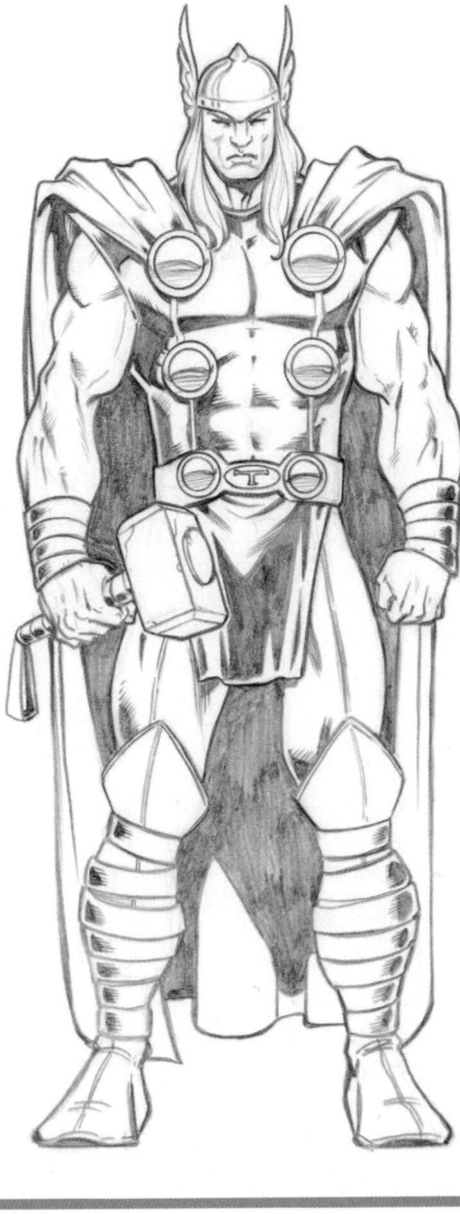

about each other rise to the surface and take over. And all it takes is a slight mental nudge from Loki, preventing them from really "hearing" each other, giving way to their suspicions. Next thing you know, they're battling each other furiously (Iron Man uses magnetic repulsion to separate Thor from his hammer, knocking it into a crevasse, managing to delay its return long enough to inadvertently cause Thor to revert to Don Blake, so he's distracted in trying to get his hammer back.)

And suddenly they are all startled to see...

The Hulk. And he's laughing his butt off. Iron Man, Cap and Thor stop battling, seeing the laughing green monster, and he's basically saying, "What a bunch of idiots! You didn't have me to be suspicious of, so you're tearing each other apart!" Immediately the three of them converge on him, and the Hulk battles them while telling them what fools they are. "Don't'cha know anything? Don't'cha LEARN anything? This whole thing stinks of the exact thing that got you guys together in the first place, and you're dumb enough to fall for it again!"

On the Isle of Silence, Loki is freaking out. "I don't believe it! Trust is easily undercut, suspicions flared to full life easily enough. But they are united in their contempt and distrust for him, and thus they lend ear no matter how much I try to turn them away!"

The battle takes them to Hoover Dam where the Hulk, in battling them, trying to drive them away, brings his hands smashing down so hard that it creates massive vibrations. But Thor sweeps in and slams him with Mjolnir so hard that the Hulk goes crashing into Hoover Dam. This cracks the dam and water starts flooding through, endangering Boulder City. Three pronged attack: Iron Man desperately repairs the damage; Thor, using Mjolnir, keeps the flood waters back, while Captain America—through his sheer gosh-darned charisma—is able to keep the people from freaking out and stampeding each other, calming them and telling them to have confidence in the Avengers.

And the Hulk, witnessing this, is angry, saying, "Right; sure. They blame the whole thing on me. Bah," and off he leaps.

Loki is cursing up a blue streak and suddenly becomes aware there's someone behind him. He turns. It's Odin "All-Father! How did you--?" "What part of 'All Seeing' is unclear to you?" says Odin calmly. "Come here," and he reaches for him and Loki screams.

The heroes come together, the Hulk gone, and they realize that—ironically—what the Hulk said made sense. They compare notes and realize they were used. They swear to each other that they will never allow themselves to be so easily manipulated. Iron Man says angrily, "I know he's your brother and all, but I want a piece of him this time." Suddenly the ground rumbles beneath them and Thor says calmly, "I actually believe he's being tended to." Cut to Loki chained to a rock underground, a snake dripping acid on his face, as Odin says coolly, "That should attend to you for a time."

Di Vito 2012

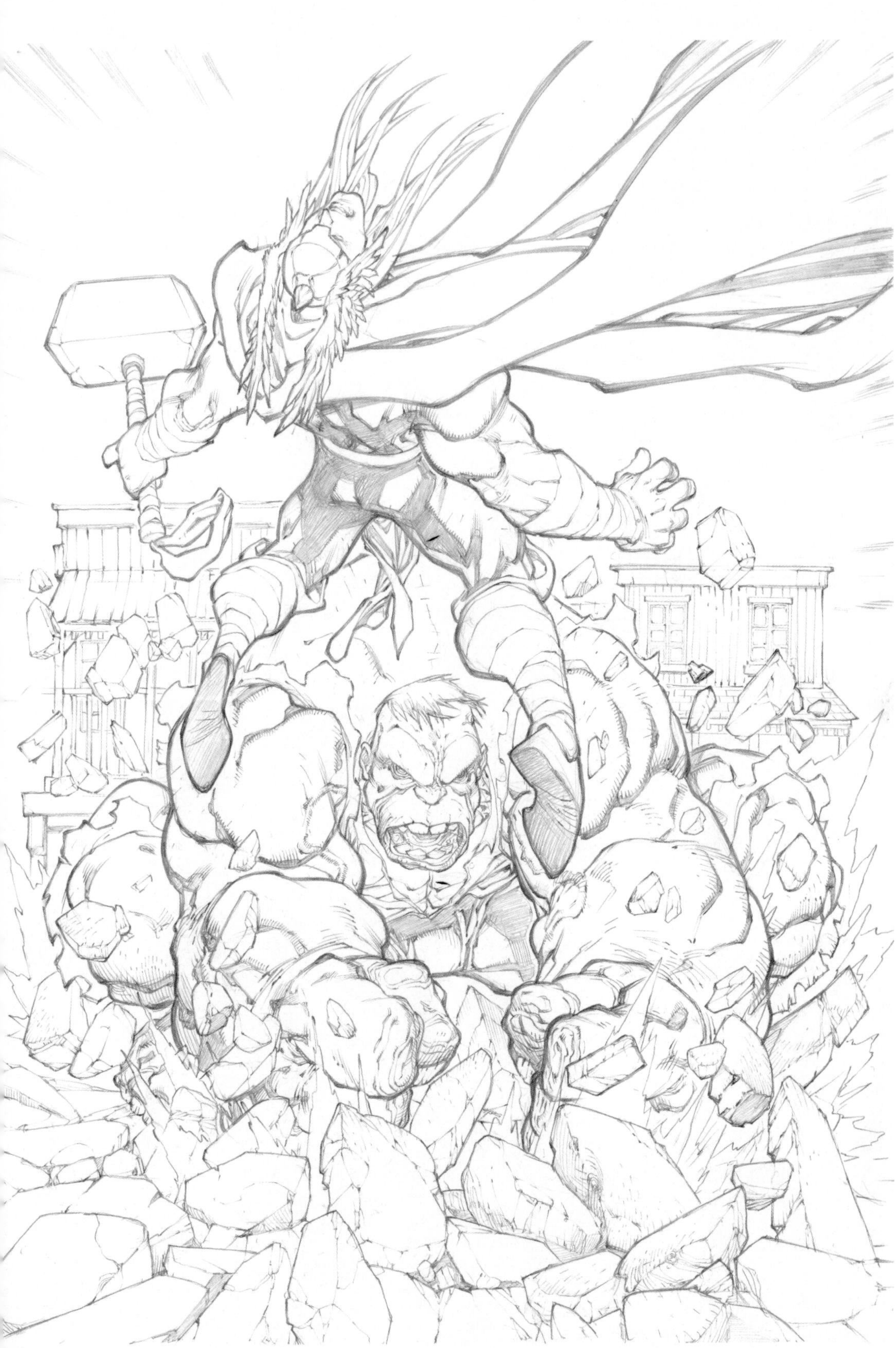

AVENGERS PIN-UP BY **ADI GRANOV**

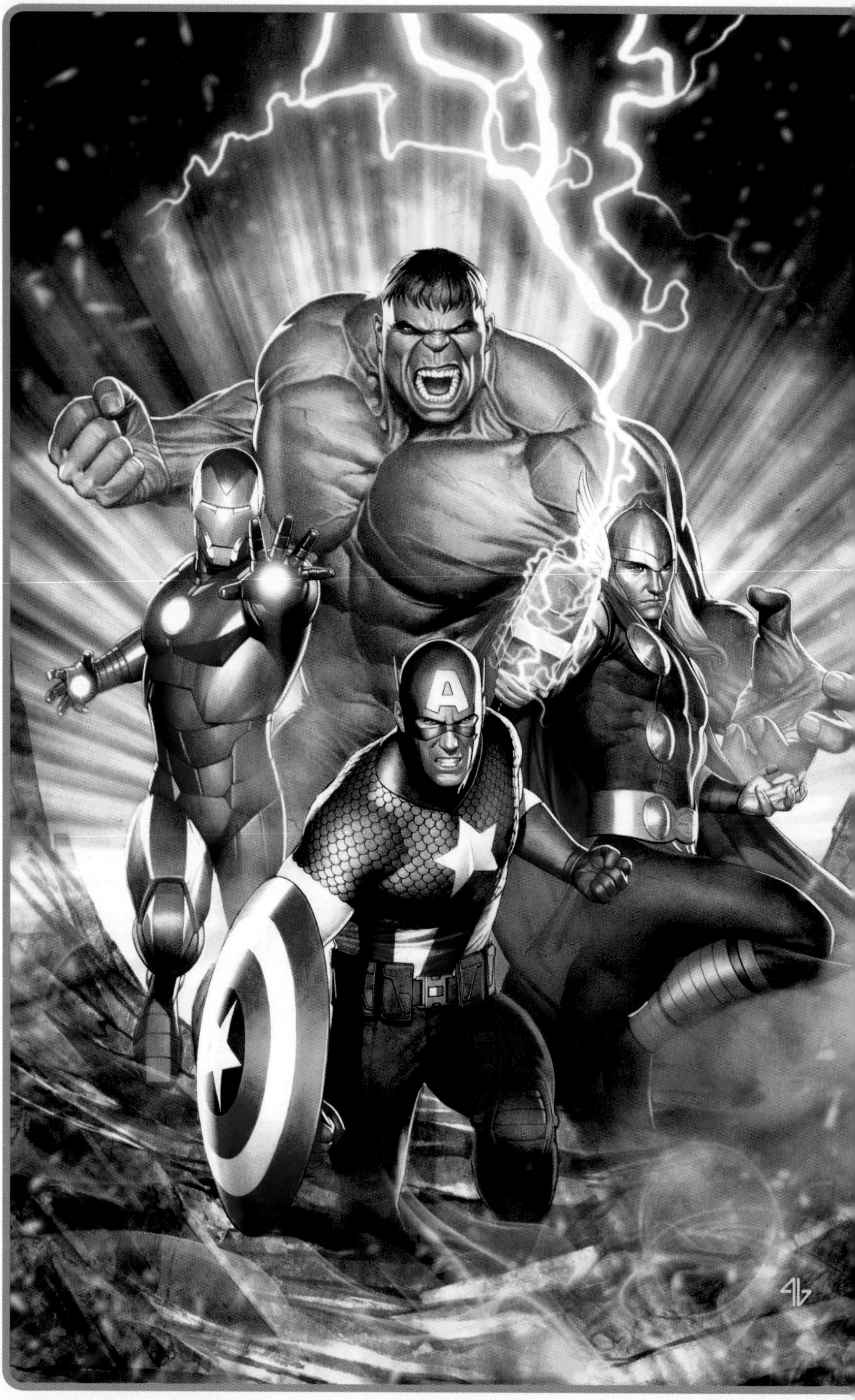

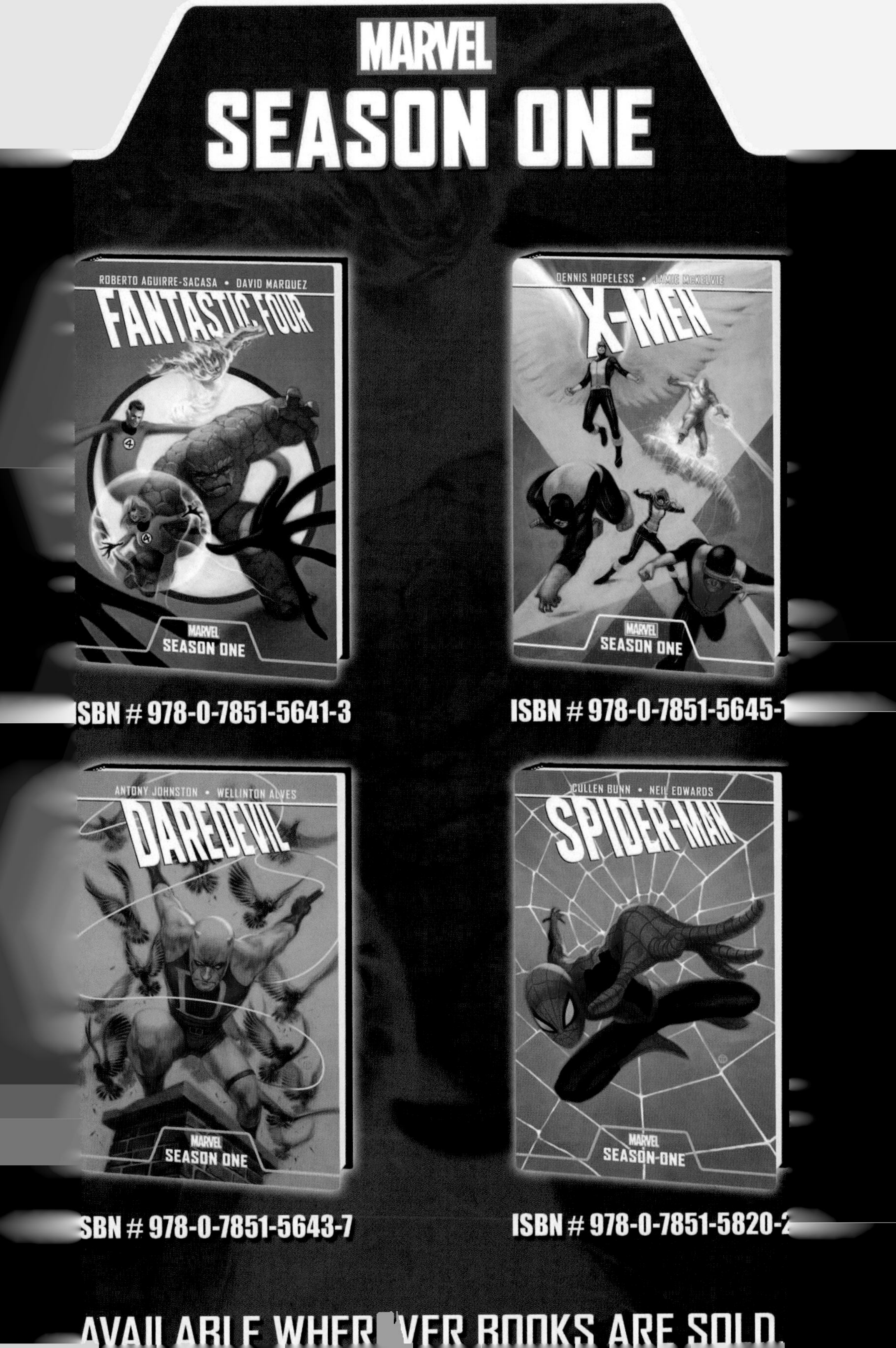
MARVEL
SEASON ONE
ROBERTO AGUIRRE-SACASA • DAVID MARQUEZ
FANTASTIC FOUR
MARVEL
SEASON ONE
DENNIS HOPELESS • JAMIE McKELVIE
X-MEN
MARVEL
SEASON ONE
ISBN # 978-0-7851-5641-3
ISBN # 978-0-7851-5645-
ANTONY JOHNSTON • WELLINTON ALVES
DAREDEVIL
MARVEL
SEASON ONE
CULLEN BUNN • NEIL EDWARDS
SPIDER-MAN
MARVEL
SEASON ONE
SBN # 978-0-7851-5643-7
ISBN # 978-0-7851-5820-
AVAILABLE WHER VER BOOKS ARE SOLD.

MARVEL
SEASON ONE

ISBN # 978-0-7851-6386-2

ISBN # 978-0-7851-6388-6

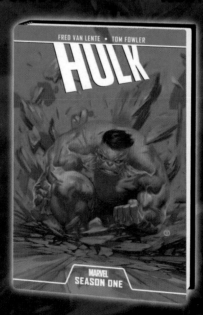

ISBN # 978-0-7851-6387-9

AVAILABLE WHEREVER BOOKS ARE SOLD